HIDDEN LONDON

DISCOVERING
THE FORGOTTEN UNDERGROUND

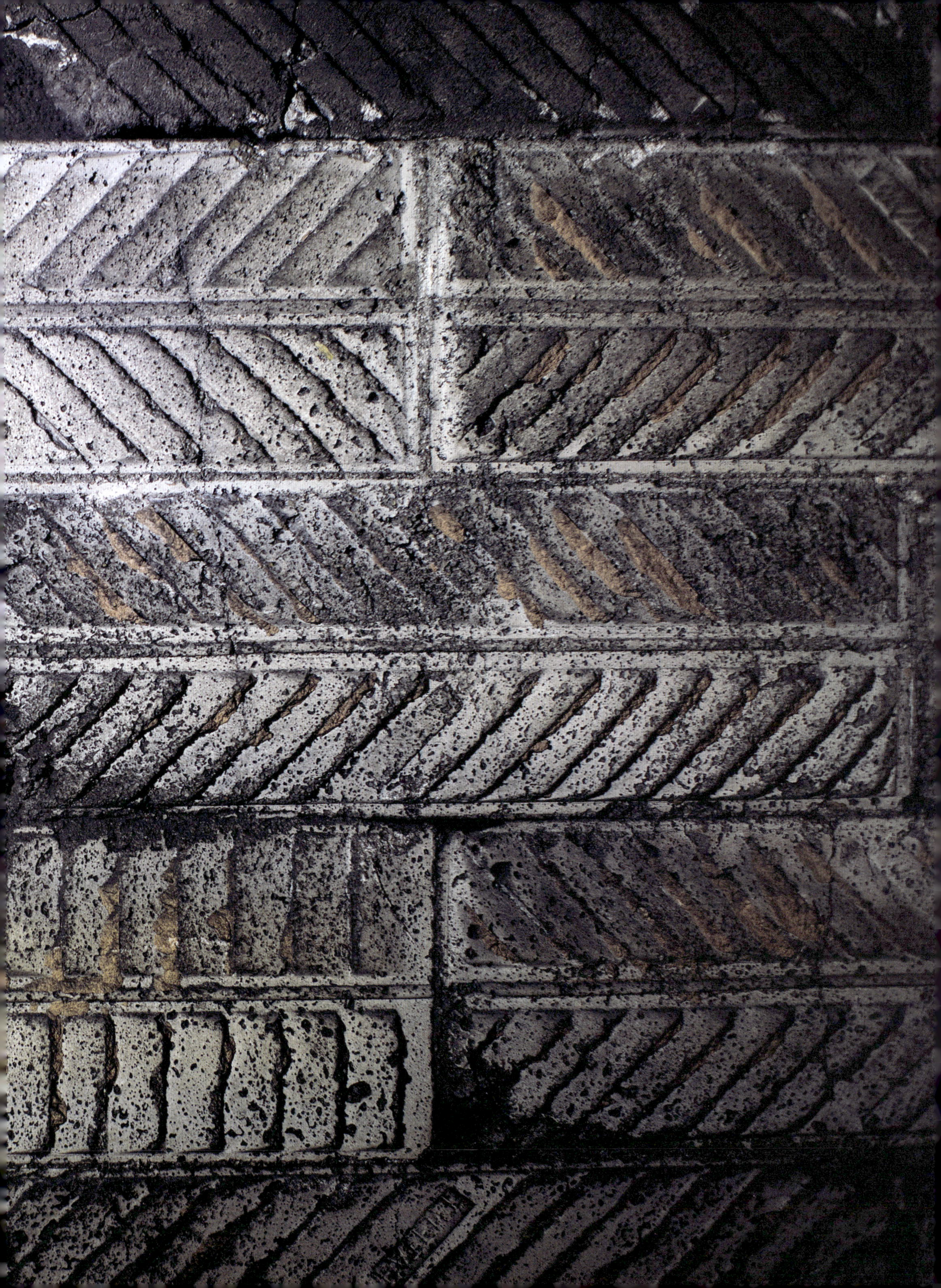

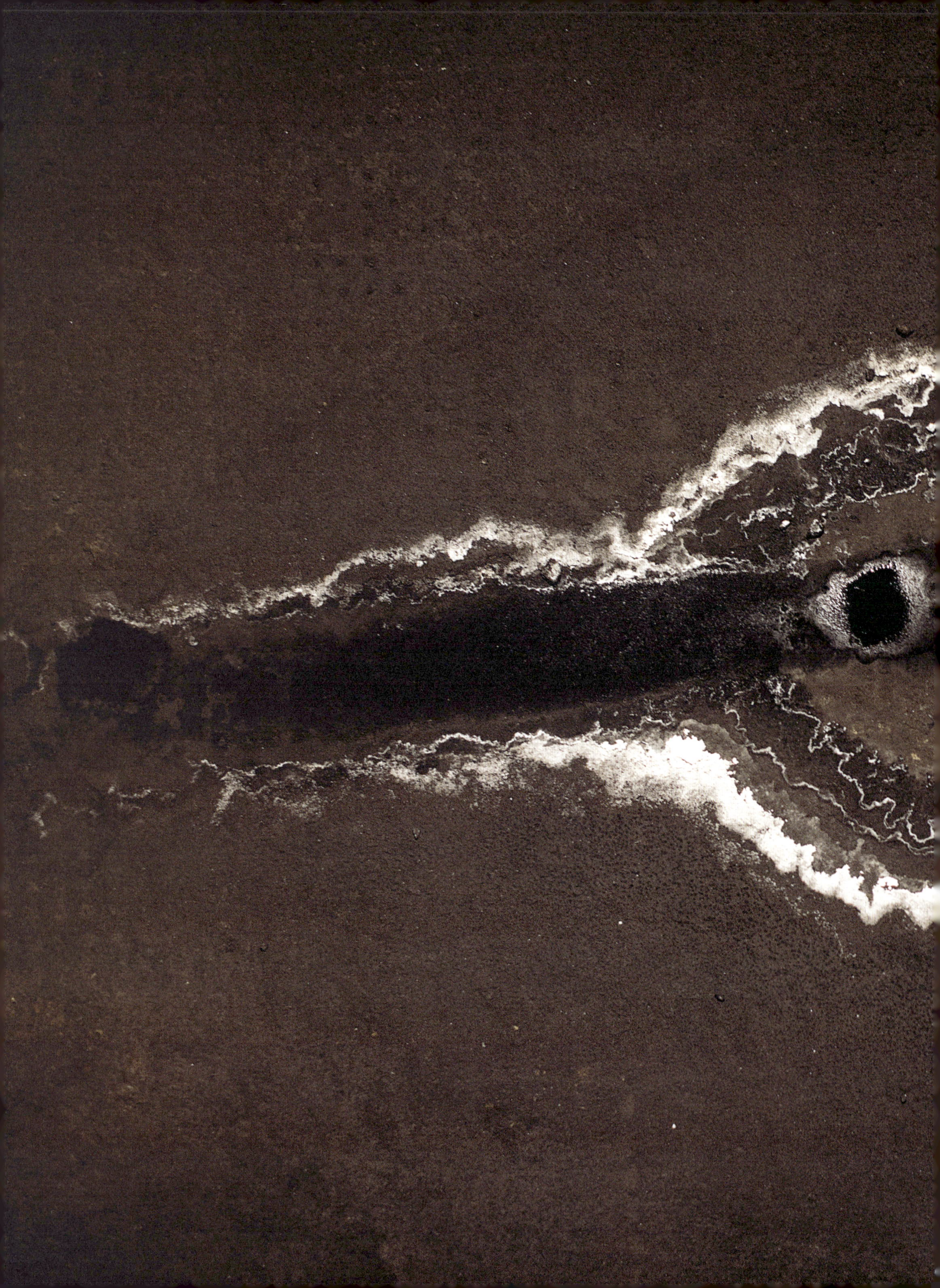

EMERGENCY EXIT

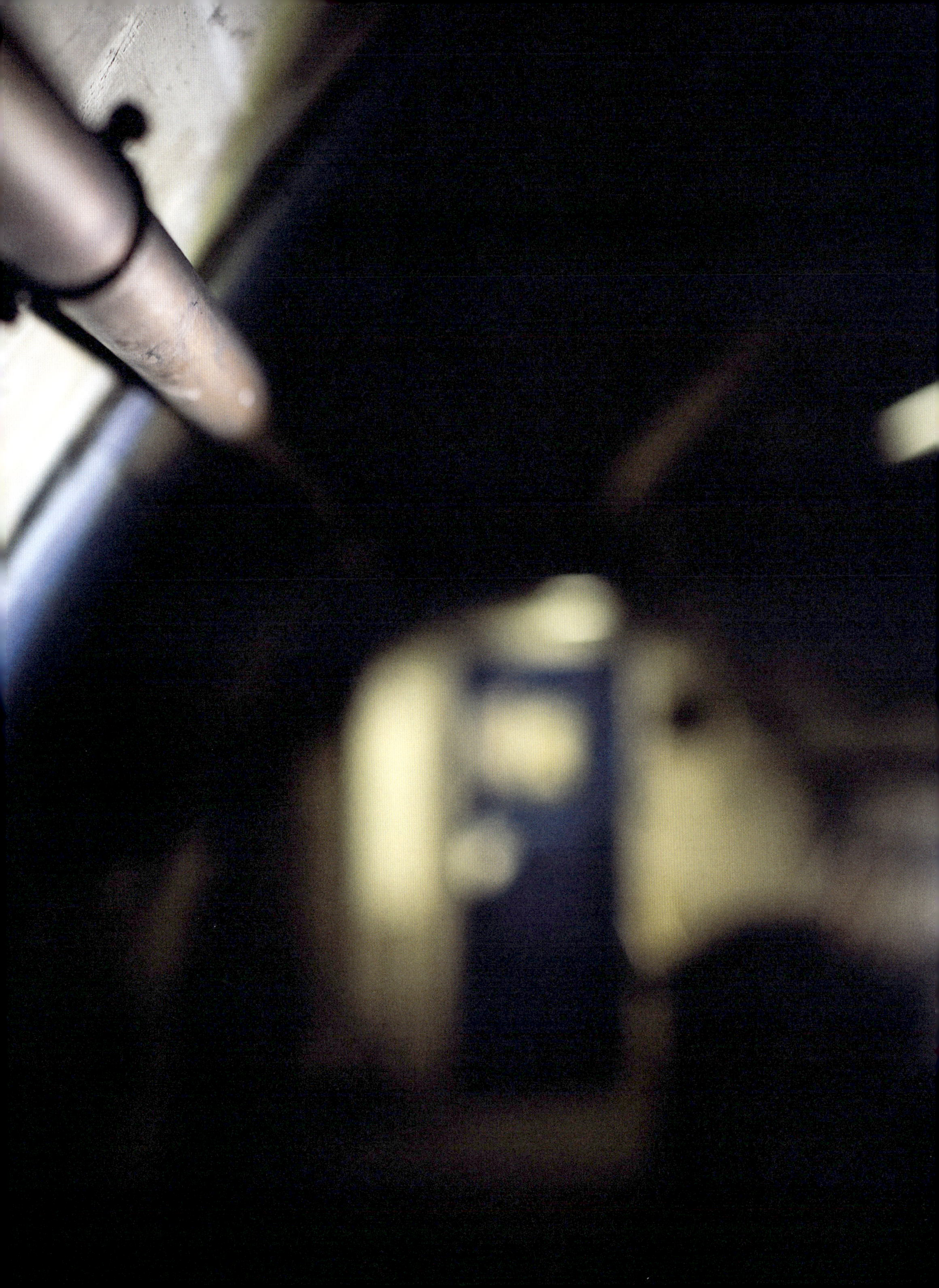

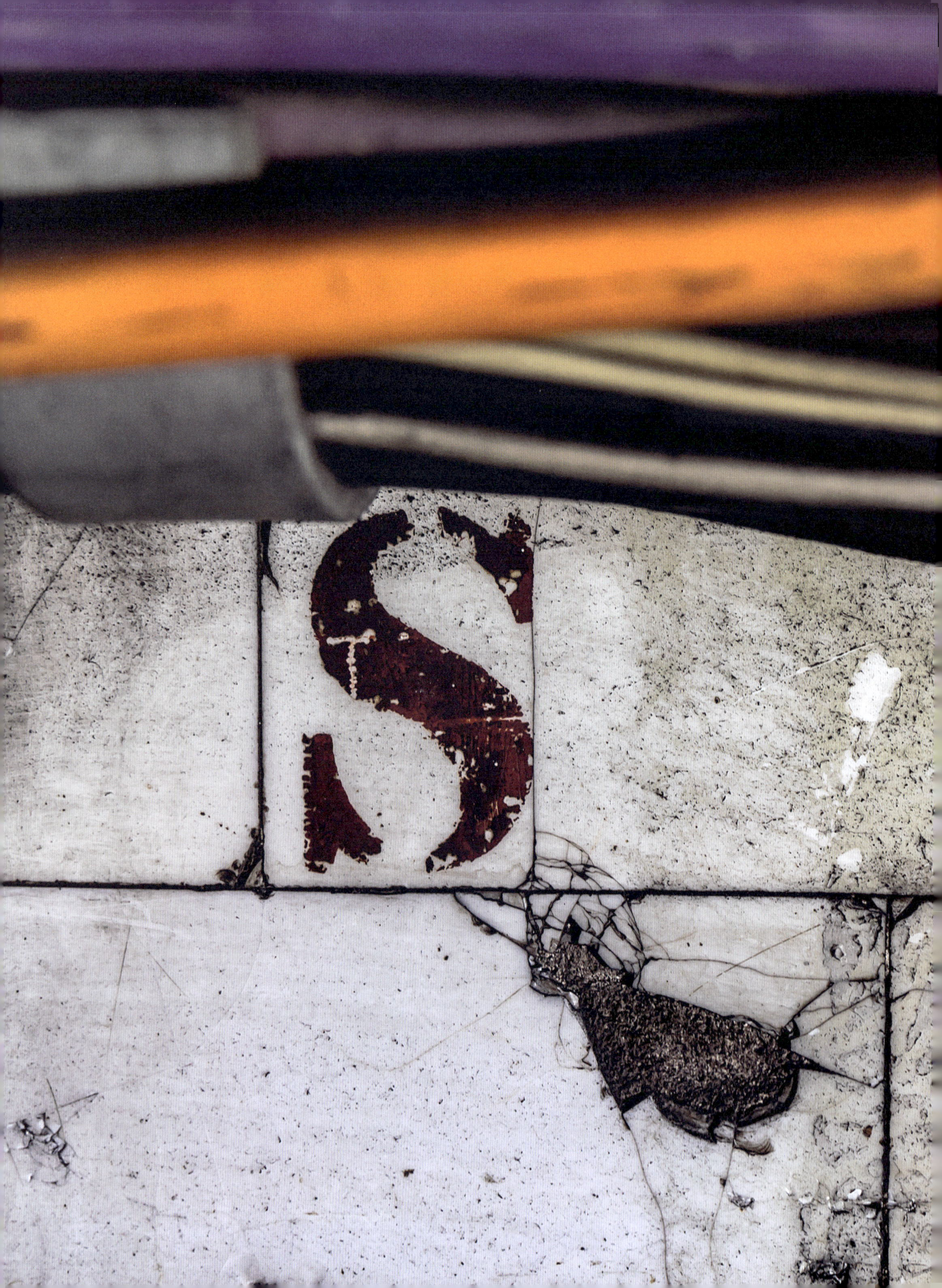
S

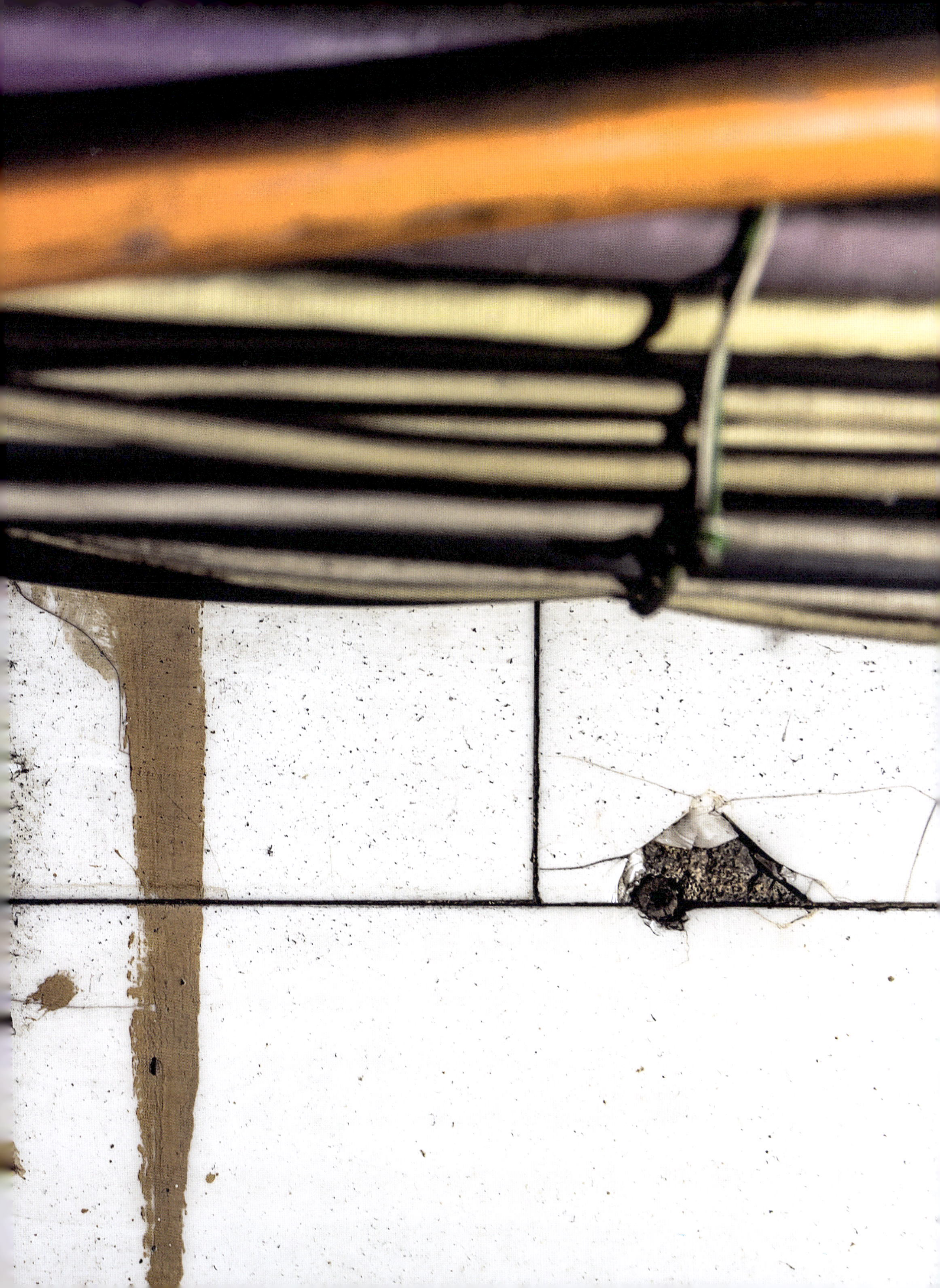

NEWELLITE
SHENTO
OLD K
LOND

SS TILES
REET
OAD
S.E.

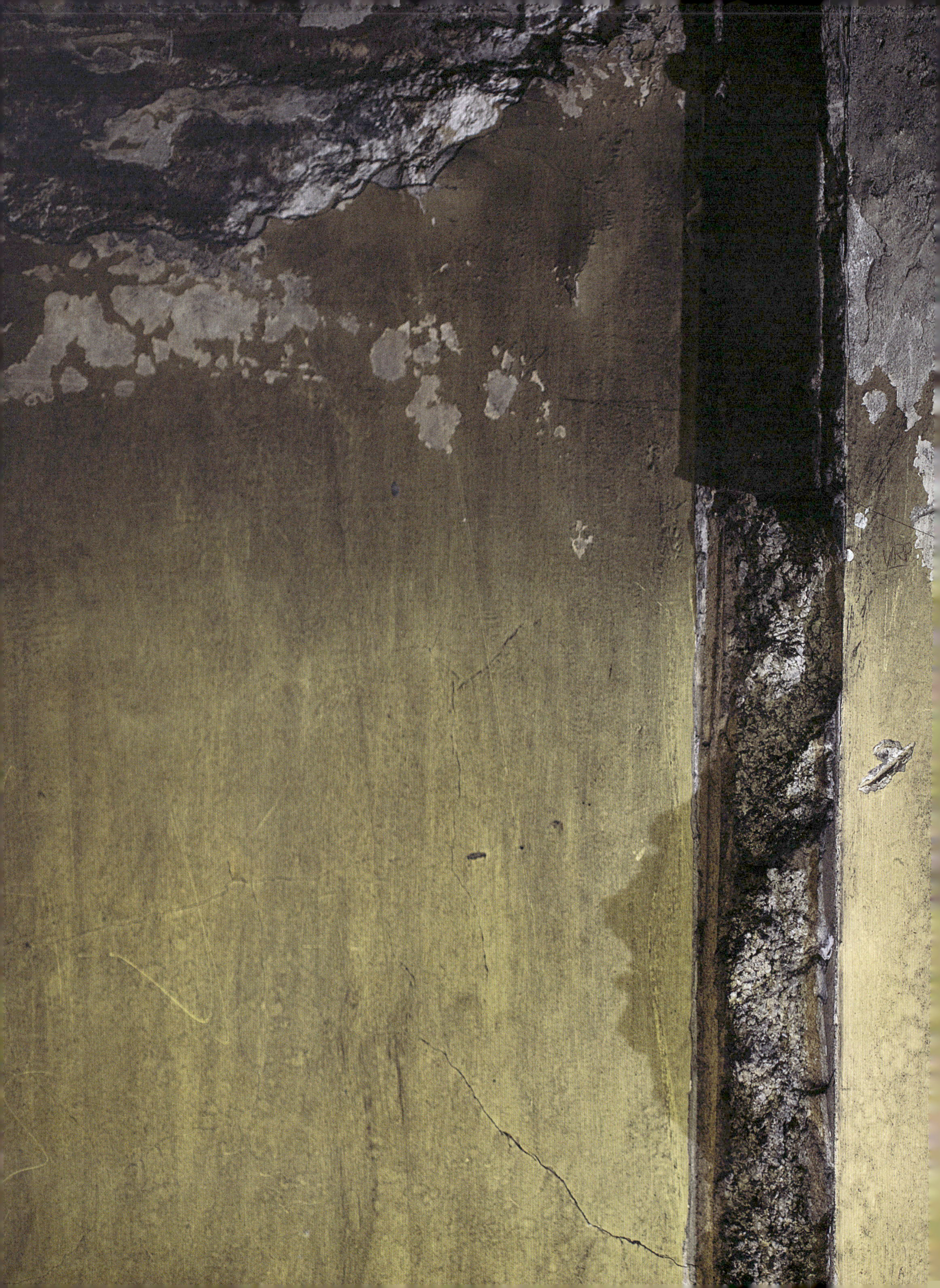

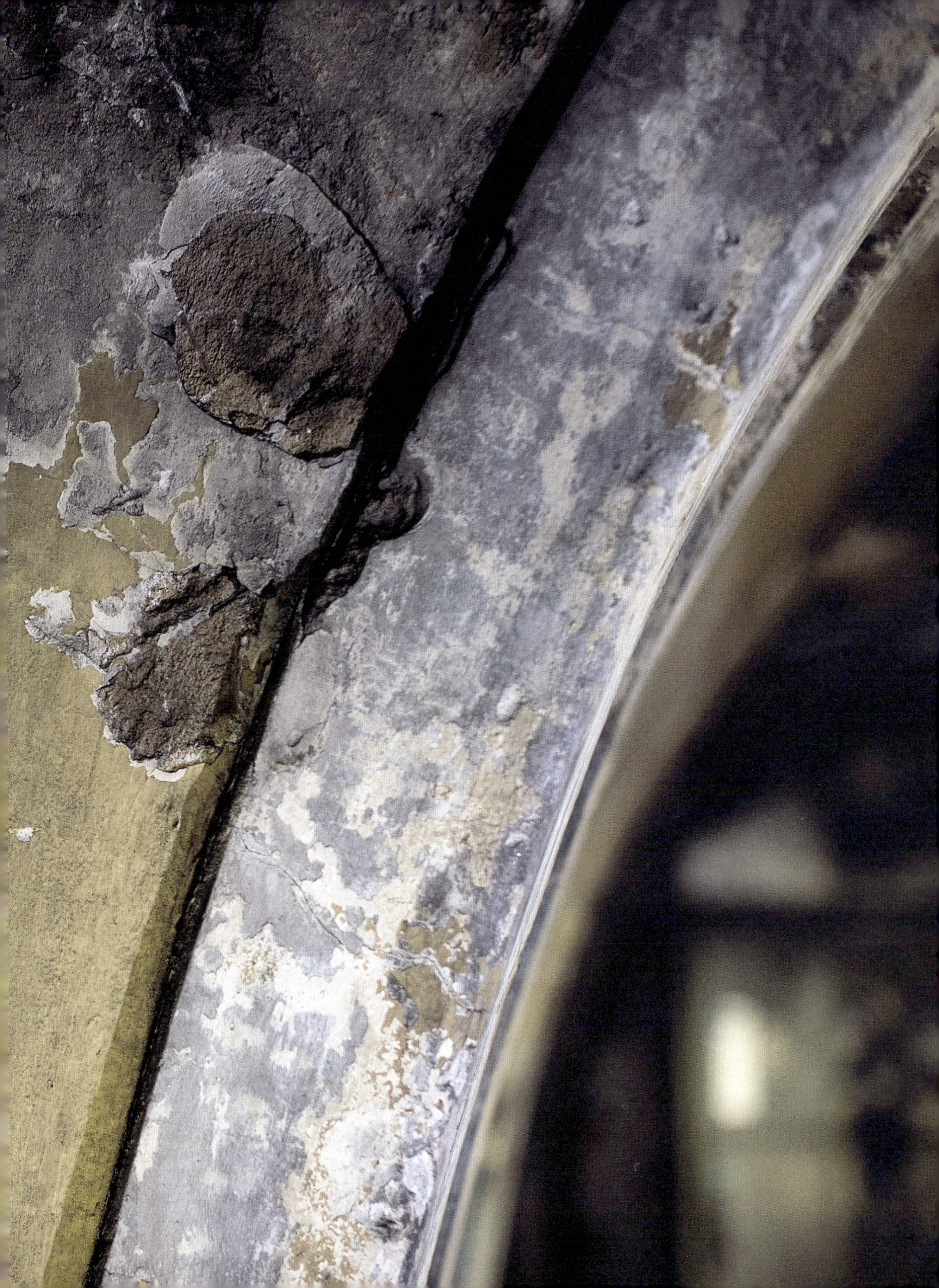

First published by Yale University Press 2019
302 Temple Street, P.O. Box 209040
New Haven CT 06520-9040
47 Bedford Square, London WC1B 3DP
yalebooks.com / yalebooks.co.uk

Text © 2019 The Authors

All rights reserved. This book may not
be reproduced or transmitted in any form
or by any means, electronic or mechanical,
including photocopy, recording or any other
information storage and retrieval system
(beyond that copying permitted by Sections
107 and 108 of the US Copyright Law and except
by reviewers for the public press), without
prior permission in writing from the publisher.

ISBN 978-0-300-245790 HB
Library of Congress Control Number: 2019939618
10 9 8 7 6 5 4 3 2 1
2023 2022 2021 2020 2019

All images © Transport for London, from the London
Transport Museum collection, except where noted
Contemporary photography: Toby Madden and
Andy Davis
Design: Praline
Copy editor: Faye Robson

Printed in China

Chris Nix is Assistant Director (Collections and
Engagement) at the London Transport Museum.
Siddy Holloway is Engagement Manager for
Hidden London and the co-creator of seven
Hidden London tours. David Bownes was head
of collections at the London Transport Museum
and Assistant Director (collections) at the
National Army Museum. Sam Mullins OBE
is Director of London Transport Museum.

CHRIS NIX, SIDDY HOLLOWAY AND DAVID BOWNES WITH SAM MULLINS

HIDDEN LONDON

DISCOVERING
THE FORGOTTEN UNDERGROUND

LONDON TRANSPORT MUSEUM IN ASSOCIATION WITH YALE UNIVERSITY PRESS

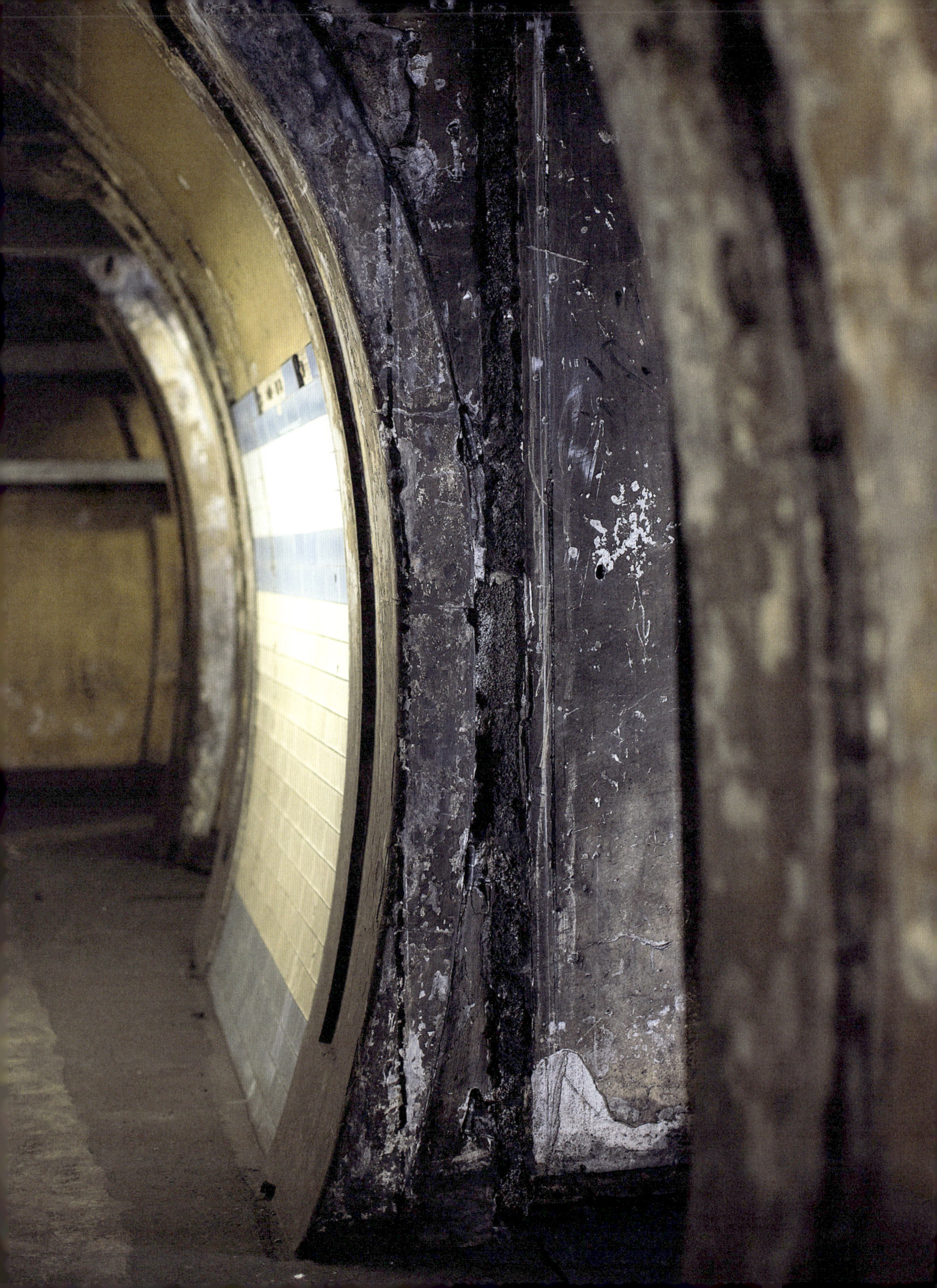

CONTENTS

19
FOREWORD

23
INTRODUCTION

37
KING WILLIAM STREET
THE FIRST DISUSED
TUBE STATION

109
55 BROADWAY
A CATHEDRAL
OF MODERNITY

173
HIGHGATE HIGH-LEVEL
CHANGE FOR
THE NORTHERN HEIGHTS

57
PICCADILLY CIRCUS
A NEW HEART
FOR LONDON

123
CLAPHAM SOUTH
DEEP-LEVEL SHELTER
BENEATH THE COMMON

189
THE STRAND
HOW HOLLYWOOD CAME
TO THE UNDERGROUND

79
DOWN STREET
THE SAFEST PLACE
IN LONDON

145
NORTH END
UNOPENED STATION
AND SECRET BUNKER

203
EUSTON
GATEWAY TO
THE NORTH

161
ONGAR & QUAINTON ROAD
FROM UNDERGROUND
OUTPOSTS TO HERITAGE
RAILWAYS

225
SELECT BIBLIOGRAPHY

226
INDEX

230
IMAGE CREDITS

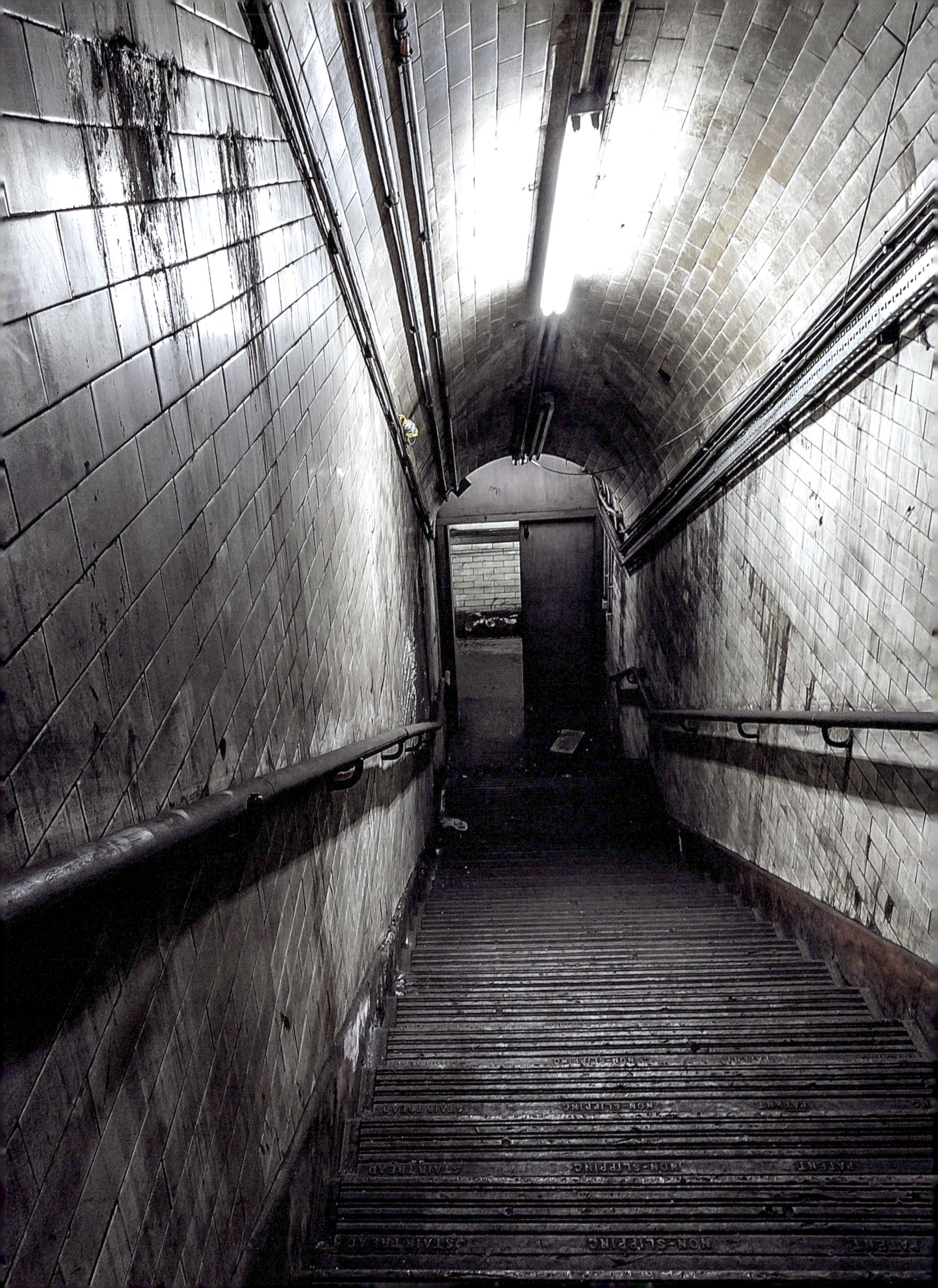
PATENT
NON-SLIPPING
STAIRTREAD

FOREWORD

London has long been shaped by its railways – ever since the Metropolitan opened as the world's first underground in 1863. By the time of the First World War, the core of today's extensive Underground network was already in place. Since then, the system has responded to London's ever-growing demands by building new lines and increasing the capacity of existing ones. We have also seen bigger stations, longer trains and platforms, more escalators and lifts, and smoother passenger journeys, with innovative signage, tickets and payment methods.

As the city's subterranean network has pushed outwards into the suburbs, and its capacity has edged upwards to five million journeys a day, old entrances, tunnels, stations and shafts have been left behind and are now sometimes hidden. This hidden London is of course a result of the pragmatic response to growth but, in the form of ghost stations, lost passages and secret spaces, it now exerts a powerful fascination and lure. I am delighted to see this hidden world shared by the London Transport Museum's tour programme and its authentic history revealed in this book.

London's richness and diversity continue to intrigue citizens and visitors alike, not least the way in which it has been shaped and reshaped by its Underground network.

Mike Brown MVO
Commissioner, Transport for London

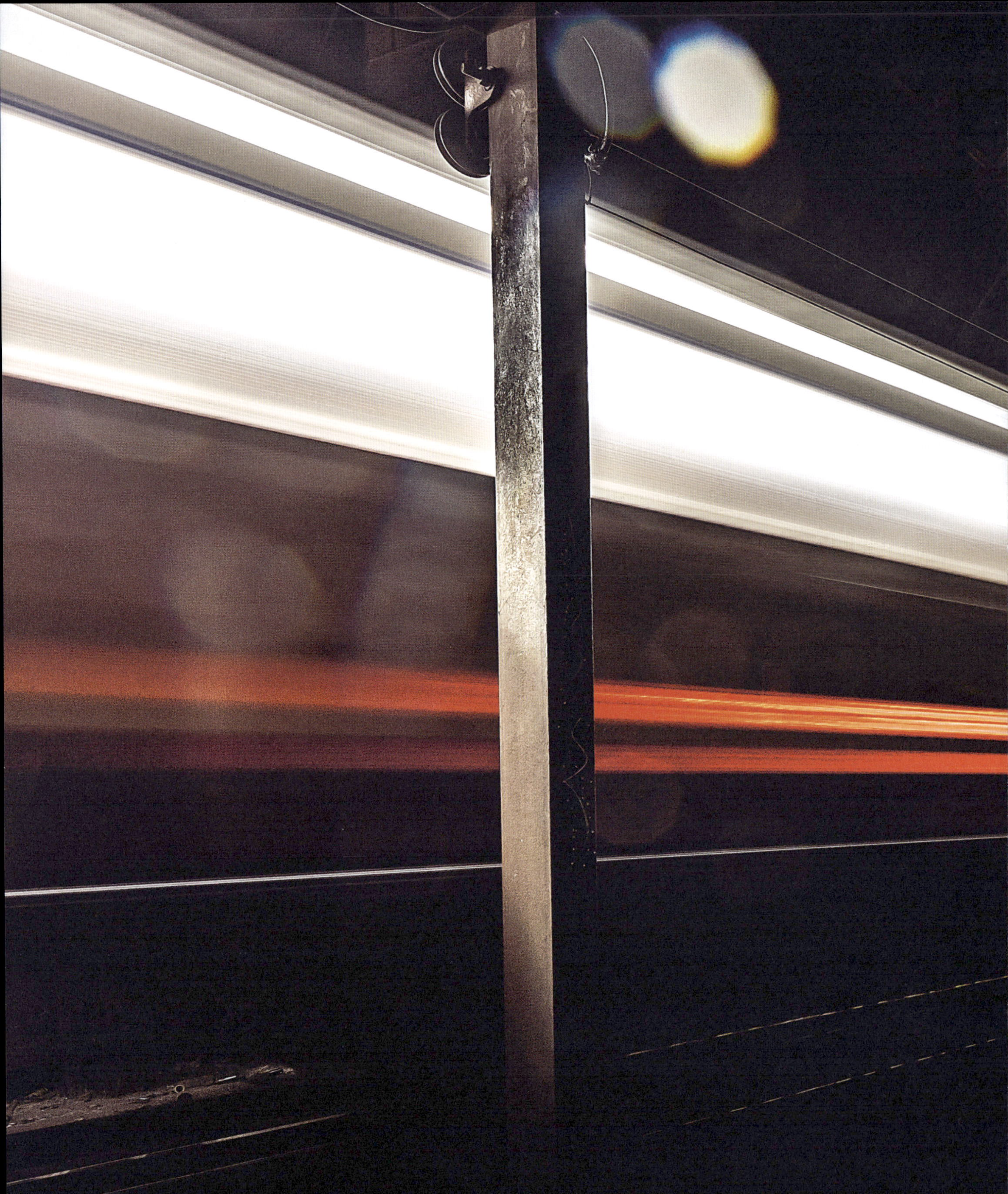

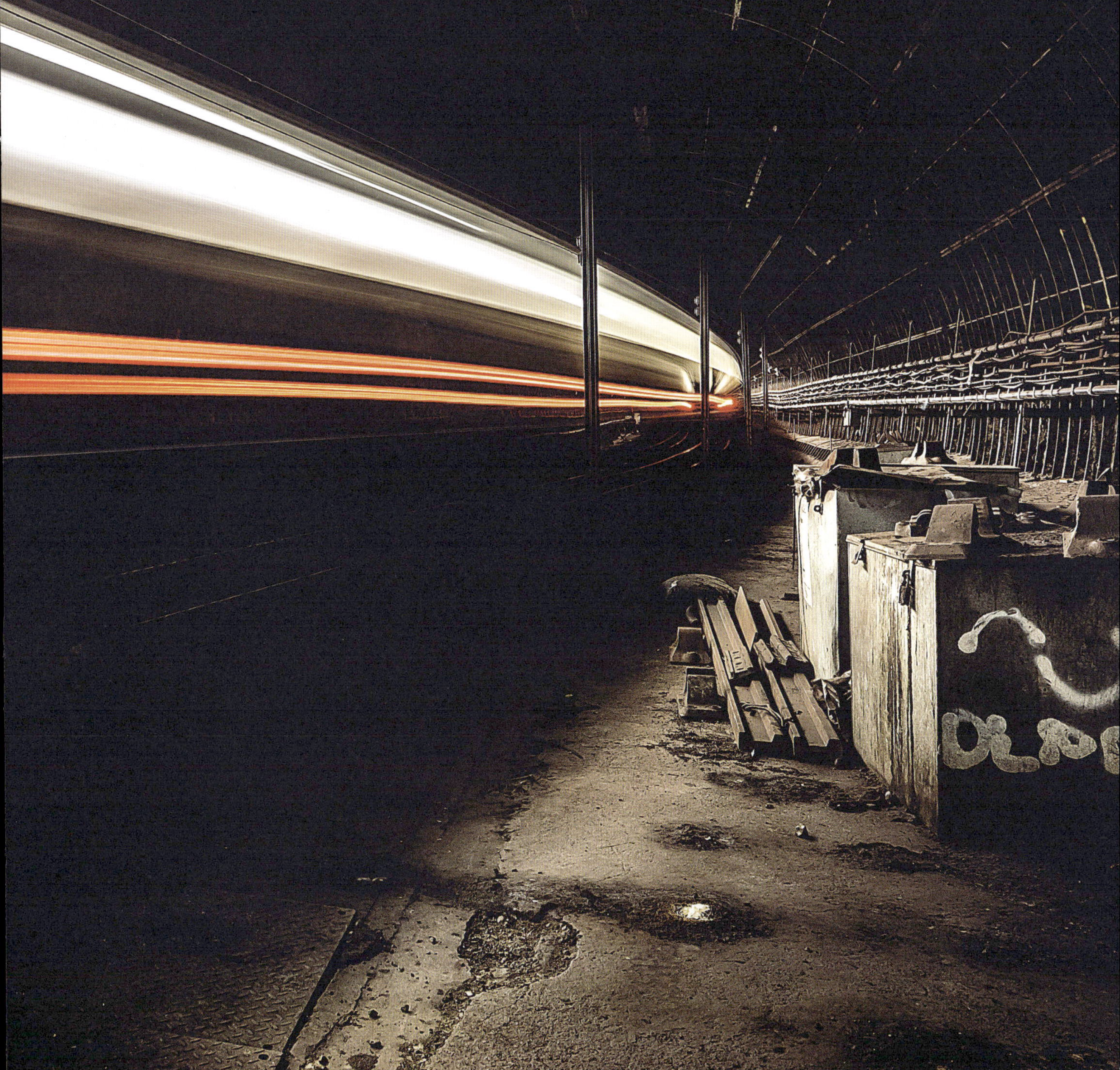

[FIG.1]   RIGHT   The access shaft for works on the Bank station upgrade project cuts through the heart of the platforms at King William Street station in 2016, allowing workers to expand and improve Bank station with minimal disruption to service.

[FIG.2]   BELOW LEFT   Those with a keen eye for detail might spot glimpses of disused stations as they pass through them while riding the Underground.

[FIG.3]   BELOW RIGHT   The exterior of disused South Kentish Town station, closed in 1924 and now repurposed as a shop. The station is also the location for a short story by John Betjeman, in which a hapless commuter is left stranded underground after inadvertently alighting at the abandoned platform during an unscheduled stop ('South Kentish Town', 1951).

INTRODUCTION

The London Underground is the lifeblood of the capital. Up to five million people use the network each day, while the famous diagrammatic map, roundel signage and 'mind the gap' announcements are icons of the modern city. Familiarity with the Underground system and its idiosyncrasies is a rite of passage that marks the true Londoner. If you know the 'Tube' (as the system is commonly known), you can access all that London has to offer. And yet, unsuspecting Londoners hurrying on their well-beaten paths are largely unaware that behind locked doors and lost entrances lies a secret world of disused stations, redundant passageways, empty lift shafts and cavernous ventilation ducts. The Tube is an ever-expanding network that has left in its wake hidden places and spaces – the flotsam and jetsam thrown up by the Underground's continuous response to the demands of the city and its commuters [FIG.1]. *Hidden London* opens up the lost worlds of London's Underground and provides a fresh insight into key stories in the city's history.

TRUTH OR FICTION? UNLOCKING THE STORIES OF HIDDEN LONDON

Disused and abandoned Underground spaces have long held a special fascination for those intrigued by what lies beneath the city's streets. Shrouded in mystery, and tantalisingly inaccessible, these strange subterranean places have become the backdrop to a good deal of urban myth and speculation. Stories abound of secret government installations and forgotten time capsules, while filmmakers and writers have reimagined the deserted Tube as the home of ghosts, aliens and even flesh-eating troglodytes descended from tunnellers trapped underground.[1] The truth, of course, is often more prosaic, but, as the case studies in this book show, the real story behind Hidden London is every bit as fascinating as the speculation and, until now, has only been partially told.

The authors of this book have been given unprecedented access to the sites discussed in the chapters that follow, and have been able to compare the physical evidence with a rediscovered wealth of surviving plans, drawings and original photographs. This has allowed new light to be shone on familiar narratives, such as that of the reuse of the closed Down Street station as Winston Churchill's secret wartime refuge (see Down Street, pp.79–107). Other, less well-known stories have also emerged: those of Cold War-era bunkers deep beneath suburban gardens (see North End, pp.145–59), fossilised passageways behind closed doors, and eerily silent platforms where trains no longer stop.

CASE STUDIES

To tell our *Hidden London* story, ten case studies have been carefully selected, revealing different types of abandonment and reuse, with sites that have shared a similar fate grouped together. Most locations are in central London,

[FIG.4] An escalator shaft and works access tunnel under construction at Bank in 2018, with modern construction techniques used on an epic scale to upgrade capacity and interchange behind the scenes at a working station.

but some can be found far from the bustling metropolis, in greenfield sites once served by the Underground network. Not all are disused stations in the strictest sense of the term. In many cases, just part of a station has become non-operational due to modification (the installation of escalators, for example) or a section of tunnel has been abandoned due to track re-routing. Occasionally, an Underground structure was built but never used, or fell into disuse shortly after opening. However, as space below ground is both expensive to make and invariably hard-won, such locations are seldom allowed to lie idle for long.

Indeed, one of the most striking features of the *Hidden London* story is the extent to which imaginative, and sometimes surprising, new uses have been found for previously abandoned sites, with these including the creation of wartime offices, air raid shelters, archival storage and facilities to effect operational improvements. Some sites have even found a new lease of life growing salad leaves for the capital's restaurants [SEE FIG.133]. This ongoing story is best illustrated by King William Street, the city terminus of the world's first deep-level tube railway, opened in 1890 but abandoned just ten years later (see King William Street, pp.37–55). Briefly repurposed as an air raid shelter in the Second World War, part of the station is used today as an underground base for engineers engaged in the massive capacity upgrade project for nearby Bank station [FIG.4].

In fact, so many Underground locations have been modified or adapted in some way that a definitive listing is near-impossible and, consequently, not all are featured in the current book. These omissions include some station closures (such as Marlborough Road on the Metropolitan line and British Museum on the Central), as well as the re-siting or abandonment of surface buildings (for example, at Uxbridge and Shoreditch).

THE ABANDONED UNDERGROUND

Although this book is primarily about the hidden spaces of London Underground, rather than being a history of the entire network, some background knowledge about how the Tube came to be is helpful in understanding why certain Underground structures ended up abandoned.[2]

The world's first underground railways were built in London by privately financed companies competing with bus and tram companies for profit. The Metropolitan Railway and the City & South London Railway (C&SLR) were both pioneering examples of Victorian technology and defined the method by which underground railways would be built across the globe. The early development of the Underground allowed London to expand rapidly. Innovations in tunnelling, traction, and lift and escalator design were driven by the success of the early Tube network. Inevitably, the revolutionary system also had lessons to learn and changes to make, which would lead to some tunnels, and even whole stations, becoming surplus to requirements.

The first section of the Metropolitan Railway was completed in 1863 using the cut-and-cover method, in which a road is dug up to create a deep cutting and track laid in the bottom, before a brick arch tunnel is built over the top and the road reinstated. This type of sub-surface railway forms the Victorian underground lines that we know today as the Metropolitan, District, Circle,

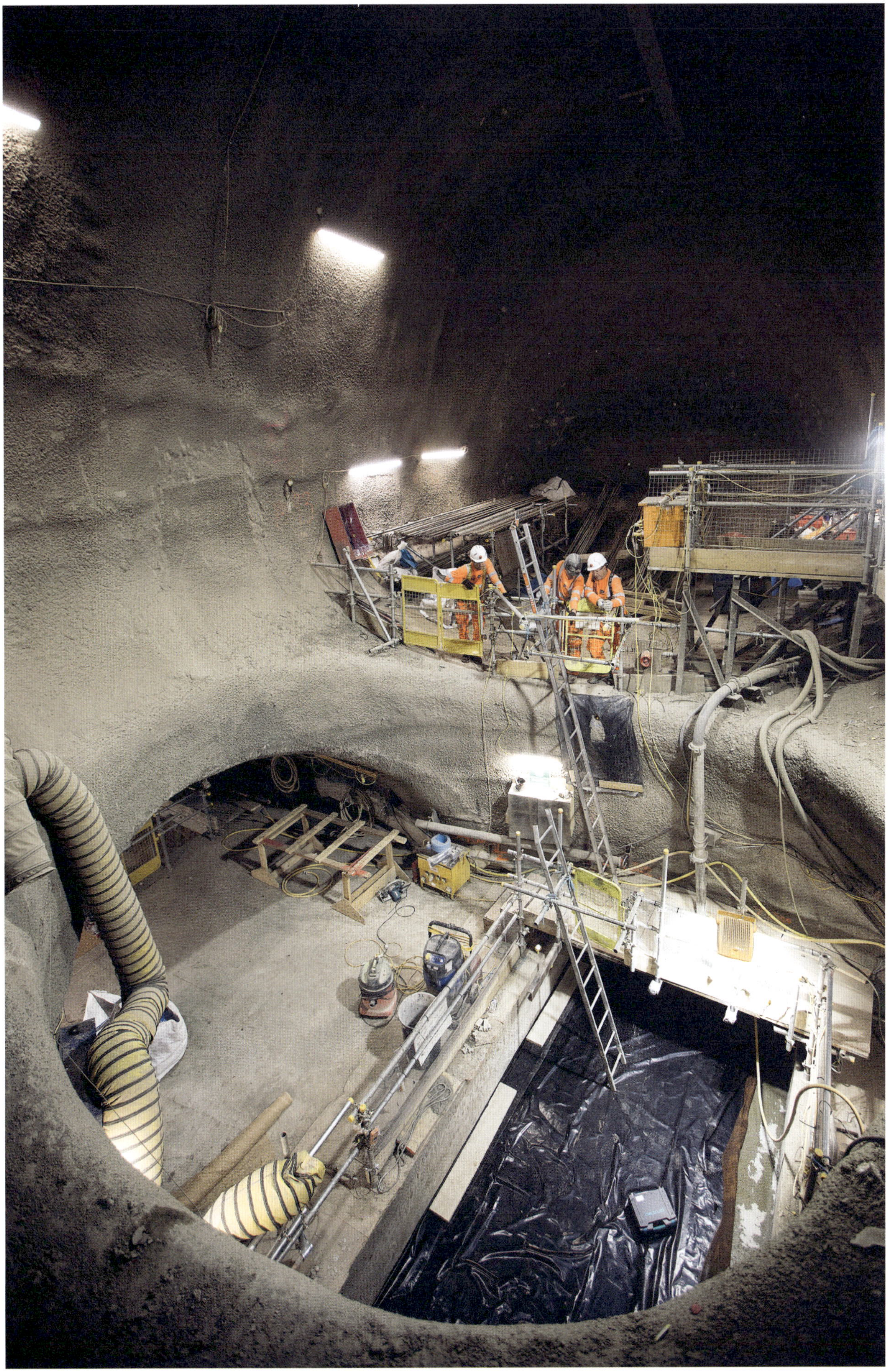

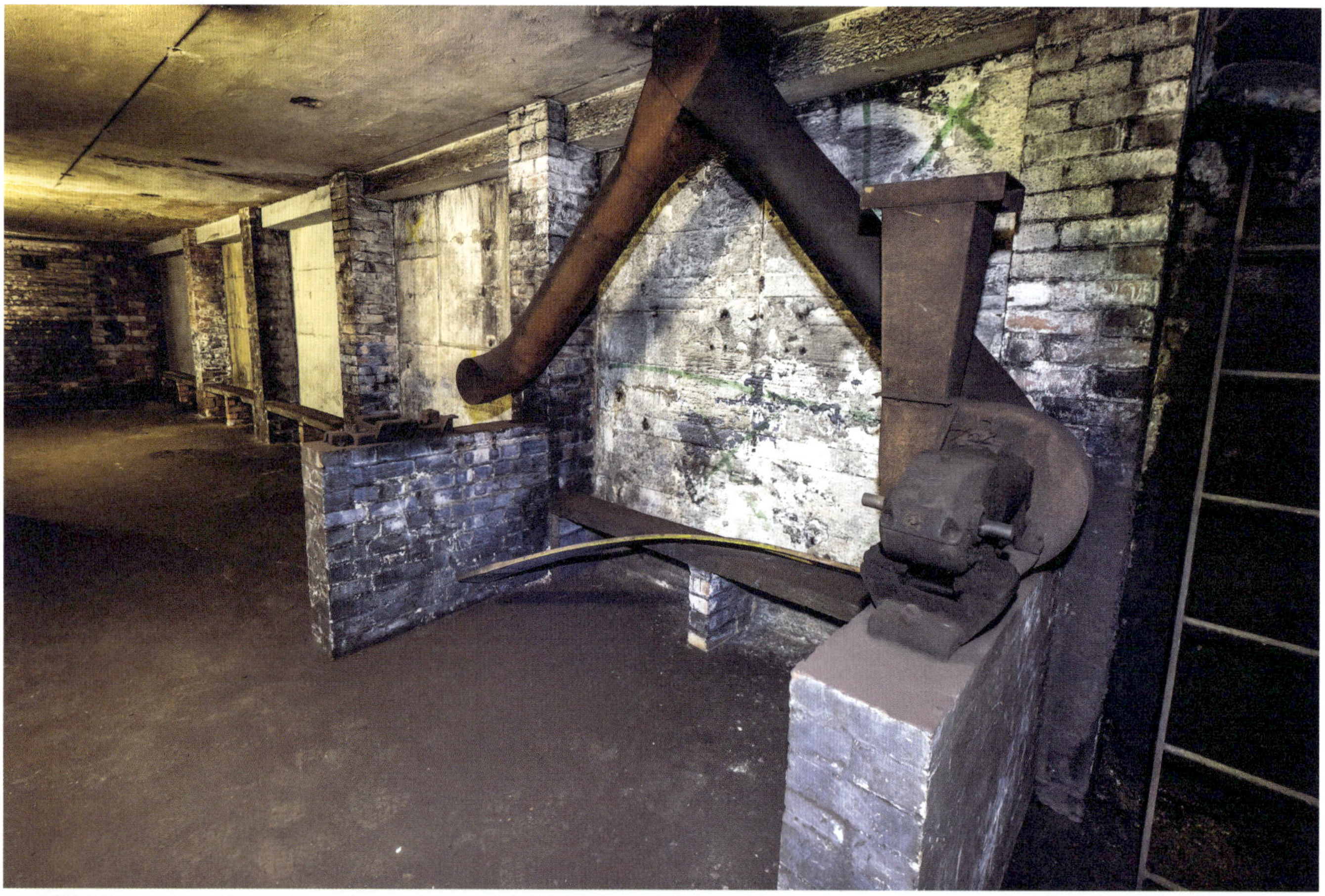

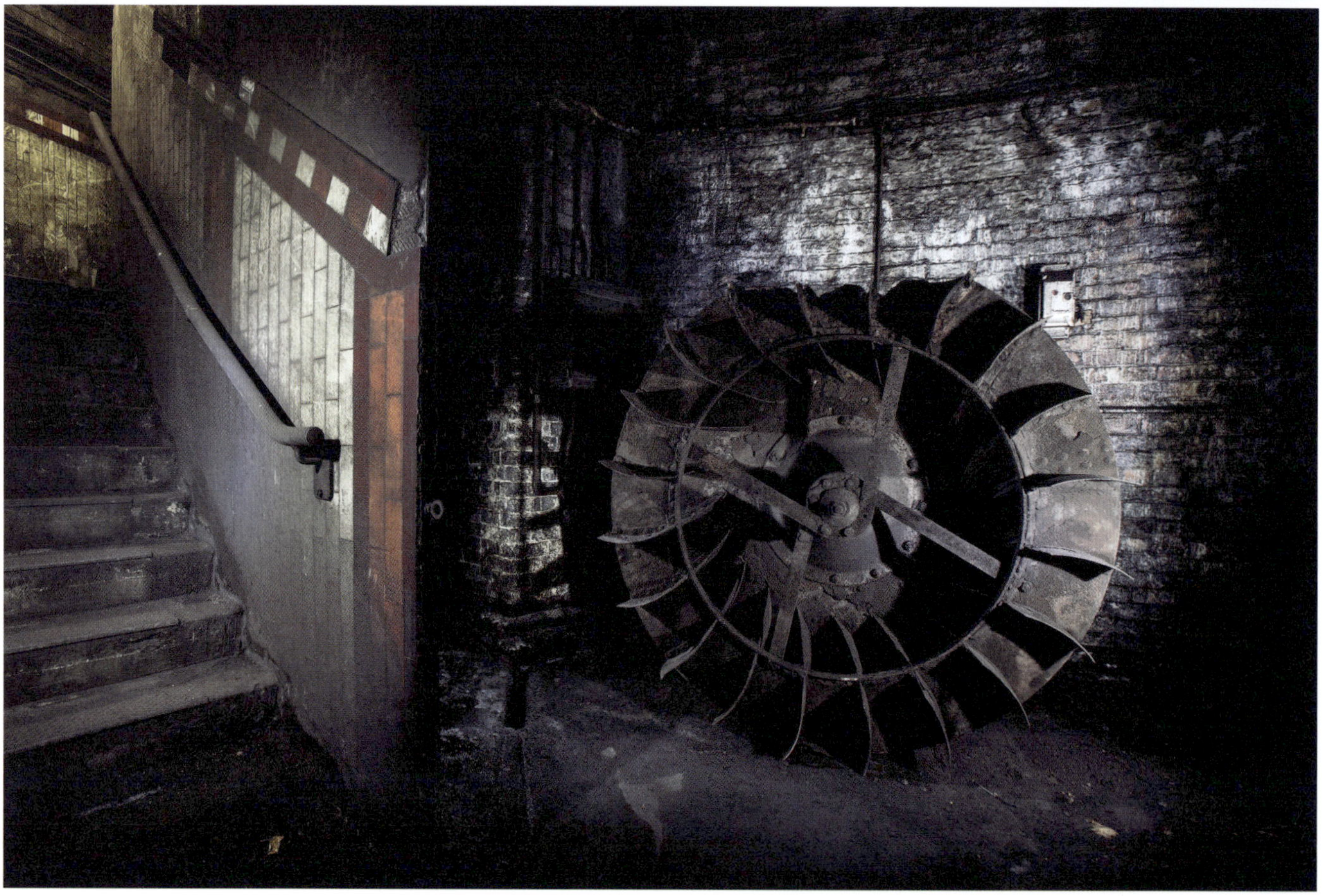

[FIG.5] ABOVE A ventilation system dating from the Second World War at Whitechapel St Marys – one of several stations where disused platforms were converted for use as civilian shelters during the war and run by the local authorities. Although just below the ground, the shelter survived a Blitz attack that destroyed the station's surface-level building.

[FIG.6] BELOW A large, redundant fan impeller in a dark corner of disused York Road station.

and Hammersmith & City. The routes were originally designed to be worked by steam-hauled trains; therefore, where possible, they were constructed in open cuttings so as to allow locomotive fumes to leave the tunnels. Stations were typically constructed as platforms in widened cuttings, each with a canopy and flights of stairs leading to a ticket-hall building at surface level. As electric locomotives replaced steam from 1905, many of these cuttings were covered over, allowing revenue to be raised from the construction of buildings above.

Ultimately, the spread of sub-surface railways was limited by the disruption they brought to busy streets during construction. In 1890 a new type of deep tube electric railway was pioneered by the C&SLR. The tunnels were dug using the new Greathead tunnelling shield, which protected miners from the collapse of the ground above while they dug and constructed the tube tunnel in cast-iron sections (see King William Street). Passenger platforms were reached by lifts, and the trains were powered by electricity – innovations that were subsequently copied by rival tube railways.

By the 1900s the race was on to criss-cross the capital, with a subterranean maze of often competing tube lines created. Many lacked the necessary financial support to bring their plans to fruition but, thanks to American investment, the basis of the modern-day central London Tube network was largely up and running by 1910.[3] It was inevitable, however, that lines originally intended to compete would create duplication and contain some innovations that would fail financially or practically. In time, some stations and parts of lines built during this period would close or be heavily modified as the rival Underground lines were grouped together under single management and extended.

The rapid expansion of London's Tube network during the Edwardian period was an enormous success, but led to unforeseen strain on infrastructure that had been built to carry far fewer people. Extensions to the modern-day Piccadilly, Northern and Central lines during the 1920s and 1930s opened vast tracts of the outer London area for much-needed housing, thus creating even greater demand for Tube services. To increase train frequency on these extended lines, lesser-used stations in central London, such as South Kentish Town and City Road, were closed. Meanwhile, to increase passenger capacity and flow, new escalator technology replaced lifts at many Underground stations (see Piccadilly Circus, pp.57–77). Many of the redundant lift shafts were, in turn, converted into ventilation shafts to supplement the original, and sometimes inadequate, ventilation systems of the first Tube stations (often limited to a single duct running down the centre of the spiral emergency stairs). In some cases, entire disused stations, such as York Road, were converted to create extra ventilation and make the Tube more comfortable [FIG.6]. Disused passageways and rooms were also used to house new, and more modern, power and signalling equipment, with the result that original station features have often been preserved in these hidden spaces.

The most famous reuse of abandoned Underground spaces, however, emerged during the Second World War, when several were re-equipped as civilian air raid shelters or for other wartime use [FIG.5].[4] Londoners had previously sought shelter in the Tube during the sporadic bombing raids of the First World War, when aerial warfare was limited in both scope and destructive capacity (though 1,413 people lost their lives from aerial attacks between 1914 and 1918). In the changed circumstances of the post-war era, however, with rapid advancements in bomber aircraft design, attention turned to how the Tube network might be utilised to provide civilian shelter during a potentially much more deadly conflict. As early as May 1929, Frank Pick, then managing director of London Electric Railways, received a secret request from the War Office Committee of Imperial Defence to consider how London Tubes could be used as shelters and for the purposes of evacuation.[5] Specifically, he was asked to consider which parts of the Underground could be adapted as shelters, how many people could be accommodated, how emergency telephones and cables could be installed and how people could be rapidly evacuated to the suburbs in the event of war.

Pick was given only 12 days to gather the information but replied in just two, with a plan to use stations on the Bakerloo, Piccadilly, Northern and Central lines as adapted shelters. Along with disused stations such as Down Street, those with abandoned lift shafts and passageways were also identified and ranked in three categories according to their depth and the degree of protection they could offer from aerial bombardment. Pick's plan goes on to detail some of the modifications that would need to be made, including the provision of toilet facilities. Interestingly, Aldwych was identified as one station that could be completely closed for use as a shelter for up to 7,000 people; it, in fact, became one of the best-known wartime shelters, despite having fallen into partial disuse as an actual station by this time.

[FIG.7] Along with health-and-safety notices, a shrine to Saint Barbara, the patron saint of tunnellers, can usually be found in underground construction sites. Here, at Bank, it seems that the construction workers have asked the saint to consider an additional request.

[FIG.8] ABOVE LEFT The distinctive exterior of a disused station, designed by architect Leslie Green, is still recognisable at Hyde Park Corner, despite having been incorporated into a hotel facade.

[FIG.9] ABOVE RIGHT Tiled wall at Piccadilly Circus station, stamped with the supplier's mark of W.B. Simpson & Sons, London, and made by Maw and Company. The colour scheme seen in the background of this photograph is unique to the station.

[FIG.10] BELOW At York Road station, the Edwardian ticket hall tiling design – with a border of green, glazed relief tiling – can still be seen against the red, cream and pink passageway.

[FIG.11] This backfilled passageway with drainpipe was the first clue that further research into the tunnels at Euston might yield an interesting story.

However, Frank Pick and the Underground management remained, initially, opposed to the concept of using the operational Tube network for impromptu civilian shelters, which they regarded as a failure of planning on the part of government.[6] Besides, Pick argued, the Tube would need to keep running during the war, moving war workers and soldiers, unimpeded by civilian shelterers. This view was initially shared by Churchill's wartime government, who were fearful of creating a 'shelter-mentality' that would encourage Londoners to forsake their wartime commitments, and possibly serve as a catalyst for civil unrest. In the event, public pressure resulted in most operational, deep-level Tube stations being opened for civilian shelter once the Blitz began in 1940, with neither the feared 'shelter-mentality' nor civil unrest materialising. As planned, some disused stations were leased for wartime use, while additional capacity was achieved by repurposing unfinished stations, such as Highgate and Bethnal Green, and by closing and converting Aldwych and constructing purpose-built, deep-level shelters at key points.

The post-war development of the Tube network continued to see new lines built and redundant sections abandoned or reused. The London Passenger Transport Board ('London Transport') had been established in 1933 as the world's largest public urban transport authority. As a single authority, it could concentrate on the work of improving the system and rationalising earlier planning anomalies in response to passenger usage. As the chapter on the Strand (pp.189–201) shows, however, changes in transport policy could still result in short-lived and abandoned schemes, as when the Jubilee line was rerouted during construction of the new extension.

PIECING TOGETHER THE PHYSICAL EVIDENCE

The disused, abandoned and repurposed locations referred to in this book have left behind a wealth of physical evidence, and many strange features – some common to multiple sites, others rare or unique – exist outside the usually well-ordered passenger environment of the Underground, adding to the 'otherness' of Hidden London. These have the power to surprise and delight even the most experienced explorer of the subterranean world.

Tiles were used throughout the early Underground stations as a practical, hardwearing decorative finish that was easy to wash down and keep clean.[7] Fragments and entire sections of original tiling can still be seen in situ at several closed locations, sometimes accompanied by traces of original posters and other notices. The Edwardian Tube station facades designed by architect Leslie Green were clad in tiles supplied by the Leeds Fireclay Company. These large tiles of oxblood-red colour clad the steel building frame and were designed to look like structural blocks. The names of each of the stations, along with the entrance and exit signs, were picked out in individual, tiled letters and often highlighted with gold leaf. These distinctive frontages help us to identify closed Underground station buildings, even when their names have been covered and the buildings adapted for other uses [FIG.8].

The ticket halls of stations built in the early 1900s were adorned inside with a cream-and-green tiling scheme, with a band of green tiles featuring a design in relief of pomegranate or acanthus leaf [FIG.10]. In the passageways and platform

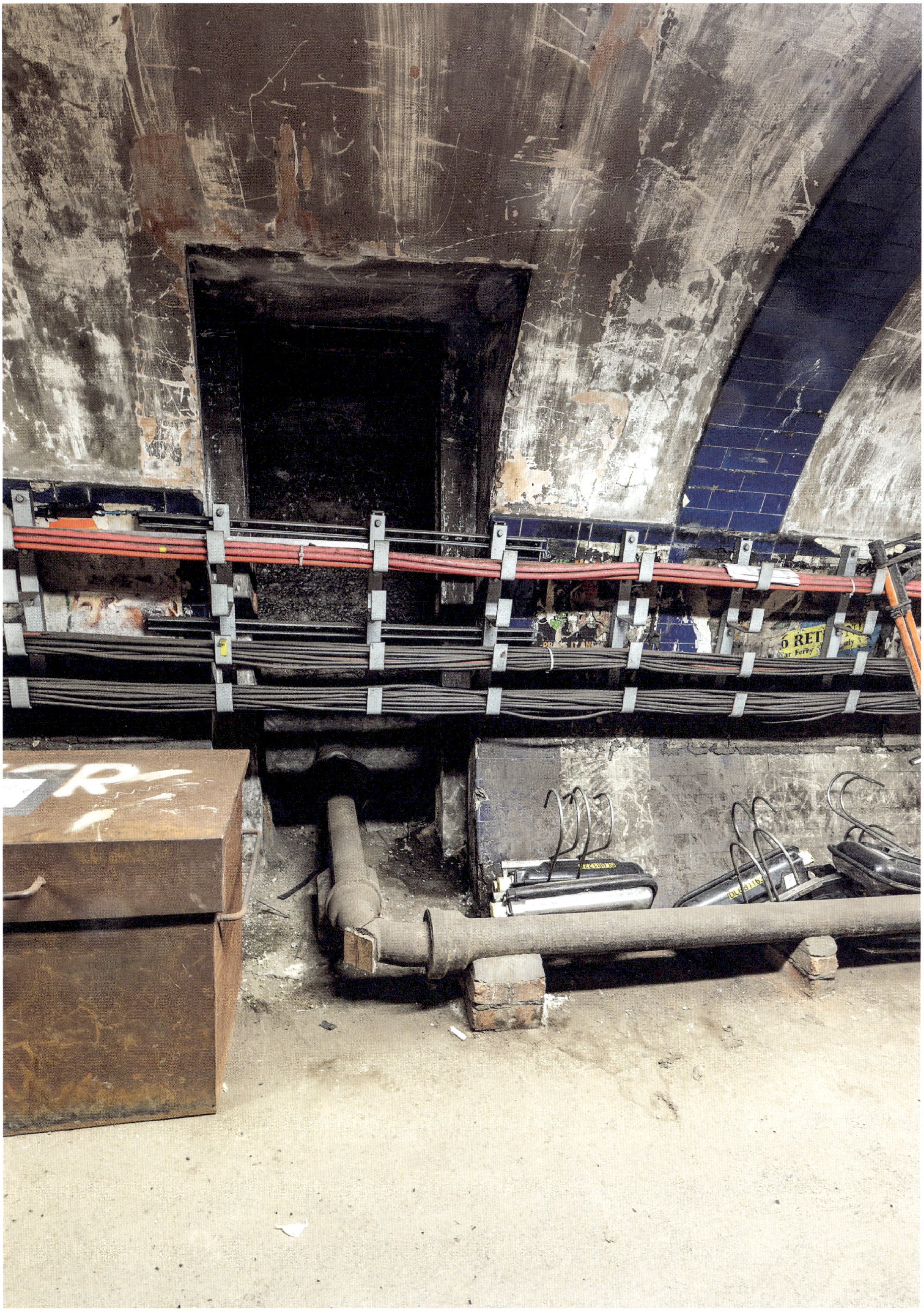

tunnels, glazed ceramic tiles were used to create unique colour patterns, helping customers to recognise their destination. At each station, there are usually one or two tiles with the names of the tile supplier and maker fired into them. Referred to as the 'maker's tiles', these are normally found near the lift shafts [FIG.9].

Even when objects have been removed completely, it is often possible to identify what was once in place from the impressions left behind, known as 'witness marks'. Wall-mounted office clocks, for example, which were installed in stations during the Second World War, leave a distinctive circular pattern, despite having been in situ for just a handful of years. The ghostly traces of Underground tiles are even easier to spot from the 'keystone' cement combing patterns used to hold them in place. In this case, the remaining marks are so distinctive that it is possible to estimate the date of the missing tiles from the marks they leave behind.

Some of the most innocuous looking spaces can have the most interesting stories, uncovered by an examination of the physical evidence. At Euston, for example, an initial site visit revealed an unusual doorway in a passageway; it did not appear on the original station plans and had been crudely backfilled with concrete [FIG.11]. Further research revealed the secret history of an additional piece of tunnel built for war service, reused as part of the construction of the Victoria line (see Euston, pp.203–21). At Down Street, the research team used physical witness marks and evidence of services to map out rooms that had been constructed for a secret Second World War bunker and subsequently demolished. The original London Transport plans for the conversion had been scrapped long ago but comparative analysis of the construction techniques used at Down Street and a similar facility in the neighbouring Dover Street bunker allowed the team to determine the layout. A further study of equipment used at Clapham South deep-level shelter confirmed the purpose of the remains of sanitary equipment at Down Street, allowing us to discover the function of individual rooms.

More familiar to cavers than commuters, stalagmites and stalactites are common features in abandoned underground tunnels. They are created from water seepage, which dissolves mineral deposits as it flows. As the water drips and partially evaporates, the deposited minerals slowly build up – growing downwards from the ceiling as stalactites and upwards from the floor as stalagmites.

In operational stations, the tunnels are fitted with decorative linings designed to seal or drain away any minor leaks and drips, but in disused stations or unlined tunnels these subterranean formations are free to develop. The most common of these are calthemite straws: delicate, hollow structures that develop slowly in the warmth of Underground tunnels, but more quickly than they would in a cave [FIG.12]. The merest touch is enough to break them, but undisturbed, in still air, these straws can develop to an impressive length and very occasionally reach the ground, where they join up with the stalagmites beneath them.

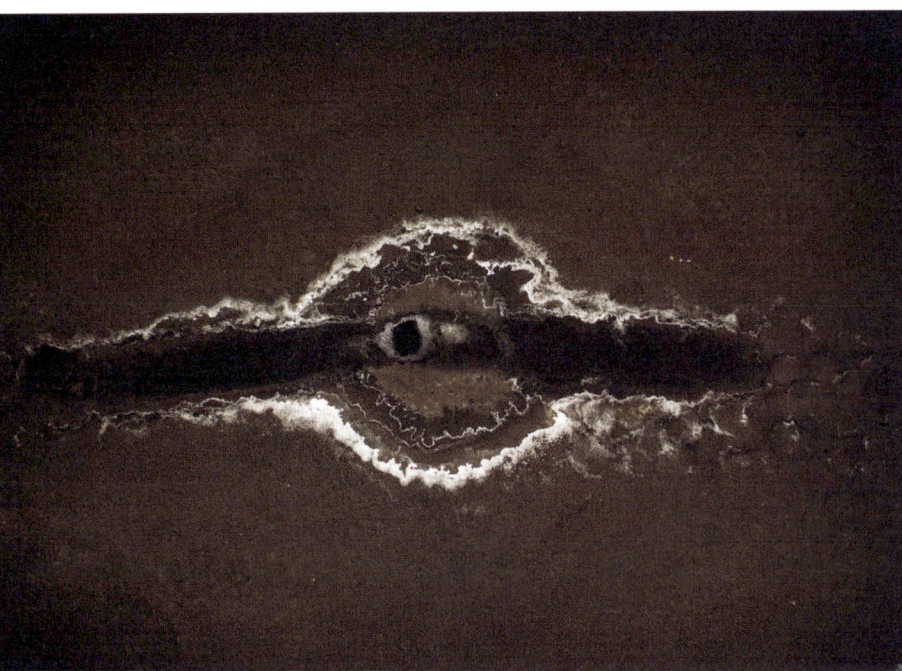

[FIG.12] ABOVE LEFT Calthemite straws, such as this one at King William Street, can take decades to form but shatter at the slightest curious touch.

[FIG.13] ABOVE RIGHT The air flow in tunnels, caused by train movement or fans, can sometimes direct water and create unexpected patterns. Here, at Down Street, a single drip from the ceiling has gradually drawn on the floor what could be seen as a London Underground 'bullseye' roundel.

COMPANY NAMES

The story of the various privately owned railway companies that created the early Underground, and their later amalgamation to form the unified system we know today, is a complex one and outside the scope of the current book. Tube lines are normally referred to in this book by their modern names (the Northern or Piccadilly lines, for example), rather than the operating company, or legal entity, that first built them. Some information about these pioneering companies is useful, however, in understanding how the network evolved:

UNDERGROUND ELECTRIC RAILWAYS OF LONDON LTD (UERL): Often shortened to 'the Underground' or 'Underground Group', this private company existed from 1902 to 1933 and included most of the deep tube railways, the sub-surface District Railway and many of the principal London tram and bus operators.

METROPOLITAN RAILWAY: Opened in 1863, the Metropolitan was the world's first underground railway. It remained independent of the Underground Group until the amalgamation of the two in 1933.

LONDON PASSENGER TRANSPORT BOARD (LPTB): Formed in 1933, the LPTB (or LT, for short) was the result of amalgamating several public transport organisations to create a publicly accountable body for London's underground railway, bus and tram network. The title 'London Transport' was retained for almost 70 years, despite successive changes to the entity's governing body.

TRANSPORT FOR LONDON: In 2000 London Transport became part of the newly formed Transport for London, responsible to the elected Mayor of London, with an enlarged remit to include river services, taxis and private hire, street management and some overground railways.

There were also over 130 independent mainline railway companies in Britain by about 1910. The majority of these were grouped together by the government in 1923 to form the 'Big Four': London & North Eastern Railway (LNER), Great Western Railway (GWR), Southern Railway (SR) and London, Midland & Scottish Railway (LMSR). All four had extensive London networks and worked closely with the Underground. In 1948 the mainline railways were nationalised to create British Railways, which survived until privatisation in the 1990s.

HIDDEN LONDON TOURS

London Transport Museum launched the Hidden London tour programme in 2015 as an expansion of the previous, curator-led walking tours of disused Underground stations. The knowledge of museum staff and volunteers, together with the support of Transport for London, has allowed previously inaccessible spaces to be opened up through tours led by expert guides. The tours are rooted in a sense of curiosity and founded on new primary research, industrial archaeology and privileged access for exploration. Each of the tours has a different narrative, but all address the common themes of why the respective sites were built, why they became disused, how they have been used and modified since, who was there and what interesting things survive to be seen or experienced.

For more details about the current range of tours available, please visit ltmuseum.co.uk.

[FIGS 14 & 15] The atmospheric passageways of Aldwych station, as experienced on a Hidden London tour.

1   In addition to the unconfirmed, and often outlandish, claims regarding secret government reuse of Underground spaces, abandoned stations have provided the backdrop for several works of fiction, including *Underground* by Tobias Hill (1999) and 'South Kentish Town' by John Betjeman (1951, fig.3), and films such as *Death Line* (1972), the latter featuring the flesh-eating troglodytes mentioned above. Redundant underground locations appear even more often on film and in television dramas, re-skinned as real or fictitious locations. For a comprehensive list of both, see http://www.nickcooper.org.uk/subterra/lu/lufilmtv/lufandtv.htm, accessed 17 December 2018.

2   The best detailed history of the Tube is by Desmond F. Croome and Alan A. Jackson, *Rails Through the Clay: A History of London's Tube Railways* (Capital Transport, 1993). There are many other excellent accounts of the Underground's fascinating story, from general surveys to specific histories exploring the different railway companies, rolling stock, the system's design heritage and its social history. One of the most accessible of these is David Bownes, Oliver Green and Sam Mullins, *Underground: How the Tube Shaped London* (Penguin, 2012), which was produced in conjunction with the 150th anniversary of the Underground in 2013.

3   The complex business of funding the early Tube is admirably and clearly explained in Stephen Halliday, *Underground to Everywhere: London's Underground Railway in the Life of the Capital* (Sutton Publishing, 2001). For a more general introduction to the importance of American financial support, and especially the influence of the Chicagoan entrepreneur Charles Tyson Yerkes, see Bownes, Green and Mullins 2012, pp.81–9.

4   The best account of Tube sheltering is provided by John Gregg in *The Shelter of the Tubes: Tube Sheltering in Wartime London* (Capital Transport, 2001), while Andrew Emmerson and Tony Beard give an overview of the use made by government agencies of abandoned Underground locations in *London's Secret Tubes* (Capital Transport, 2009). For background information regarding transport planning during the war, and a social history-focused account of Tube sheltering, see Bownes, Green and Mullins 2012, chpt. 4.

5   TFL Archive (LT 000527/002/002).

6   For an account of Pick's antipathy to the suggestion, see Bownes, Green and Mullins 2012, pp.154–62.

7   For a comprehensive history of the tiling patterns used at Tube stations, see Douglas Rose, *Tiles of the Unexpected Underground: A Study of Six Miles of Geometric Tile Patterns on the London Underground* (London, 2007).

Watertight doors must be kept closed at all times - contact PREMISES AND STRUCTURES-INSPECTION ENGINEER auto 38628 for access

No smoking

KING WILLIAM STREET

THE FIRST DISUSED TUBE STATION

[FIG.16] PREVIOUS The sealed tunnel entrance leading from King William Street station under the Thames.

[FIG.17] ABOVE A cutaway illustration showing how construction of the City & South London railway began in 1886. In a breathtaking example of Victorian engineering self-confidence, work was carried out directly under the Thames, with a shaft sunk from Old Swan Pier (on the north bank) to a point well below the river bed. All equipment, including the tunnelling shields, was sent down the shaft and assembled underground, with twin tunnels, one above the other, driven in each direction.

Deep beneath London's historic banking district lie the decaying remains of the world's first Tube terminus: King William Street, bypassed and abandoned in 1900 as the network expanded. The connecting, small-bore tunnels running under the Thames, which once transported thousands of passengers every day to their jobs in the City or homes in the suburbs, were abandoned at the same time and now echo with the sounds of ships' propellers overhead. The tunnels are an unreal-seeming place, where fragile calthemite straws hang precariously from rusting tunnel rings and where relics from the nineteenth century show how this forgotten space was occasionally woken to serve a new purpose.

The most dramatic of these interventions was the refurbishment of the station and sections of tunnel for use as an air raid shelter during the Second World War – a process that stripped away many, but not all, of the original Victorian fixtures. In 2018, almost 130 years after construction, the future of King William Street came to be bound up with the capital's latest civil engineering project, the massive subterranean upgrade of Bank station.

WORLD'S FIRST ELECTRIC UNDERGROUND RAILWAY

It all started so well. On Tuesday 4 November 1890, the Prince of Wales boarded the inaugural train of the world's first deep-level, electric tube railway at King William Street station. Everything about the railway, named the City & South London (C&SLR), was modern and progressive [FIG.17].[1] From the hydraulically powered passenger lifts to the specially designed electric locomotives running in tunnels 23 metres (75 feet) below street level, this was cutting-edge urban transport for the new century. At the royal reception later that day, the company chairman called it a 'masterpiece of engineering genius'.[2] A month later, the first passenger trains began running from suburban Stockwell in south London to the King William Street terminus in the heart of the City. The journey of nearly five kilometres took just 18 minutes and, with one flat fare for all, it was both quicker and cheaper than taking the bus, tram or steam railway.

Contemporary newspapers were full of praise for the convenience of the service and the clean, neatly laid out stations, lit by gas and glazed with white reflective tiles bordered by tiles bearing a brown leaf pattern.[3] Comparing King William Street with the sulphurous stations on the rival, steam-hauled underground (opened in 1863), one editorial commented that the former 'stands for civilisation, the others for barbarism'.[4]

Passengers entered the station via the ground floor of an existing building on the corner of Arthur Street (now Monument Street), which housed both the booking hall and railway company headquarters. Below ground, the platforms were reached by two hydraulic lifts, with a spiral staircase installed for emergencies. Yet, despite the convenience of the services, the modernity of the stations and the favourable press response, things did not go as planned at the City terminus.

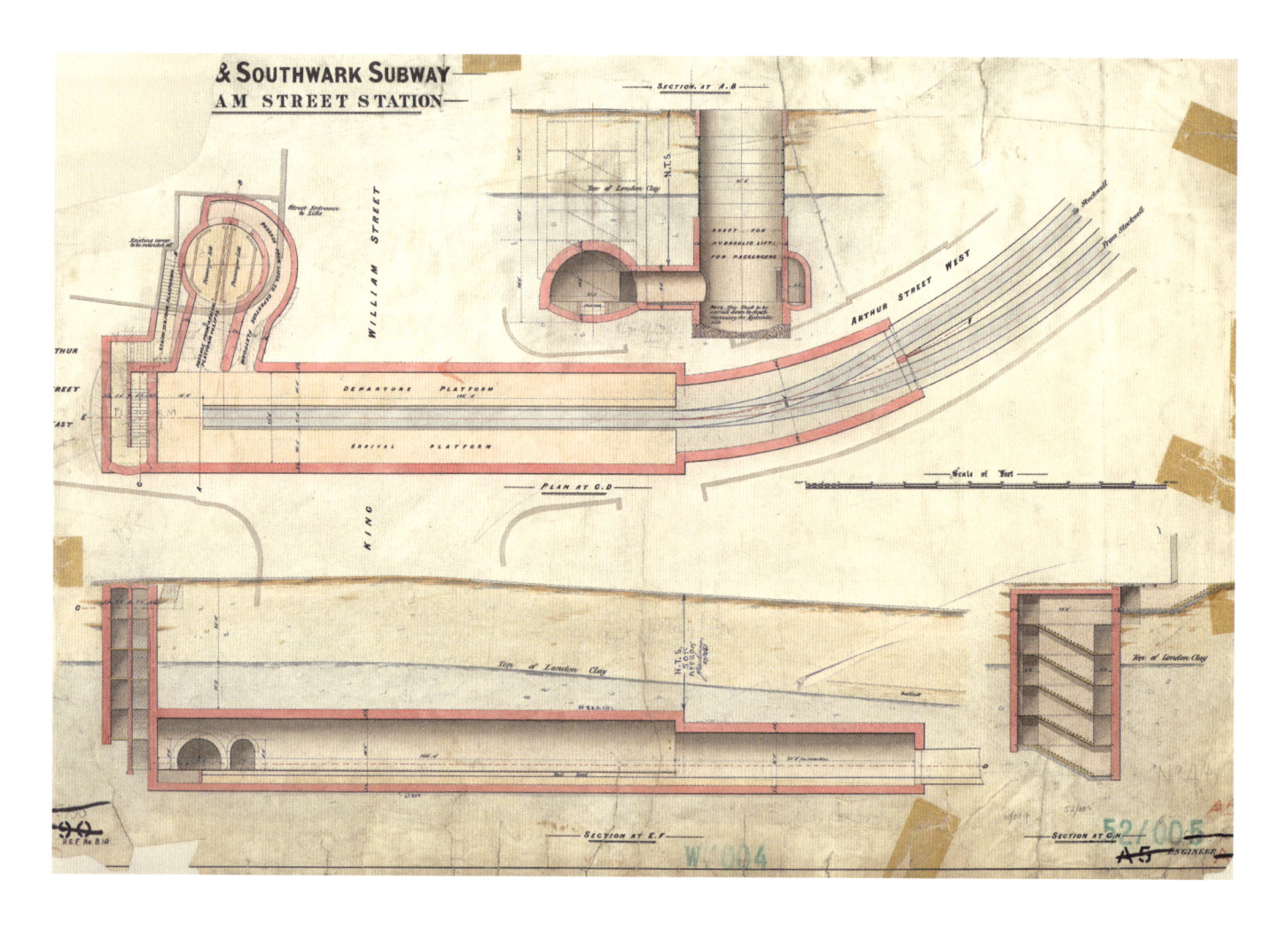

[FIG.18] A recently rediscovered engineering drawing showing King William Street as built in 1890, including the original crossover junction leading to a single-track platform for both arrivals and departures. This bottleneck arrangement was to cause severe operational problems later.

'AN ENGINEERING FAILURE'

The problem for the world's first deep-level tube railway was that it applied several new technologies for the first time and thus suffered the fate of many pioneers, who have been forced to learn from costly mistakes. The railway had been built using revolutionary tunnelling techniques developed by the engineer James Henry Greathead.[5] As this was an untested method, parliament had insisted that the railway follow the route of public thoroughfares as far as possible to avoid potential damage to existing buildings. On the north side of the river this meant following the narrow Swan Lane on its approach to King William Street, with the result that the tunnels here were built with steep gradients and sharp curves that were to cause severe operational difficulties from the day of opening [FIG.18].[6]

At the planning stage, this had not concerned the engineers greatly, as the railway was intended to be cable-hauled – a technology that could handle steep inclines. However, contemporary developments in electric traction convinced the promoters to switch to electricity during the construction phase. This required the invention of an entirely new type of electric locomotive and the construction of a coal-fired power station at Stockwell to generate the required wattage. Both projects represented a significant challenge in Victorian London and demanded innovative solutions.

[FIG.19] BELOW LEFT A drawing from 1890 of the King William Street terminus, showing the original single-track bay, flanked by two platforms for departure and arrival. The station layout was reconfigured with a central platform and two tracks in 1895.

[FIG.20] BELOW TOP RIGHT The street-level entrance to the station at No.46 King William Street, 1890s. Unlike other surface stations on the line, which were purpose-built with a distinctive architectural style, the booking office at King William Street was installed in an existing office building.

[FIG.21] BELOW BOTTOM RIGHT Driver Thomas Pemberton photographed in 1922 with one of the original City & South London locomotives he drove on the day of the royal opening. The engines were built by the Salford firm of Mather & Platt.

As it turned out, the steep curves and gradients at King William Street were simply too much for the early electric motors to cope with, and trains would often grind to a halt at the bottom of the approach. Embarrassingly, this happened during the Prince of Wales's inaugural trip. Drivers had been warned in advance to request assistance from a spare locomotive if they had trouble making the ascent. On this occasion, however, the foreman in charge instructed driver Thomas Pemberton merely to roll back down the incline and have another go. It did not work, and a protocol was subsequently introduced to allow the locomotive from the next train to be decoupled and allowed to help push the stranded train into the station [FIG.21].[7] That such instruction was necessary hardly inspired confidence in Greathead's 'masterpiece of engineering genius'.

The short and poorly thought-out platform layout at King William Street also caused operational difficulties [FIGS 18 & 19]. Overcrowding was common, especially when trains were delayed making the run up to the station. As the lifts continued to disgorge passengers, the situation could quickly turn ugly. In March 1891, for example, 'City gentlemen and others of a somewhat rough class' found themselves in conflict with station staff as they tried to escape the dangerously busy conditions.[8]

At the half-yearly board meeting in February 1892, Charles Mott, the company chairman, conceded that King William Street station and the approaching tunnels had been 'an engineering failure'.[9] Although improvements could be made, the restricted layout limited options and, in the end, a scheme was approved to build an entirely new stretch of tunnel from the new Borough station (south of the river) to Moorgate, bypassing King William Street altogether.

In the meantime, some modifications were made to the station, including the addition of a ladies' waiting room and left luggage office at street level – both unnecessary echoes of traditional railway operation, presumably insisted on by genteel passengers travelling into town. Below ground, capacity remained limited, while passenger numbers continued to grow, reaching 15,000 a day by 1895.

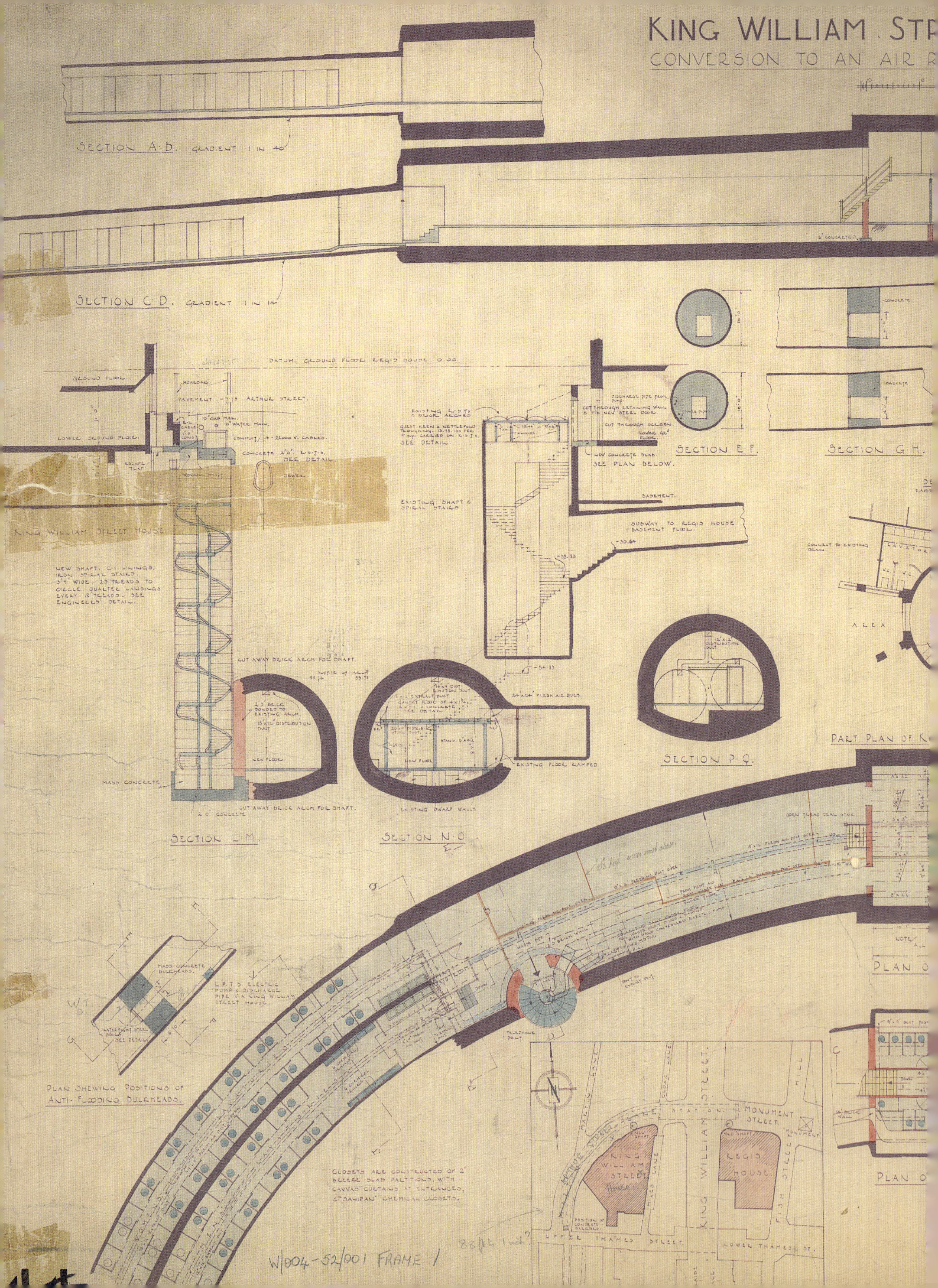

KING WILLIAM
CONVERSION TO AN AIR
SECTION A.B. GRADIENT 1 IN 40
SECTION C.D. GRADIENT 1 IN 14
DATUM. GROUND FLOOR REGIS HOUSE 0.00
GROUND FLOOR
LOWER GROUND FLOOR
PAVEMENT. ARTHUR STREET.
KING WILLIAM STREET HOUSE
NEW SHAFT. C.I. LININGS. IRON SPIRAL STAIRS. 3'9" WIDE. 23 TREADS TO CIRCLE. QUARTER LANDINGS EVERY 12 TREADS. SEE ENGINEERS' DETAIL.
EXISTING SHAFT & SPIRAL STAIRS
SUBWAY TO REGIS HOUSE BASEMENT FLOOR.
BASEMENT.
NEW CONCRETE SLAB SEE PLAN BELOW.
CUT AWAY BRICK ARCH FOR SHAFT.
MASS CONCRETE
NEW FLOOR
EXISTING FLOOR RAMPED
EXISTING DWARF WALLS
SECTION E.F.
SECTION G.H.
SECTION L.M.
SECTION N.O.
SECTION P.Q.
PART PLAN OF
PLAN SHEWING POSITIONS OF ANTI-FLOODING BULKHEADS.
MASS CONCRETE BULKHEADS.
CLOSETS ARE CONSTRUCTED OF 2" BREEZE SLAB PARTITIONS, WITH CANVAS CURTAINS AT ENTRANCES, 2" "DAWIPAN" CHEMICAL CLOSETS.
KING WILLIAM STREET
REGIS HOUSE
MONUMENT STREET.
UPPER THAMES STREET.
LOWER THAMES ST.
W/004-52/001 FRAME 1

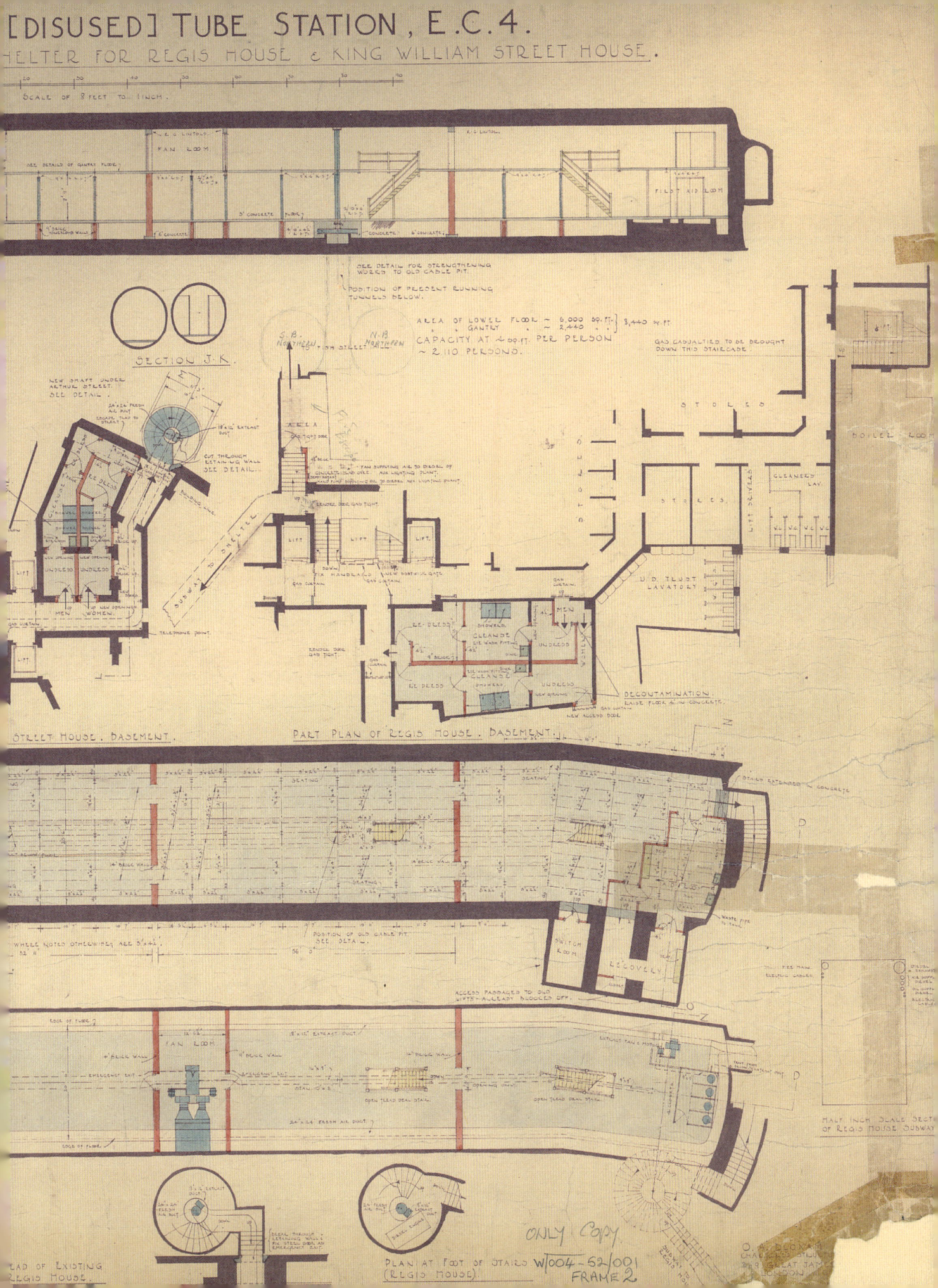

[DISUSED] TUBE STATION, E.C.4.
SHELTER FOR REGIS HOUSE & KING WILLIAM STREET HOUSE.

[FIG.22] PREVIOUS King William Street station air raid shelter conversion drawing, 1940. Among the many fascinating details are the gas decontamination chambers installed in the basements of the adjoining office blocks, together with the new station access shaft sunk in Arthur Street for workers at King William Street House.

CLOSURE

Work on the replacement route from Borough to Moorgate began in 1896 and the line was ready for passengers by 1900. Intermediate stations were conveniently situated at London Bridge (for interchange with the mainline railways) and at Bank, close to the original King William Street terminus. The latter, together with the original tunnels under the Thames, was now completely bypassed and officially closed on 25 December 1900. This was the first stretch of the Underground to close in London.

Railway Magazine was incensed. 'The present disused railways of the City & South London Railway under the Thames is [sic] apparently forgotten. How much unremunerative capital is sunk in it?' asked the magazine's editorial two months after the closure.[10] Perhaps surprisingly, there was very little comment from daily newspapers, possibly because the replacement stations at Bank and Moorgate were better situated for commuters. It had, however, been a costly mistake for the railway company, which looked for alternative ways to recoup its investment in the now-disused tunnels.

ATTEMPTED REUSE

An obvious solution was for the cross-river section to become part of a new transport scheme. This had seemed possible briefly when an associated company, the City & Brixton Railway, obtained permission to take over the line in 1898, but the plans came to nothing. Similarly, suggestions made over ten years later that the disused space could be used for cultivating mushrooms or as a bonded store failed to attract much interest.[11] It seems that the railway was holding out for a more lucrative offer from a utility company grateful for the opportunity to lay cables under the Thames at a cut-price rate. Again, no offer came.

By 1914, the tunnels were being used primarily to store surplus railway stock and engineering supplies. The onset of war with Germany the same year caused a brief moment of panic for the Underground authorities, when the editor of *Railway and Travel Monthly* alleged that the tunnels might be used as a base for enemy agents. This resulted in a thorough, and fruitless, police search of the area. It also led to the removal of the track (supposedly in the interests of safety), while entrances to the old station and tube tunnels were securely sealed.[12]

For the next 15 years the line was regularly inspected by engineers, but otherwise allowed to slowly decay. By now, the C&SLR had become part of the much larger Underground Group (see p.33), and in 1930, the company decided the time had come to dispose of the station and tunnels by sale or lease.[13] A special tour was laid on for selected journalists as a prelude to the sale [FIG.24], led by the transport historian and Underground employee Charles Lee. What these visitors found was a staggering time capsule of the Victorian era as it was left at the moment the station was closed 30 years earlier [FIGS 23, 25, 26]. As Lee described it, for readers of the *Railway Magazine*:

> The present means of access is through what was formerly the emergency staircase, and this is reached from a cellar under 46, King William Street, the premises which constituted the booking office of the original terminal station. Descending this gloomy circular stairway by the light of two

acetylene flares, our party reached the old platform level with the feeling of having turned back a page of history and recalled those sensations, forgotten by the present generation, which were experienced by the inaugural party through this, the world's first electric tube railway, some forty years ago. As now existing, the old station still retains sufficient traces of its former equipment to enable a fair idea to be gained of its working condition, although the tracks have been entirely, and the platform partially, removed. At the platform level the station consists of a circular brick tunnel, with a centre platform and the sites of the lines on either side. Openings give access to the old lift shaft, which formerly contained two hydraulic lifts. The shaft has been covered over and the top portion now is utilised for shop premises. Remains of gas fixtures are a reminder that the stations were lighted by gas during the first ten years of the railway's existence, electricity being introduced gradually thereafter at first only on the newer stations. The 'King William Street' station names are still in position in two or three places. At the end of the platform are the remains of the signal box still containing its 22 hand-operated levers. Three of the two-position semaphores are in position. One, at least, of which it may be hoped will be preserved in the company's museum. Beyond the station, the brick tunnel ceases and the line enters the two iron tubes. Our party proceeded along the left-hand tube. The point where the other tube crosses over is easily noticed and the two tracks are connected by an iron ladder.[14]

The press were less impressed. Noting the inaccessible location and dank conditions, the Leeds Mercury concluded that 'there is hardly likely to be very brisk competition for the two tunnels', adding that even London County Council had rejected the site for storage.[15] The assessment proved prescient, and further attempts to find a buyer were dropped.

The station and tunnels might have remained mothballed had not world events intervened. As the threat posed by Nazi Germany became ever more apparent, attention began to turn to how Londoners might be protected from aerial attack in the event of a new conflict. Against this background of growing concern, one journalist from the Star newspaper visited the disused station in early 1936. After considering several alternative uses for the space, including a dance hall and wine cellars, he made a more accurate prediction: it would make an ideal bombproof air raid shelter.[16]

THE KING WILLIAM STREET SHELTER

The suggestion was not immediately taken up, as the European crisis lurched from seeming resolution and back again. The outbreak of war in September 1939, however, provoked a renewed sense of urgency, and the abandoned station and tunnels were now viewed as offering potential air-raid protection for the office blocks above. The original surface building had long since been replaced by Regis House and, in early 1940, the owners took out a lease from London Transport to convert the disused underground space for staff use.

Considerable work was required to turn the dilapidated station into an air raid shelter [FIGS 22 & 27], including the installation of a second floor in the station

[FIG.23] RIGHT A poster hoarding for the auctioneer Douglas Young, frozen in time when King William Street closed in February 1900. The photograph was taken on a press visit to the abandoned station in 1930.

[FIG.24] BELOW *The Daily Mirror* was one of several newspapers invited to visit the disused station in 1930 as part of the publicity surrounding the proposed sale.

Wednesday, April 2, 1930   THE DAILY MIRROR   Page 5

OLD STATION AND DERELICT TUNNELS UNDER THE THAMES FOR SALE

The old King William-street station, once the terminus of London's first electric tube, running from King William-street to Borough, now for sale.

Abandoned subways of the line, which pass under the Thames above London Bridge, and, with the station, await a purchaser. An offer was made some time ago by a prospective mushroom grower.—("Daily Mirror" photographs.)

[FIG.25] ABOVE The remains of the platform and wooden signal box, 1930. Incredibly, two rusting semaphore signals, complete with lamps, are still in place above the departure and arrival bays, although the track has long been removed.

[FIG.26] RIGHT A murky view of the station tunnel, with most of the Victorian painted station name still legible, 1930.

[FIG.27] ABOVE A press photograph of the former station tunnel during conversion, 16 March 1940. Described as being a 'luxury shelter', a First Aid post and ventilation unit can be seen at the back of the picture. The posters are an odd mix of government propaganda and pre-war travel publicity.

[FIG.28] RIGHT A wartime government information poster by Fougasse (Cyril Bird), photographed in situ at King William Street during an enthusiasts' tour organised by London Underground in 1977.

tunnel to provide additional space. Toilet blocks were built into the old running tunnels, together with an air ventilation system and kitchen.[17] A new entrance shaft was also sunk in Arthur Street to give direct access from the basement of a second office block, King William Street House, which shared the shelter.

In June 1940 London Transport's staff magazine, *Pennyfare*, reported that the completed shelter could accommodate 2,000 office workers and had cost about £20,000 to convert.[18] But not everyone was happy with the way the conversion had been managed. The following September, at the height of the aerial bombardment known as the Blitz, the *Daily Herald* criticised the City Corporation (and, by implication, London Transport) for permitting such a strategically positioned shelter to remain in private hands. According to the paper, the shelter was being used primarily by the owners of Regis House and King William Street House to carry on 'a proportion of their normal business activities' during the day, rather than providing night-time shelter for those in need.[19] The point was reiterated a month later when the *Daily Herald* called on the Corporation to order the owners to open the shelter for the general public.[20] However, it remained in private hands for the duration of the war and appears to have been used only by office staff and their families, who chose to shelter in the City at night.

After the war, the tenancy was retained, and the converted station continued to be used for document storage well into the 1970s. With no need for structural modifications, many of the wartime adaptations and fixtures, including morale-raising propaganda posters, remained in place until relatively recently [FIG.28].

THE SOUTHWARK SHELTER

South of the river, the outbreak of war in 1939 resulted in similar negotiations between Southwark Council and London Transport regarding the possible conversion of the disused Tube tunnels abandoned at the same time as King William Street station. The twin tunnels under the Thames were regarded as highly vulnerable to a direct hit from high explosives and had been blocked off with concrete plugs at the time of the Munich Crisis a year earlier.[21] Now, with the very real threat of aerial attack and without enough deep-level shelters to protect citizens, Southwark Council proposed a scheme for converting nearly a kilometre of disused tunnels into one of London's largest public shelters, capable of accommodating 8,000 people. The plan was approved by the Minister of Home Security, Sir John Anderson, in December 1940 and work began a month later. Surprisingly, given its status as a publicly-owned body and the supposedly shared endeavour of wartime emergency, London Transport charged the council £100 annual rent and insisted that all works would be reversed as a condition of handover once the crisis had passed.[22]

Conversion work, which included the addition of eight new entrances, an air-conditioning plant, electricity, seating, toilets, first aid posts and a strong room for council papers, was expected to take three months and cost about £40–50,000. In the event, the works proved far more extensive than initially estimated, and the final bill came to £105,628 in January 1943.

The shelter opened to the public on 24 June 1940, six days after the start of the Blitz. By August, thousands of people were sleeping in the tunnels every night. Wardens and staff were provided by the council, while charitable organisation The Salvation Army undertook catering duties from February 1941. The shelter remained in use throughout the war, continuing to host Londoners even after the immediate threat of air attack had subsided.

After the war, the tunnels again fell into disuse, although they were maintained by the council until 1960, when they were refurbished and returned to London Transport. In 1968 and 1969 a section of the disused tunnel was reused for a ventilation system installed as part of the London Bridge station upgrade.

KING WILLIAM STREET IN MODERN TIMES

Since its short-lived reincarnation as a private air raid shelter, the abandoned King William Street station has held a special fascination for those interested in subterranean London. Intrigued by its snapshots of the Victorian era and wartime London, later visitors were struck by how much physical evidence remained, undisturbed by the passage of time. One such visitor was the explorer Ranulph Fiennes, who included the station in a documentary made for the BBC in 1971.[23] Another was the journalist Handel Kardas, who described the unnerving experience of entering 'another world of old, musty tunnels and twisting stairways' for a 1992 article in *Railway World*.[24] Among the relics still in situ at that time were sections of original, nineteenth-century tiling [FIG.31] and structures installed during the Second World War, such as the two-tier station shelter, ventilation units, wartime notices and toilet blocks [FIGS 29 & 30].

It was not just wartime memorabilia that struck visitors as unusual. The disused tunnels running under the Thames had an atmosphere all of their own, which changed depending on the tide [FIG.32]. This, combined with the noises of rivercraft above, created a disconcerting environment, as one filmmaker discovered on a visit in 1989:

> Strange, eerie, thin layers of mist would form, hanging in the air and catch you unawares when your torch lit them. On the upper level you can see the brick dome that holds back the Thames. At low tide, it felt like being in a submarine waiting to be depth charged, looking up, following the sound of the pleasure boat propwash [sic] slowly getting louder and louder until it was right above you, then fading as it passed.
>
> This, combined with the long delay echo of our voices coming back at us down the tunnel from the concrete bulkhead on the other side of the river, spooked all of us and raised hairs on the back of your neck. Then your torch would go out![25]

By the early twenty first century, most of the wartime posters had disintegrated due to changes in how the space was ventilated, while part of the old southbound running tunnel was cut through during the Jubilee line extension works at London Bridge. In an echo of the C&SLR directors' initial aims for the disused tunnels, cables and fibre optics have been installed along part of the route.

Nowadays, the station itself is a construction site, traversed at the south end by an excavation shaft installed as part of the £500 million upgrade of nearby Bank station. The work, which will result in a new Northern line tunnel and

[FIGS 29 & 30] Wartime fittings at King William Street still in situ during a visit prior to the Bank Tube upgrade. The photograph above shows part of the ventilation plant. The image below shows the mezzanine floor installed above the original platform, with water closets on either side.

[FIG.31] The original emergency stairway installed by the City & South London Railway, complete with Victorian tiling. Following the removal of the lifts, this stairway (accessed via Regis House basement) became the principal way of reaching the disused station.

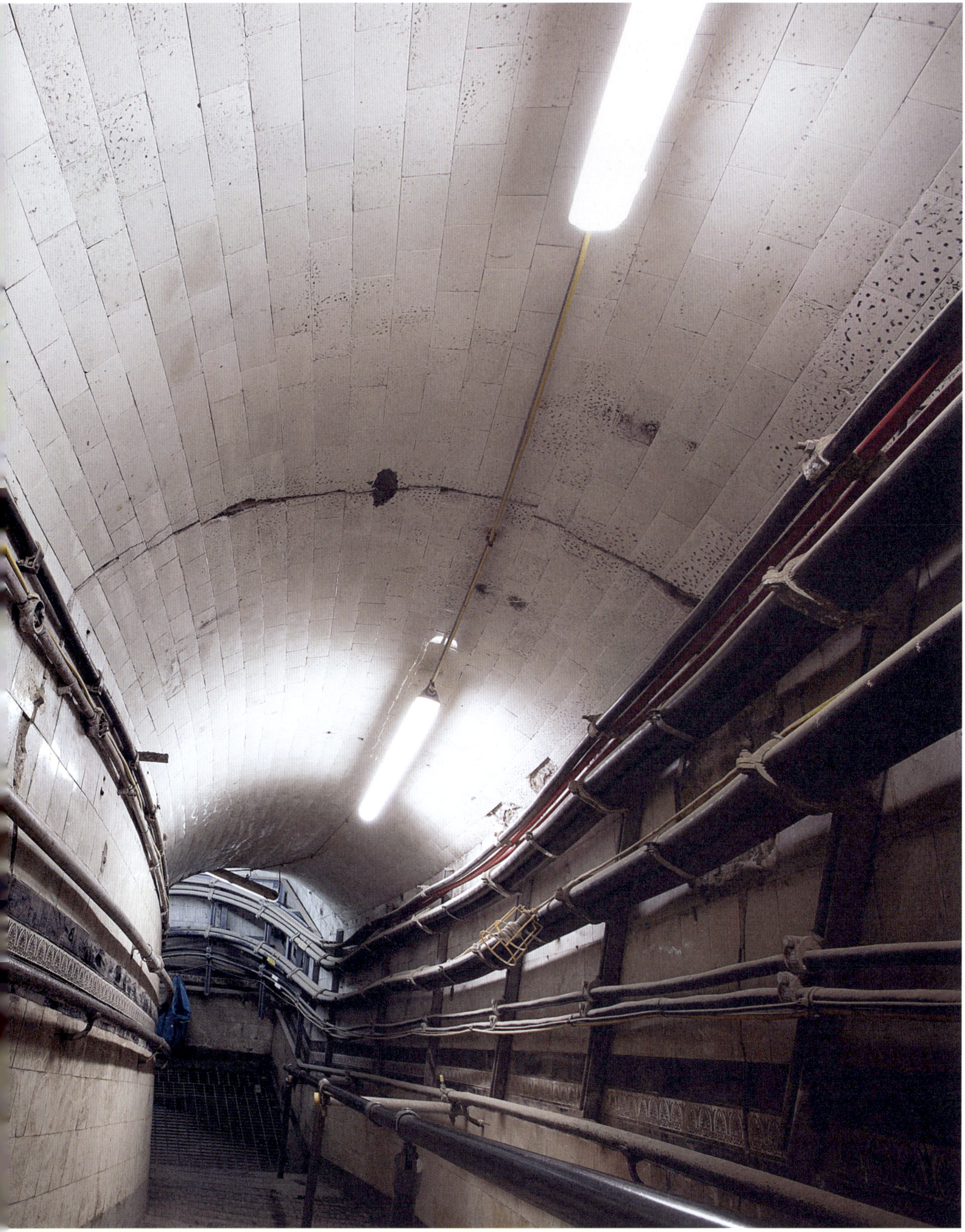

[FIG.32] One of the tunnels under the Thames. The original gradient markers on the tunnel wall record just how steep the approach to the station was at this point, rising 1 in 14 and 1 in 36.

better interchange between lines, is due to be completed in 2020. To facilitate greater access and provide storage for contractors, some of the wartime infrastructure at King William Street has been demolished, although this is scheduled to be reinstated once work is completed.[26] Above ground, the original Regis House was demolished in 1995 and subsequently replaced by a new building of the same name. The location of London's first closed Tube station is now recorded by a blue plaque on the side of a building in Monument Street.

1 For an excellent account of the history and construction of the City & South London Railway, see Printz P. Holman, *Amazing Electric Tube: History of the City and South London Railway* (London Transport Museum, 1990).
2 The royal opening was widely reported by national and regional newspapers. The quote here is from the *Leighton Buzzard Observer*, 11 November 1890, p.6.
3 See, for example, a report on the front page of the *South London Post*, 8 November 1890.
4 *Bristol Mercury*, 7 March 1890, p.3.
5 For Greathead's own account of constructing the C&SLR, see James Henry Greathead, 'The City & South London Railway', *Proceedings of the Institution of Civil Engineers*, vol. cxxiii (1896).
6 For a detailed account of construction at King William Street, see J.E. Connor, *London's Disused Underground Stations* (Capital Transport, 2012), pp.6–13.
7 The incident was recalled by Thomas Pemberton in a retrospective interview with the Underground's in-house magazine, *T.O.T. Staff Magazine*, October 1922, p.7.
8 *Salisbury Times and South Wilts Gazette*, 7 March 1891, p.7.
9 Quoted in the *St. James's Gazette*, 3 February 1892, p.13.
10 *Railway Magazine*, February 1901.
11 Ibid.
12 *Railway and Travel Monthly* [1914], quoted in Connor 2012, p.10.
13 The sale/lease was widely published, with illustrated articles appearing in, for example, the *Daily Mirror*, 2 April 1930, pp.4–5, and the *Sphere*, 12 April 1930, p.74.
14 *Railway Magazine*, September 1930.
15 *Leeds Mercury*, 1 April 1930, p.4.
16 *Star*, 17 March 1936, quoted in Peter Bancroft, *The Railway to King William Street and Southwark Deep Tunnel Air Raid Shelter* (Nebulous Books, 1981), p.5.
17 Running tunnels are tunnels built solely for train operation, as opposed to station tunnels, which house the Underground platforms.
18 *Pennyfare*, June 1940, p.66.
19 *Daily Herald*, 26 September 1941, p.5.
20 *Daily Herald*, 16 October 1941, p.4.
21 Desmond F. Croome and Alan A. Jackson, *Rails Through the Clay: A History of London's Tube Railways* (Capital Transport, 1993), pp.267–8.
22 For the best, and most comprehensive, account of the construction and use of the Southwark air-raid shelter, see Bancroft 1981.
23 Reported in *London Transport Staff Magazine*, June 1971, p.15. The film was broadcast as part of a documentary entitled 'Underground London' in the BBC's *World About Us* series.
24 *Railway World*, April 1992, pp.44–5.
25 Interview with Rob Lansdown, regarding a visit to King William Street in 1989, made as part of the production process for a short film for the London Transport Museum (private correspondence, 19 November 2018).
26 'Bank Station Capacity Upgrade – fact sheet 3', TfL, 2014, http://content.tfl.gov.uk/bcsu-factsheet3-arthur-street-worksite.pdf, accessed 28 January 2019.

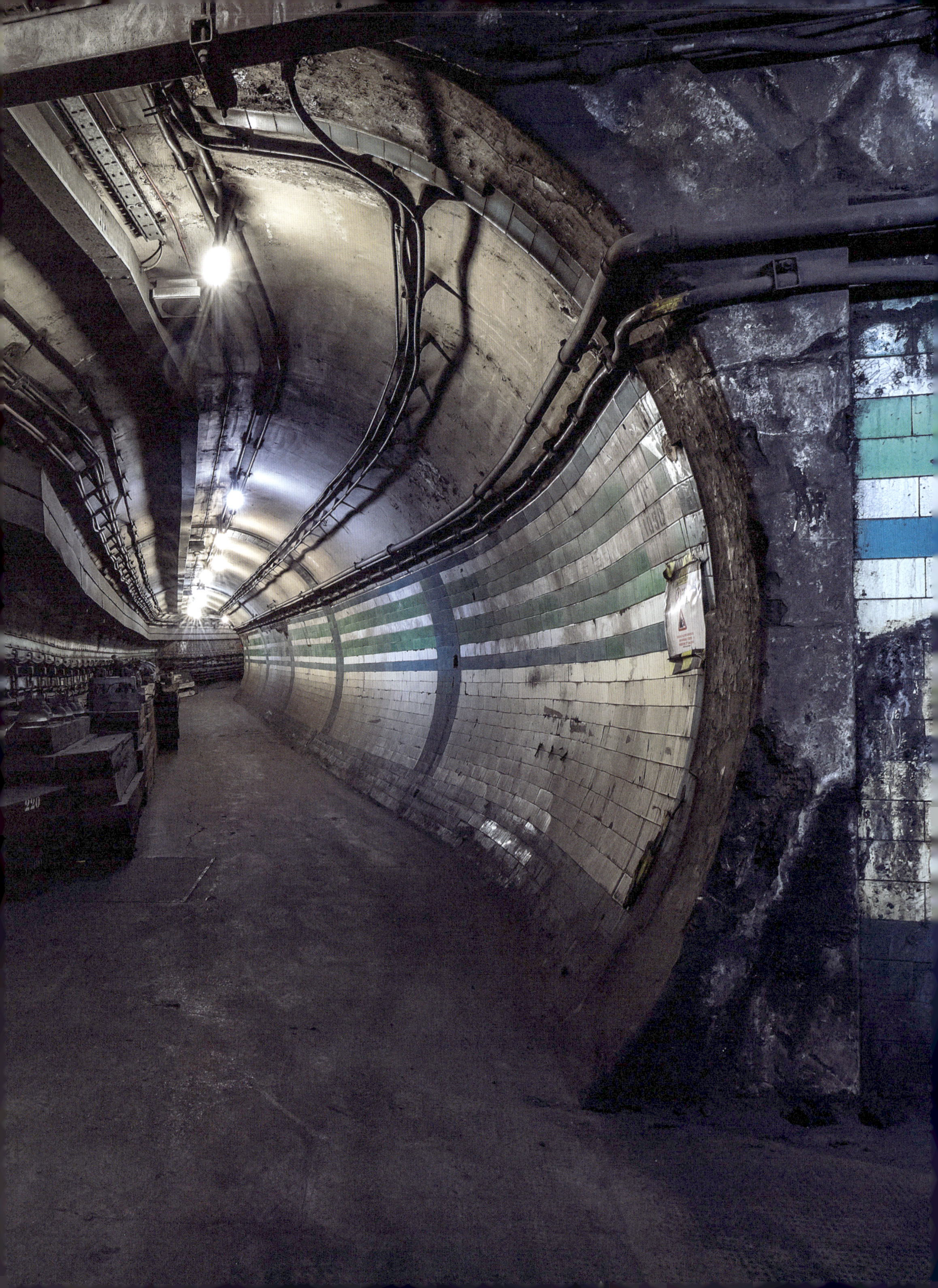

PICCADILLY CIRCUS

A NEW HEART FOR LONDON

[FIG.33] PREVIOUS As well as providing ventilation and housing vital services for the successful running of the Tube, the old passageways and tunnels at Piccadilly Circus are used by London Underground to store materials and tools.

[FIGS 34 & 35] Piccadilly Circus is one of the finest examples of a station originally built with lifts, but later modernised with escalators. The station opened in 1906 serving the Bakerloo and Piccadilly lines. Designed by Leslie Green, the station had three entrances: on Piccadilly Circus itself (above), Haymarket, and Jermyn Street (right), leading to a shared booking hall. The station facades and original booking hall survived until the 1980s, when the whole block was demolished.

The rapid expansion of deep-level tube railways in early-twentieth-century London was enabled by three new technologies: the Greathead tunnelling shield, electrically powered trains and passenger lifts.[1] Lifts were crucial for transporting passengers rapidly between surface-level station buildings and platforms deep below. Passenger use of the Tube had steadily increased in its first few years of operation but numbers boomed during and after the First World War, with millions using the system each day. To cope with increased demand, a new technology, the escalator, was introduced.

The first escalator on the Underground was installed at Earl's Court station on 4 October 1911, allowing passengers to connect quickly between the Piccadilly and District lines. A report in the *London Daily News* suggests that, initially, the public were somewhat suspicious of these moving staircases, regarding them as dangerous and unsafe. Representatives from the paper were sent to test them out. They tried – and failed – to injure themselves and the published report served to reassure the public that the new technology was not only safe, but actually offered many advantages over the use of lifts:

> Its carrying capacity is nearly 12,000 an hour and it never stops. It takes four fast working lifts to carry anything like that number, and the delay to passengers is considerable. In a curious way the staircase too is preferable; it gives no sense of shock of upward or downward motion, as a lift does.[2]

As well as offering a smoother ride and carrying more passengers, the escalator could also be used as an emergency staircase in the event of a power failure, rendering many emergency spiral staircases redundant as well.

Central London stations like Piccadilly Circus, which previously operated with lifts, had escalators installed from 1911, after the successful installation at Earl's Court, to manage increased traffic and to improve passenger flow. As escalators require an incline of around 30 degrees, the vertical shafts, landings and connecting passageways built for the lifts were now unfit for purpose. In some cases, entirely new station entrances had to be built, some distance away from the originals. Thus, the introduction of escalators brought with it a swathe of station reconfigurations and, in some cases, closures, all of which left a significant number of hidden, defunct underground passageways and shafts.

Many of these disused spaces survive as forgotten pockets of history, sitting just beyond the reach of unsuspecting passengers, hurrying by on their daily commute. Piccadilly Circus is one of London's most famous landmarks and its Tube station is an excellent example of a site where escalator installation left large spaces idle. When Piccadilly Circus Underground station reopened in December 1928, it was branded 'A New Heart for London'.[3] With a brand new, ticket hall and escalators replacing the old lifts and entrances, it brought a modern, even luxurious, experience to travellers on the Tube. This reflected Frank Pick's belief that London Transport's purpose was not just to move people around but to civilise the city.

The other stations covered in this chapter have all been selected because they share a history of adaptation and reuse. Much of the original architecture, although hidden, remains in place. Other examples can be found across the modern Tube network but, in many cases, little of interest remains of the original features.[4]

[FIG.36] NEXT The eight lifts at Piccadilly Circus were housed in four shafts sunk to different depths. This diagram of c.1904 shows the Piccadilly line lifts and passageways, as well as the joint emergency staircase, shared with the Bakerloo line, that led to the surface. Traffic at the station was 1.5 million passengers a year in 1907, but by 1922 that number had risen to 18 million.[5] It became apparent that the existing booking hall, lifts and long passageways were not adequate, and a brand new booking hall was planned underneath Piccadilly Circus itself, with escalators to convey passengers to the Underground platforms below.

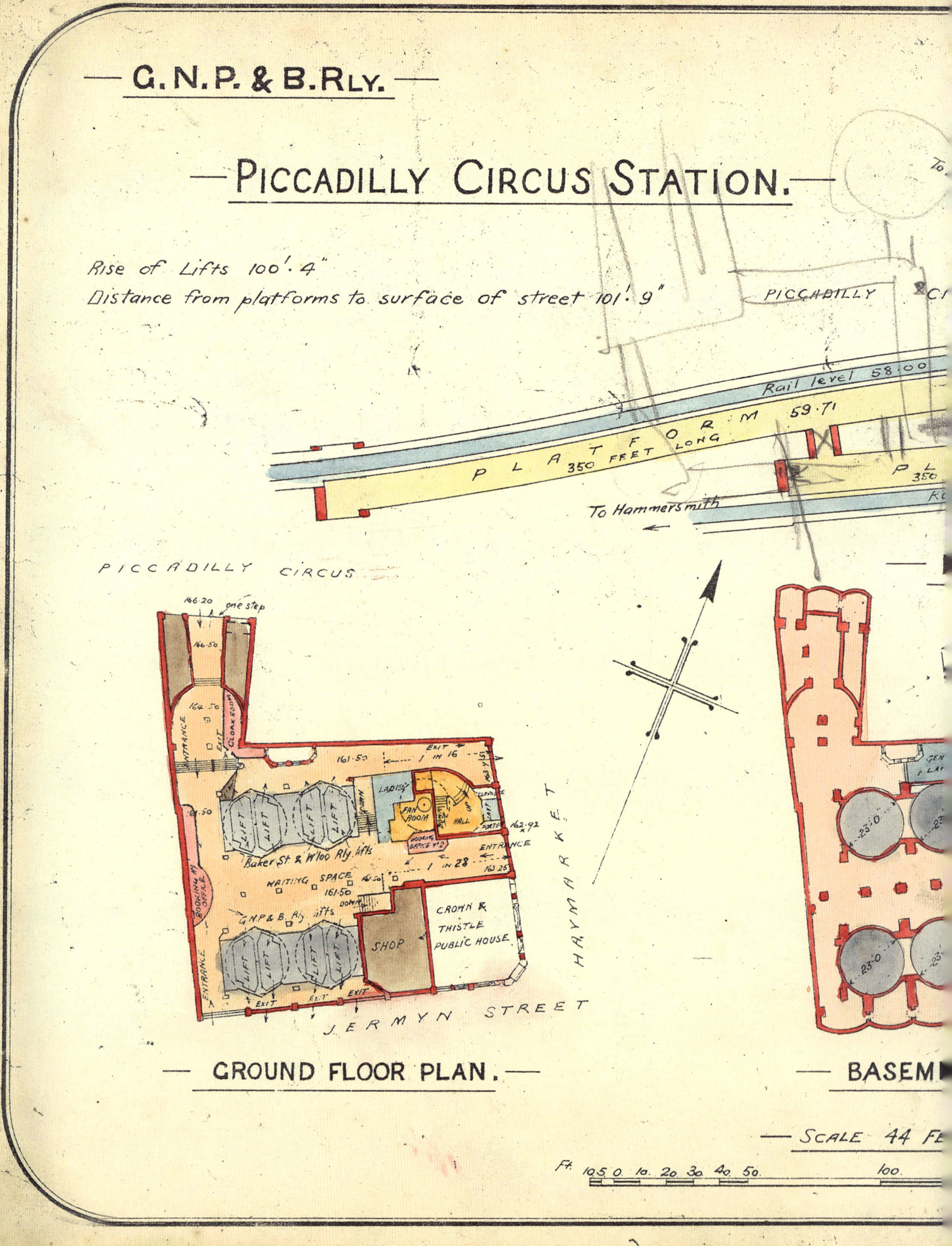

G.N.P. & B. Rly.

Piccadilly Circus Station.

Rise of Lifts 100'. 4"
Distance from platforms to surface of street 101'. 9"

Rail level 58.00
PLATFORM 59.71
350 FEET LONG
To Hammersmith

PICCADILLY CIRCUS

146.20 one step
164.50
CLOAK ROOM
161.50 EXIT 1 IN 16
LADIES
FAN ROOM
BOOKING OFFICE N°2
Baker St & W'loo Rly. lifts
WAITING SPACE 161.50
G.N.P & B. Rly. lifts
162.92
ENTRANCE 1 IN 28 161.25
SHOP
CROWN & THISTLE PUBLIC HOUSE
BOOKING OFFICE
EXIT EXIT EXIT
JERMYN STREET
HAYMARKET

GROUND FLOOR PLAN.

BASEM[ENT]

Scale 44 FE[ET]
Ft. 10 5 0 10. 20. 30. 40. 50.   100.

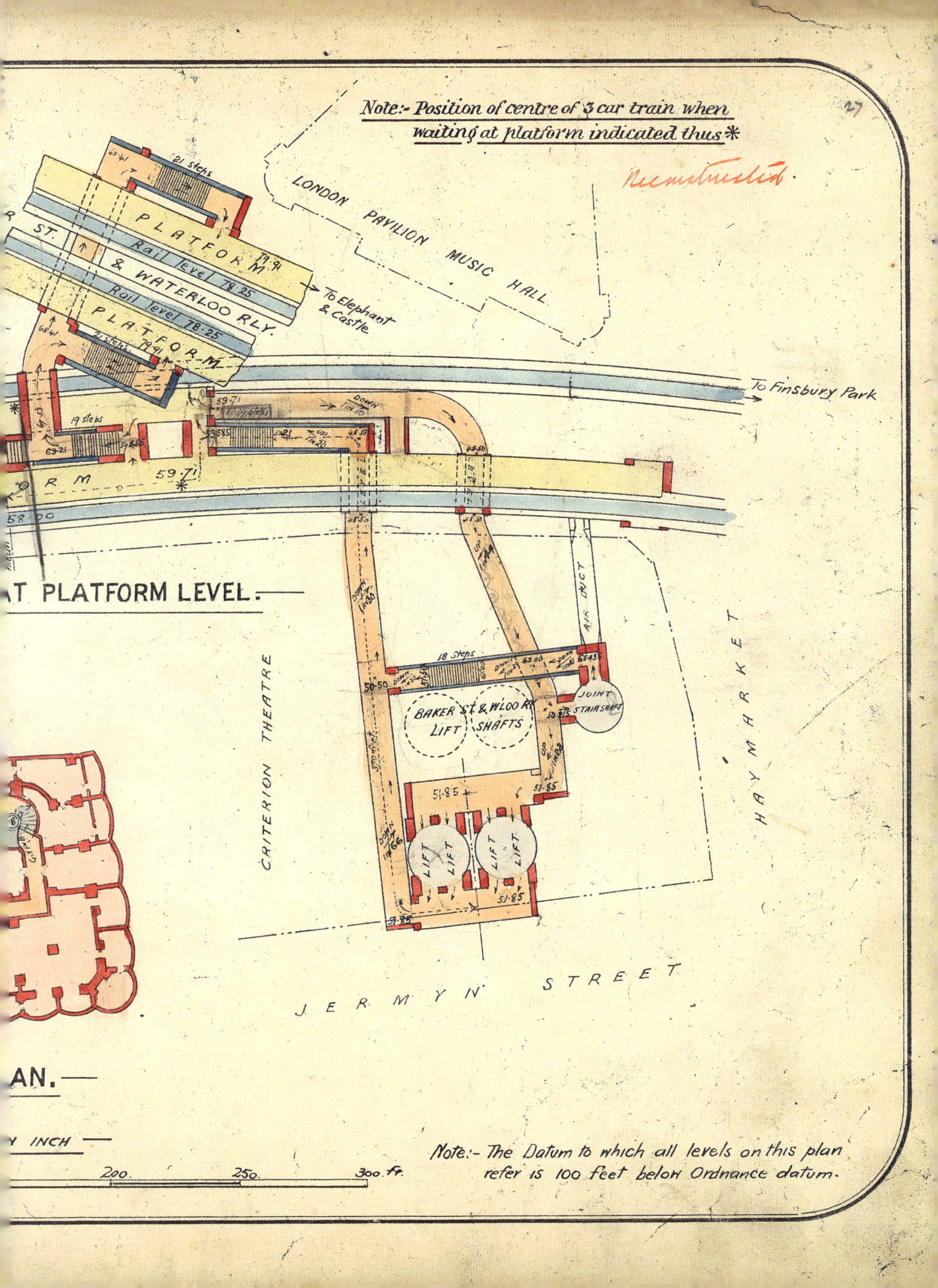

Note:- Position of centre of 3 car train when waiting at platform indicated thus ✱

Reconstructed.

LONDON PAVILION MUSIC HALL

PLATFORM
BAKER ST. & WATERLOO RLY.
Rail level 78.25
PLATFORM
Rail level 78.25
→ To Elephant & Castle

To Finsbury Park

CRITERION THEATRE

BAKER ST. & W'LOO RY LIFT SHAFTS

JOINT

LIFT LIFT LIFT

HAYMARKET

JERMYN STREET

AT PLATFORM LEVEL.

Note:- The Datum to which all levels on this plan refer is 100 feet below Ordnance datum.

[FIG.37] ABOVE When first opened in 1906, the large booking hall at Piccadilly Circus served the Bakerloo and Piccadilly lines. Each line was accessed by four lifts, controlled by lift operators. In January 1914, Piccadilly Circus became the first Underground station to receive two automatic, landing-operated lifts, quickly followed by two more.[6] This reduced staffing costs and improved passenger flow at a time of rising passenger numbers, especially during the First World War.

[FIG.38] OPPOSITE BELOW Before construction, the proposed station design had to be meticulously tested, due to the difficult nature of the site. A full-size mock-up of the booking hall was erected at the Earls Court Exhibition Centre, so that engineers could establish the best layout for the booking hall and 11 escalators. The booking hall's flat ceiling was constructed with steel girders and joists to support the immense weight of the traffic above and the famous Shaftesbury Memorial Fountain (incorrectly known as 'Eros' by many visitors).[7]

[FIG.39] ABOVE Douglas MacPherson's 1928 'stomach diagram' shows the complexity of the newly constructed station below Piccadilly Circus.

[FIG.40] ABOVE Commercial postcards promoted the idea of the new booking hall at Piccadilly Circus, opened on 10 December 1928, as a triumph of modern architecture. The upgraded station was designed by architect Charles Holden and used materials including bronze and travertine marble from Tivoli, Italy. The same materials were used for the Underground's head office building at 55 Broadway, opened in 1929, which was also designed by Holden. The booking hall featured shops, train indicators to show the reliability of the service and a grand mural of the world, with London at its centre. The former station entrances closed the following year.

[FIG.41] RIGHT During the Second World War, Piccadilly Circus was used for civilian sheltering. All available space was pressed into use, including passageways in the disused part of the station. Here, in a photograph taken in September 1940, shortly after the Blitz began, shelterers are sleeping on the escalators, as the platforms are already full and overcrowded.

[FIG.42] RIGHT Initially, conditions for the thousands of overnight shelterers were poor and problems grew as there were no sanitary arrangements. Cubicles with chemical toilets were installed in the disused passageways and provided a temporary solution.[8] The toilets were emptied into a holding tank and the waste was pumped up to the sewers using compressed air. The unpleasant job of emptying the buckets normally fell to station staff, as seen here. The sewage ejection tank at Piccadilly Circus was housed in the shaft left by the removal of the emergency stairs.

[FIG.43] BELOW Piccadilly Circus was a shelter not just for civilians. Valuable paintings from the Tate, the London Museum (now part of the Museum of London) and other collections were stored in disused passageways during wartime. Here, in February 1946, the paintings *Wake* by Edward Burra (left) and *Nymph and Young Girl Dancing* by William Etty (right) are shown being returned to their respective institutions.

[FIGS 44 & 45] ABOVE After escalators were fitted in the 1920s, former lift shafts, landings and passageways at the station were closed to the public. The emergency staircase was removed and the shaft converted to provide ventilation to both lines, as aided by a large extractor fan (above left) and an opening cut into the wall at platform level, covered with a grille through which air could freely flow (right).

[FIG.46] BELOW As well as providing ventilation and housing vital services for the successful running of the Tube, the old passageways and tunnels at Piccadilly Circus are used by London Underground to store materials and tools.

KNIGHTSBRIDGE

[FIG.47] RIGHT Knightsbridge station opened on 15 December 1906, on the Piccadilly line. From the booking hall, four lifts descended to a lower landing, with further passageways and stairs leading to the platforms. Major changes were made to the station in the early 1930s and a new, circular, sub-surface booking hall opened on 18 February 1934.

[FIG.48] ABOVE LEFT After the station was rebuilt with escalators, passageways leading to the lifts and the lift shafts themselves were abandoned. The shafts, like so many others on the Piccadilly line, were converted to provide passive ventilation. During the Second World War, Knightsbridge station was designated a shelter, able to accommodate up to 700 civilians. It was also equipped with provisions for London Transport staff, all while the station remained in operational use.[9] After the war, the passageways were used for ventilation once again and, occasionally, for storing engineering materials and equipment.

[FIG.49] ABOVE RIGHT The disused passageways and lift shafts of Knightsbridge station are being given new life in 2020. Knightsbridge is to be upgraded to make it step-free as a part of the Mayor's 2018 Transport Strategy. This step-free route will reopen the disused areas of the station that have been closed to the public since 1934 and two lifts will be installed in the old lift shafts leading to a brand-new entrance on Hooper's Court, close to the location of the original 1906 station. This is a rare example of a disused lift shaft being re-used for its original purpose.

HYDE PARK CORNER

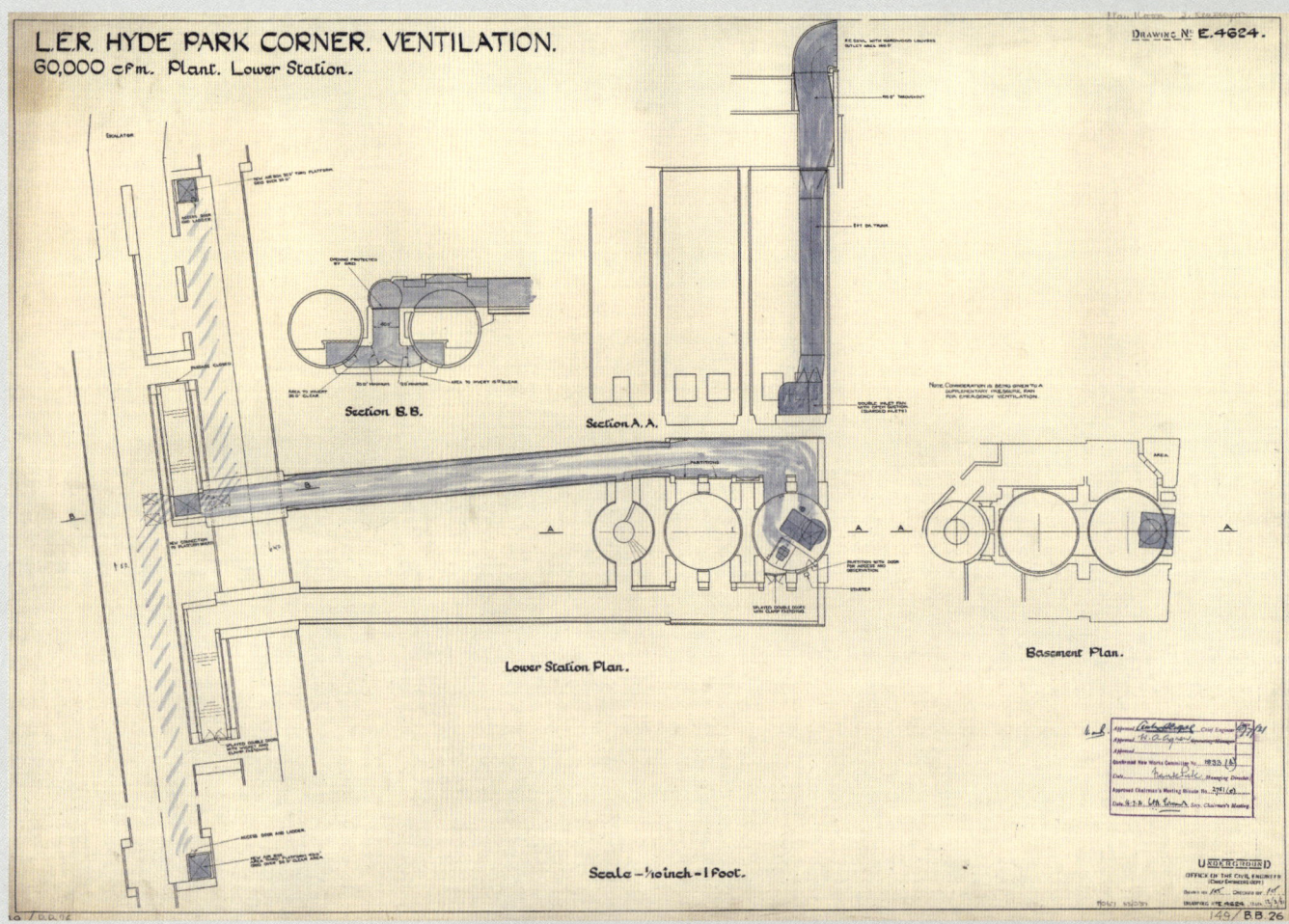

[FIG.50] ABOVE Hyde Park Corner opened in 1906 with three lifts and a spiral staircase. As traffic increased in the 1920s, the station was redesigned to include escalators and another purpose was found for the closed passageways and lift shafts. This diagram from 1931 shows one of the shafts converted into a fan chamber, to circulate air to the poorly ventilated Piccadilly line.

[FIG.51] RIGHT Today, the lift shaft still houses fans that help ventilate the Piccadilly line. This door marked 'FANS' dates from 1932 when the equipment was installed.

OXFORD CIRCUS

[FIGS 52 & 53] BELOW The first Tube station called Oxford Circus opened on the Central line on 30 July 1900 (below left) and as it looked in 1906 (below right). Located on the eastern corner of the intersection of Argyll Street and Oxford Street, the entrance to the single-storey building led to a booking hall with four lifts to take passengers down to the platforms.

[FIG.54] BOTTOM By 1914, the Central and Bakerloo lines had been joined under the Underground Group. Oxford Circus became one of the first stations to be fitted with escalators, which were opened on 9 May 1914, along with a brand new concourse booking hall in the basement.

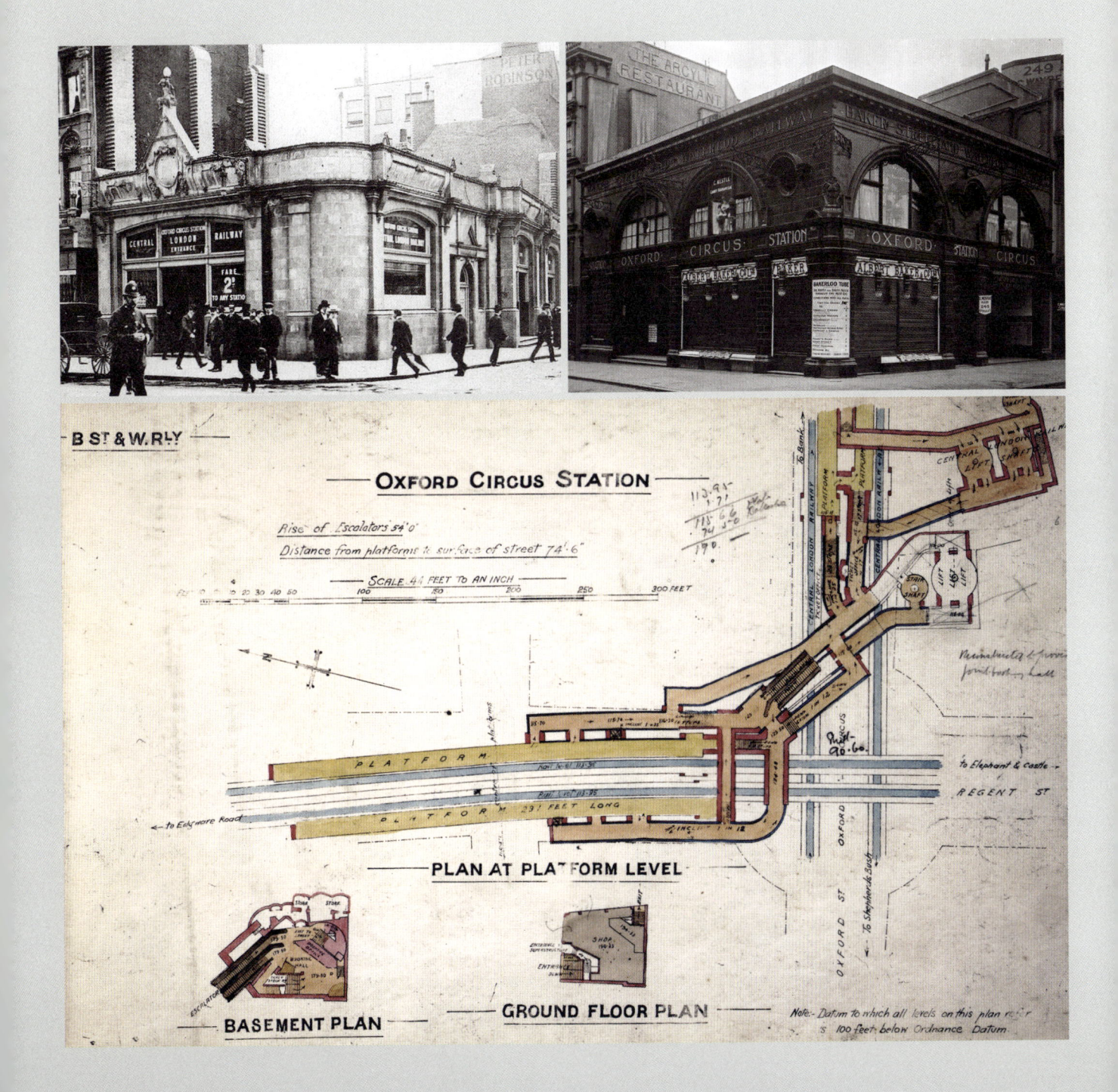

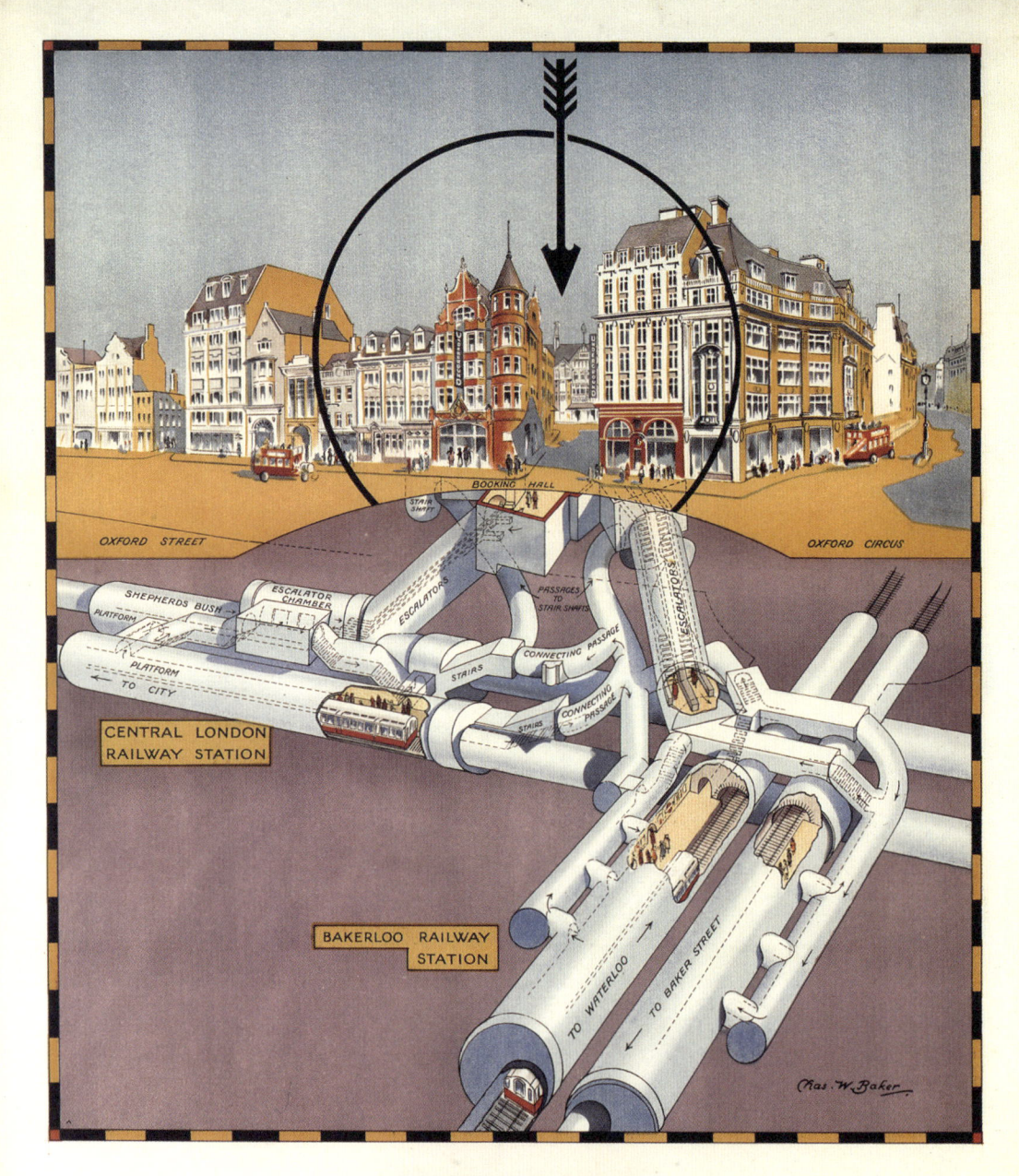

UNDERGROUND

OXFORD CIRCUS
THE NEW STATION
WILL BE COMPLETED ABOUT END OF JUNE

TRY IT AND SAVE TIME

[FIG.55] OPPOSITE Further modifications were made to Oxford Circus station in 1925, to provide a new sub-surface booking hall and escalators.

[FIGS 56 & 57] TOP AND ABOVE LEFT The 1925 works left the emergency staircases of the Bakerloo (above) and the Central line (below) disused. These spaces, with the staircases removed, now function as ventilation shafts and storage areas, but their original tile finishes and fittings can still be seen.

[FIG.58] ABOVE RIGHT Major redevelopments took place at the station between 1963 and 1969 because of the construction of the Victoria line, which opened on 7 March 1969. This long, deep ventilation tunnel, which helps extract foul air from the station, was built as part of the redevelopment.

ANGEL

[FIG.59] BELOW The narrow City & South London Railway island platform at Angel around 1901. It was not until Angel station was fitted with escalators in 1993 that the opportunity was also taken to replace the island platform layout. A new northbound platform tunnel was constructed, and the island platform filled in on one side to create a wide southbound platform.

[FIG.60] OPPOSITE ABOVE The abandoned lift shafts (just seen on the left) and passageways at Angel, closed to the public in 1993. On the walls, some advertising and original tile features remain.

[FIG.61] OPPOSITE BELOW A Northern line train rejoins the original northbound tunnel at Angel. The line originally travelled through the position of the photographer.

[FIG.62] NEXT The lift shafts at Finsbury Park station belonged to the Great Northern and City line, which opened the station in 1904. The Piccadilly line opened their own station in 1906 but connected the booking hall and platforms with staircases and subways. The station is one of only two deep tube stations (the other being Arsenal), whose platforms are reached by staircase alone. The original Great Northern & City Railway (GN&CR) lifts at Finsbury Park travelled only 8.5 metres (28 feet), the shortest distance of any lift on the Underground system. The lifts were replaced by spiral staircases in 1921.

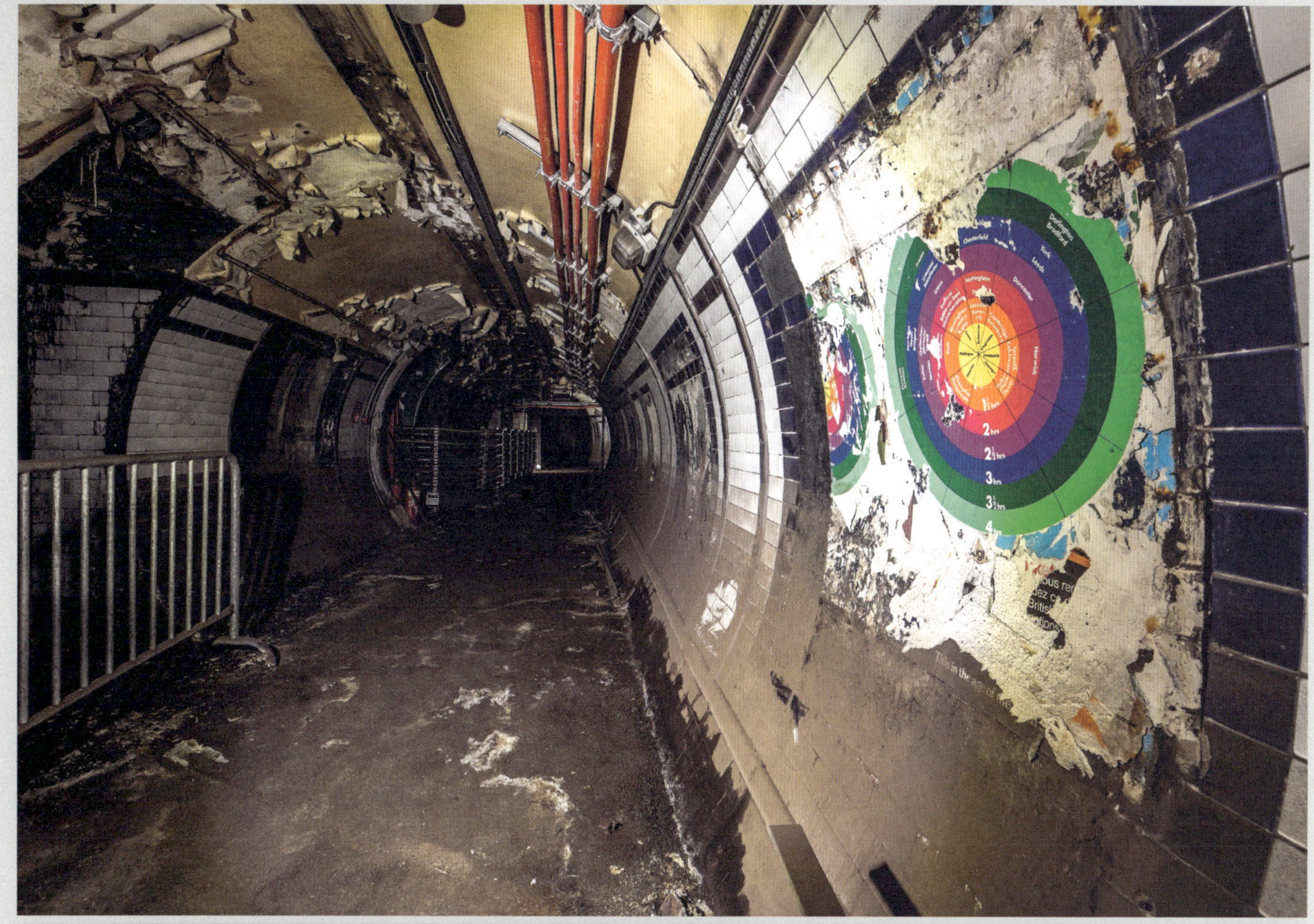

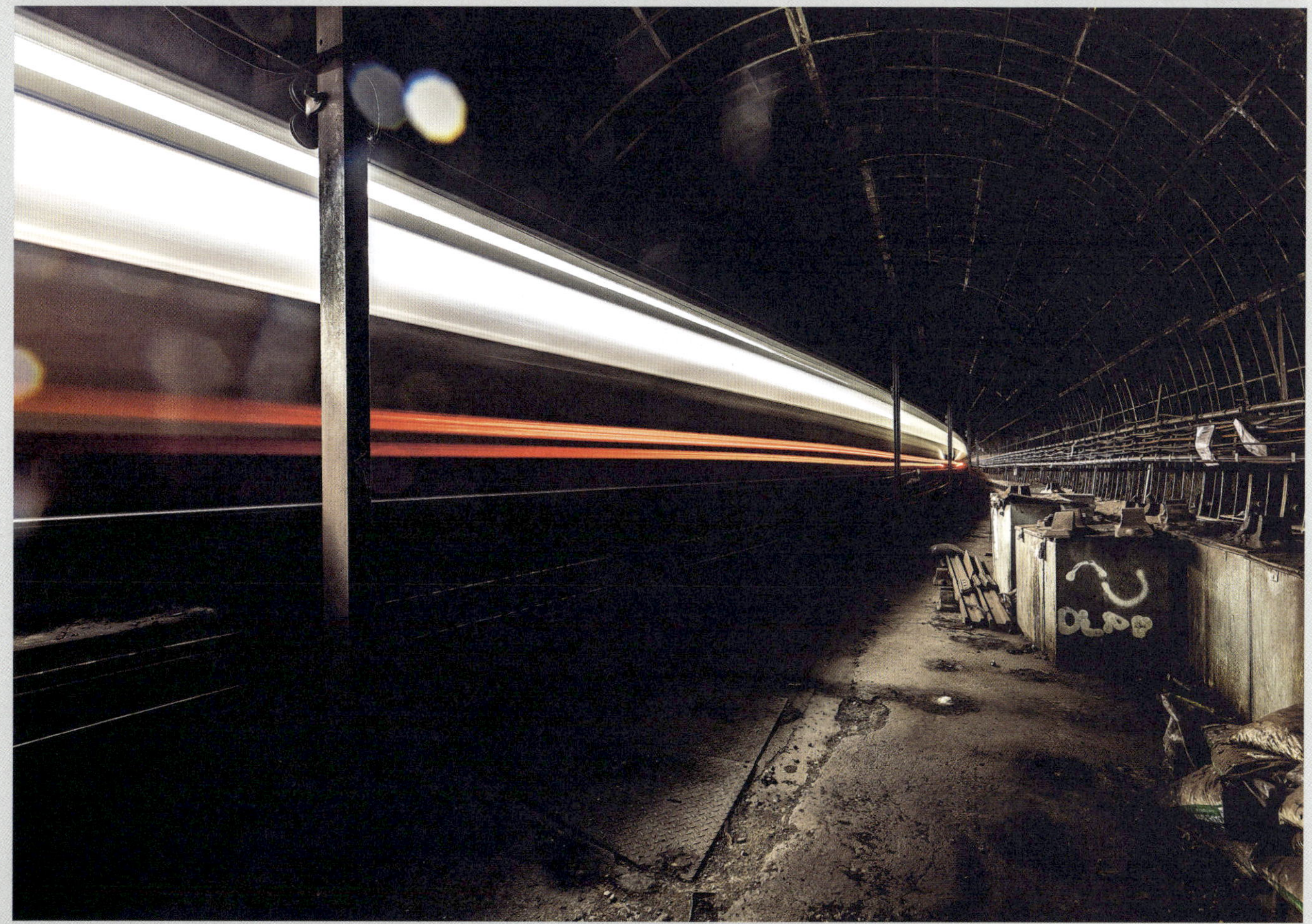

Treatment of
ELECTRIC SHOCK
ACT AT ONCE
WARNING
ISOLATE LIGHTING CIRCUITS BEFORE WORKING ON CIRCUIT AS THERE ARE EXPOSED TERMINALS

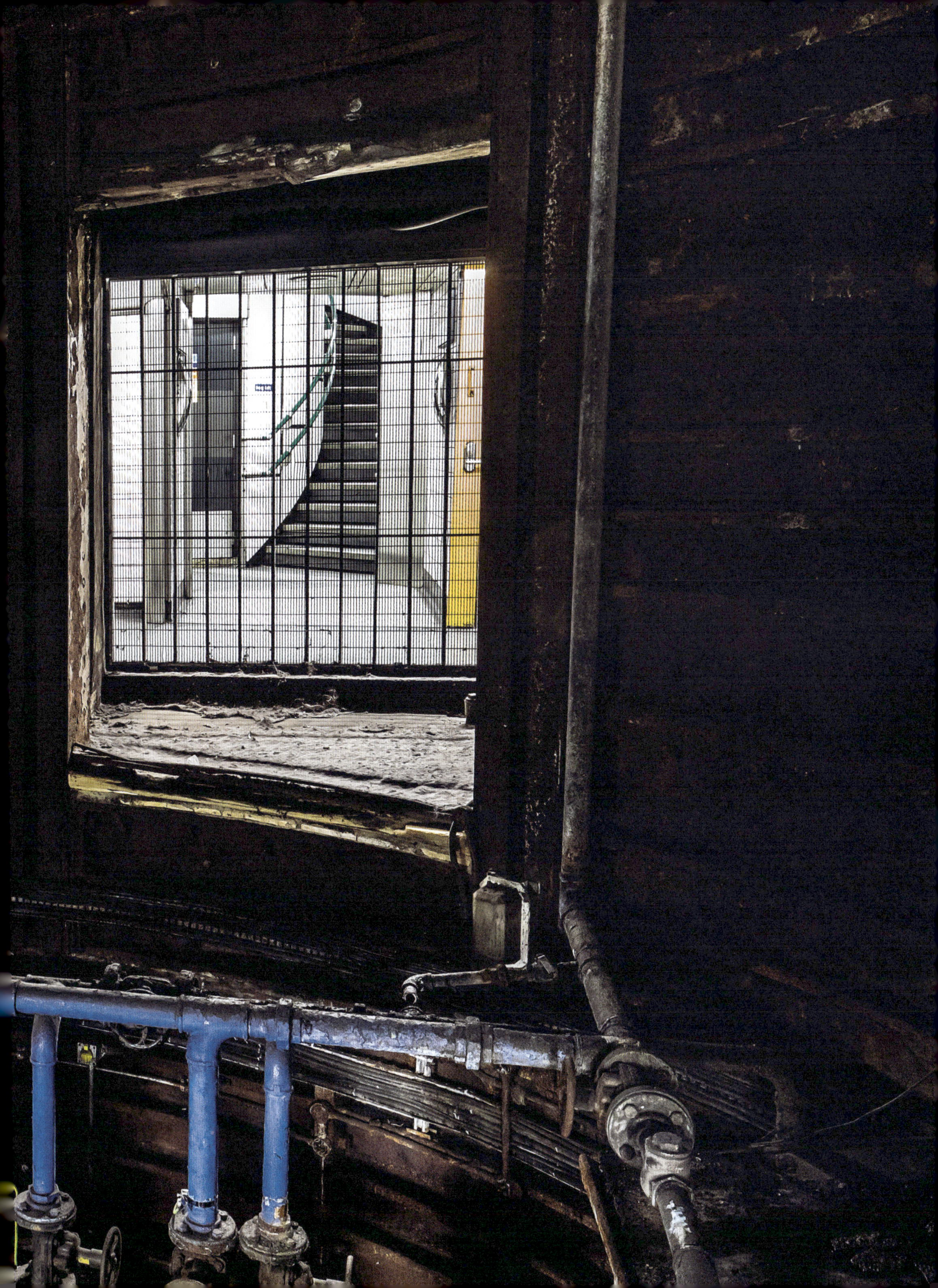

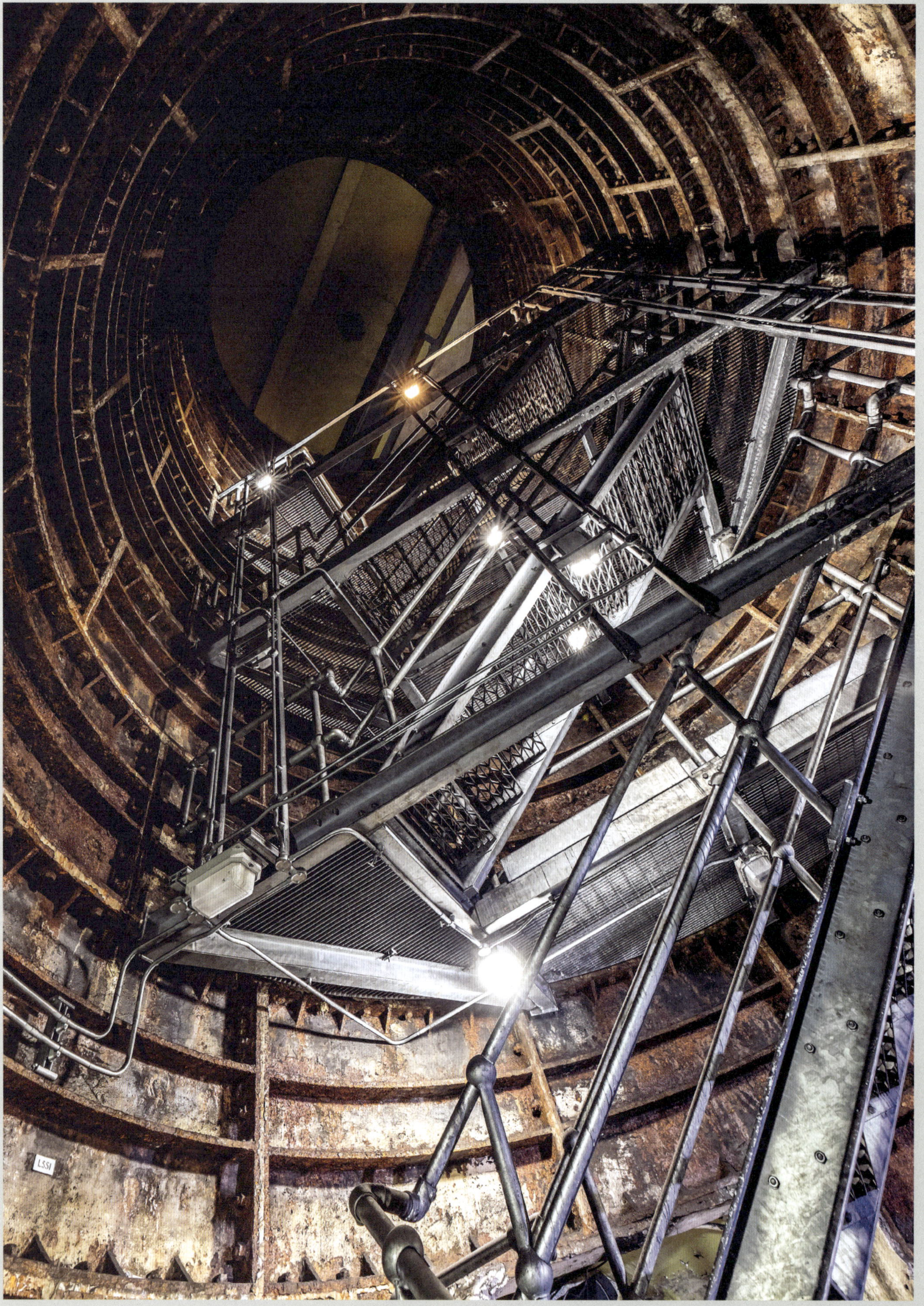
LSSI

1   Antony Badsey-Ellis, *Building London's Underground: From Cut-and-Cover to Crossrail* (Capital Transport, 2016), pp.52–64.
2   *London Daily News*, 30 September 1911, p.3.
3   Charles W. Baker, 'A New Heart For London – Piccadilly New Station' [poster for the Underground Electric Railway Company Ltd], 1928, London Transport Museum, LTM 1983/4/2584.
4   Stations on the modern Tube network that were built with lifts and later rebuilt with escalators are as follows: on the Piccadilly line, South Kensington, Dover Street, Holborn, King's Cross, Finsbury Park and Leicester Square; on the Northern line, Clapham Common, Clapham North, Stockwell, Oval, Kennington, London Bridge, Bank, Moorgate, Old Street, Camden Town, Kentish Town, Archway, Euston, Warren Street and Embankment; on the Central line, St Paul's, Chancery Lane, Tottenham Court Road, Bond Street, Marble Arch and Shepherds Bush; on the Bakerloo line, Marylebone, Trafalgar Square and Waterloo.
5   Desmond F. Croome and Alan A. Jackson, *Rails Through the Clay: A History of London's Tube Railways* (Capital Transport, 1993), p.195.
6   Croome and Jackson 1993, p.130.
7   The Shaftesbury Memorial Fountain is surmounted by a winged statue of Anteros. The fountain was erected in 1893 to commemorate the philanthropic works of Anthony Ashley-Cooper, 7th Earl of Shaftesbury and occupied the centre of the Circus. It has twice been moved from the Circus: for the reconstruction of the Underground station, between 1922 and 1931, and to preserve it during the Second World War. In 1948 it was moved back to the site but relocated to the south-eastern side of Piccadilly Circus where it stands today.
8.   Elsan toilets were buckets with a seat that contained odour neutralising and sterilising chemicals. They had to be emptied regularly by hand and the contents refreshed.
9.   Knightsbridge station, LTM 1999/42940.

[FIG.63] Baker Street station was one of the original Metropolitan Railway sub-surface stations opened in 1863. The Bakerloo line opened a separate station accessed by lifts in 1906. In October 1914, interchange between the Metropolitan and Bakerloo line stations was improved by the installation of two escalators. The lifts remained in use to carry passengers up to street level until 24 November 1940, when the original Bakerloo line station was closed to passengers. The lifts were used just one more time, on 8 May 1945, to help clear the huge crowds that attended the Victory in Europe celebrations.

TO STREET
←

DOWN STREET

THE SAFEST PLACE IN LONDON

[FIG.64] PREVIOUS The deep emergency spiral staircase at Down Street shows evidence of its wartime repurposing, with 'TO STREET' signage and the remains of a small, central lift shaft.

[FIG.65] TOP The handsome Down Street station building shortly after opening in 1907. A classic design of the Edwardian London Tube, by architect Leslie Green, it was based on a rigid steel frame, which supported lifts and gave the building sufficient strength to allow overbuilding in future. The facade was covered in oxblood-red tiles, with its name in large, gilded letters above the entry and exit bays. These features meant the closed station was still recognisably part of the Underground at street level.

[FIG.66] ABOVE LEFT A public information poster from 1932 informing passengers of the impending closure of Down Street and improved facilities at nearby Hyde Park Corner station.

[FIG.67] ABOVE RIGHT After the station closed, a tobacconist's shop was constructed in the right-hand entryway (as seen from the street). This, together with painted wooden, tiled boards that obscured the station name, helped the site to blend into obscurity (to avoid being targeted by the enemy) as construction work began on the rapid conversion of the station into the secret headquarters of the REC.

As passengers on the Piccadilly line hurry between Green Park and Hyde Park Corner, few are aware of passing through the disused Down Street station, let alone of this station's vital role in Britain's war effort between 1939 and 1945. Yet Down Street was adapted as the bunker headquarters for national railway operations during the war – a vital, secret and secure communications hub for coordinating freight, troop and passenger trains. As trains passed the former station, key figures in the national war effort met in offices and meeting rooms on the platforms and in the passageways. Dormitories, dining facilities and bathrooms were provided for staff, who worked safely below ground, interrupted only by passing trains. In October 1940, the prime minister himself, Winston Churchill, dined and sheltered here overnight as the Blitz raged above in nearby Whitehall and Piccadilly.

The devastating effects of modern aerial warfare were seared into the public imagination on 26 April 1937, when German and Italian aircraft attacked and effectively destroyed the city of Guernica in a single day of raids during the Spanish Civil War.[1] Britain had already suffered bombing from aircraft during the First World War, and civilians had reacted by seeking improvised shelter. Fortunately for the capital and the country, the government, led by those who had lived through the earlier conflict, had been discreetly planning defences

and preparing for the worst long before it became a reality during the Blitz. As the threat of war intensified, so did London Transport's efforts to strengthen its network in readiness for the expected bombardment. A catalogue of disused stations had been prepared in 1929 to answer a future emergency.[2] Down Street and stations like it would play an essential and secret role in supporting Britain's war effort by allowing essential services to be coordinated without interruption.

The rapid expansion of privately owned Tube lines in the Edwardian period led to the construction of many Underground stations across the capital. Some would prove to be financially unsuccessful due to their location, awkward design or proximity to rival stations. Four stations situated on the Piccadilly line – at Down Street, Brompton Road, Dover Street (now Green Park) and York Road – were fully abandoned or heavily modified from their original state in the early 1930s. These lesser-used stations were closed to speed up the service through the city centre following the extension of the line north and south into the suburbs. Their lifts were removed and the platforms, lift shafts and passageways became ventilation shafts for the busy Tube. Elsewhere on the line, Holborn station concealed a disused platform that had served the branch to Aldwych until 1917, when low levels of traffic on the line caused it to be closed (see The Strand, pp.189–201). At South Kensington, a 36.5-metre (120-foot) length of tunnel, built in 1903 as the beginnings of a project to build a deep-level District line, had been repurposed from 1927 as a signalling school.

London Transport saw the wartime potential of such large spaces below ground as bunkers for coordinating transport; the idea of using them as civilian shelters came later. The tunnels were typically 20 metres (approximately 66 feet) or more below ground – deep enough to provide protection from the most powerful German bombs. They were also connected by the Piccadilly line, meaning that personnel and telephone cables could easily pass between sites, safe from the air raids above. As the Blitz threatened to bring the capital to a halt, one by one the dormant stations on the Piccadilly line and elsewhere

G.N.P. & B. R^ly

Rise of Lifts 60'. 8"
Distance from Platforms to surface of stre

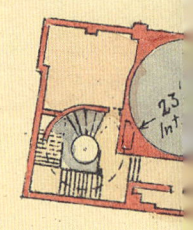

BASEMEN

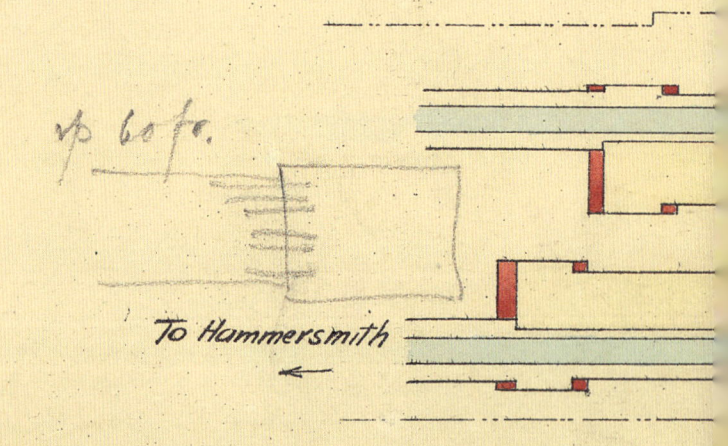

up 60 ft.

To Hammersmith ←

GREEN

FEET 10 5 0

[FIG.68] A station plan of Down Street, built by the Great Northern, Piccadilly & Brompton Railway, reveals the long passageways required to connect the platforms under Piccadilly with the remote, side-street location of the ticket hall building on Down Street.

Down Street Station

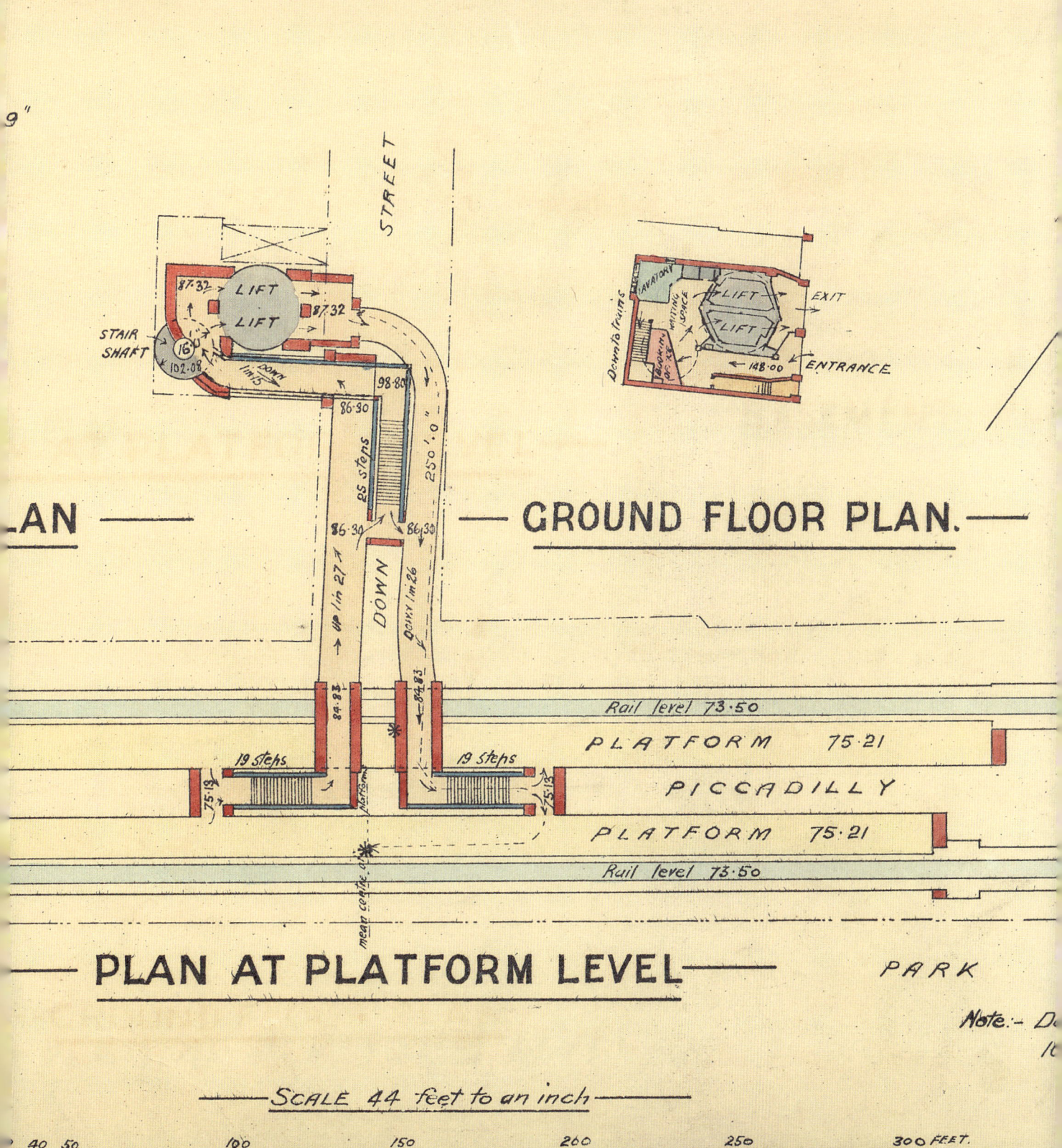

Ground Floor Plan.

Plan at Platform Level

Scale 44 feet to an inch

were called up for duty, adapted for reuse and connected to key civilian and military installations by telephone. The wartime role of these bunkers was kept secret at the time and, as their stories emerged in post-war years, they were characterised as interesting individual sites rather than as part of a resilient, distributed and connected network.

A FAILED STATION

Down Street station sits on a quiet side street in London's affluent Mayfair. Its somewhat awkward design and lengthy passageways to the platform [FIG.68] meant that it struggled to attract passengers from the day it opened in 1907 [FIG.65]. The remodelling of neighbouring stations at Dover Street (now Green Park) and Hyde Park Corner in the early 1930s, with the installation of escalators, brought the entrances of these stations closer to Down Street. This was the final blow to the station's future and, in May 1932, it was closed for passenger use and quickly converted into a humble ventilation shaft with a siding to accommodate Piccadilly line trains [FIG.66].

DOWN STREET'S FINEST HOUR

Railways were the arteries of British transport in the 1930s, and vital for the logistical effort associated with the impending war. As in the First World War, the coordination of the privately owned railway companies was overseen during the new conflict by a government department: the Railway Executive Committee (REC). Its members were drawn from the senior management of Britain's 'Big Four' mainline railways – London & North Eastern Railway (LNER), London Midland & Scottish Railway (LMSR), Great Western Railway (GWR) and Southern Railway (SR) – together with representatives from London Transport. The REC headquarters were initially run from Fielden House on Great College Street, very close to the Houses of Parliament. The chairman of the REC, Sir Ralph Wedgwood, had served with the Committee during the First World War and was aware of the need to prepare the headquarters for whatever aerial bombardment might come. He instructed the REC secretary, Gerald Cole Deacon, to make the necessary preparations. These included plans to reinforce and bombproof the basement of Fielden House to protect its large telephone exchange, essential to the coordination of the nation's railways.

By 1939, Cole Deacon had been advised by the London Metropolitan Police that the building was unsuitable for conversion as a bombproof facility due to its shallow basement. There was concern, too, that the proximity of the River Thames and Houses of Parliament made the building a potential collateral target. Cole Deacon sought alternative premises with good provision for telephone lines. Discussions with London Transport quickly led him to seek permission to convert Down Street station into underground headquarters truly fit for purpose. The design features that blighted Down Street as a passenger station – deep, lengthy passageways and discreet location – made it ideal as a bunker from which to run the nation's railways, undisturbed by the destruction wreaked above. On 28 April 1939 Frank Pick, now chief executive officer of London Transport, approved the conversion in principle and the race was on to convert the site before war was declared.³ [FIGS 69 AND 70].

A PLACE FOR EVERYTHING

Gerald Cole Deacon designed the REC headquarters to maximise the use of the available space with an efficiency reminiscent of fitting out a boat. His hand-drawn sketches were turned into construction plans by London Transport, with the installation itself built by engineering contractors McAlpine and fitted out in first-class style by LMSR's Wolverton carriage works staff. By the time war was declared on 3 September 1939, the facility was sufficiently finished to allow a skeleton staff to move in. As the works were completed over the following months, the core staff and operations of the REC moved below ground to Down Street [FIG.71].

The weeks before the site was fully completed were uncomfortable for staff, but by comparison with most civilian shelters, the REC enjoyed extremely well-appointed facilities, with air conditioning, private bedrooms, kitchen, and separate bathrooms and mess rooms for senior executives and lower ranked officers. In January 1941, the *Railway Gazette* was, surprisingly, given permission to write an article about the facility, provided with a full set of plans and allowed to take photographs throughout the site. Publication was delayed due to belated security concerns from the REC, but the article was eventually published in November 1944 and provides a remarkable record of this secret headquarters. It is notable that one photograph, captioned as the executive mess room, looks lavish for a bunker but is in fact the neighbouring mess room for lower ranking officers – a sign perhaps of some sensitivity about portraying the full grandeur of the panelled, wallpapered executive mess during a time of war.[4]

The noise of the Piccadilly line running through the station, just inches away from meeting rooms, the telephone exchange [FIG.74] and bedrooms, meant that life in the bunker was difficult for those working and sleeping there full-time. Nonetheless, the facility allowed the REC to do its job regardless of air raids and, a year after opening, its effectiveness as a bunker meant that it would protect an extremely important guest.

In early October 1940, the Blitz moved west, from the docks and East End to Whitehall. On the night of 15 October came the most sustained attack yet on the governing centre of the country. A bomb fell on the Treasury and killed three officials. The prime minister's official residence at 10 Downing Street was badly damaged, though staff were saved, having been ordered to the shelter only minutes before. A high-explosive bomb fell only a few metres from No.10 and John Martin, a duty officer that night, wrote:

> I seemed to fly down with a rush of blast, the air full of dust and the crash and clatter of glass breaking behind. There was a rush of several of us into the shelter and we tumbled on top of one another in a good deal of confusion. …The mess in the house (no.10) was indescribable – windows smashed in all directions, everything covered with grime, doors off hinges and curtains and furniture tossed about in a confused mass.[5]

[FIG.69] NEXT A London Transport blueprint reveals the final, ingenious design for the state-of-the-art national control centre, impervious to aerial bombardment or gas attack. The lower passageways and platforms provided workspace and accommodation for 40 staff. Down Street's unique landing passageway also created space for the rarest of all things in a bunker: plumbed toilets and bathing facilities.

[FIG.70] PAGES 88–89 A London Transport telephone connection diagram from 1941 shows the emergency communications network linking coordination bunkers and key control facilities, including the heavily reinforced telephone exchange in the basement of 55 Broadway (pp.109–21).

DOWN ST – DISUSED TUBE STATION

PLAN – HIGH LEVEL SUBWAY

PASSENGER LIFT

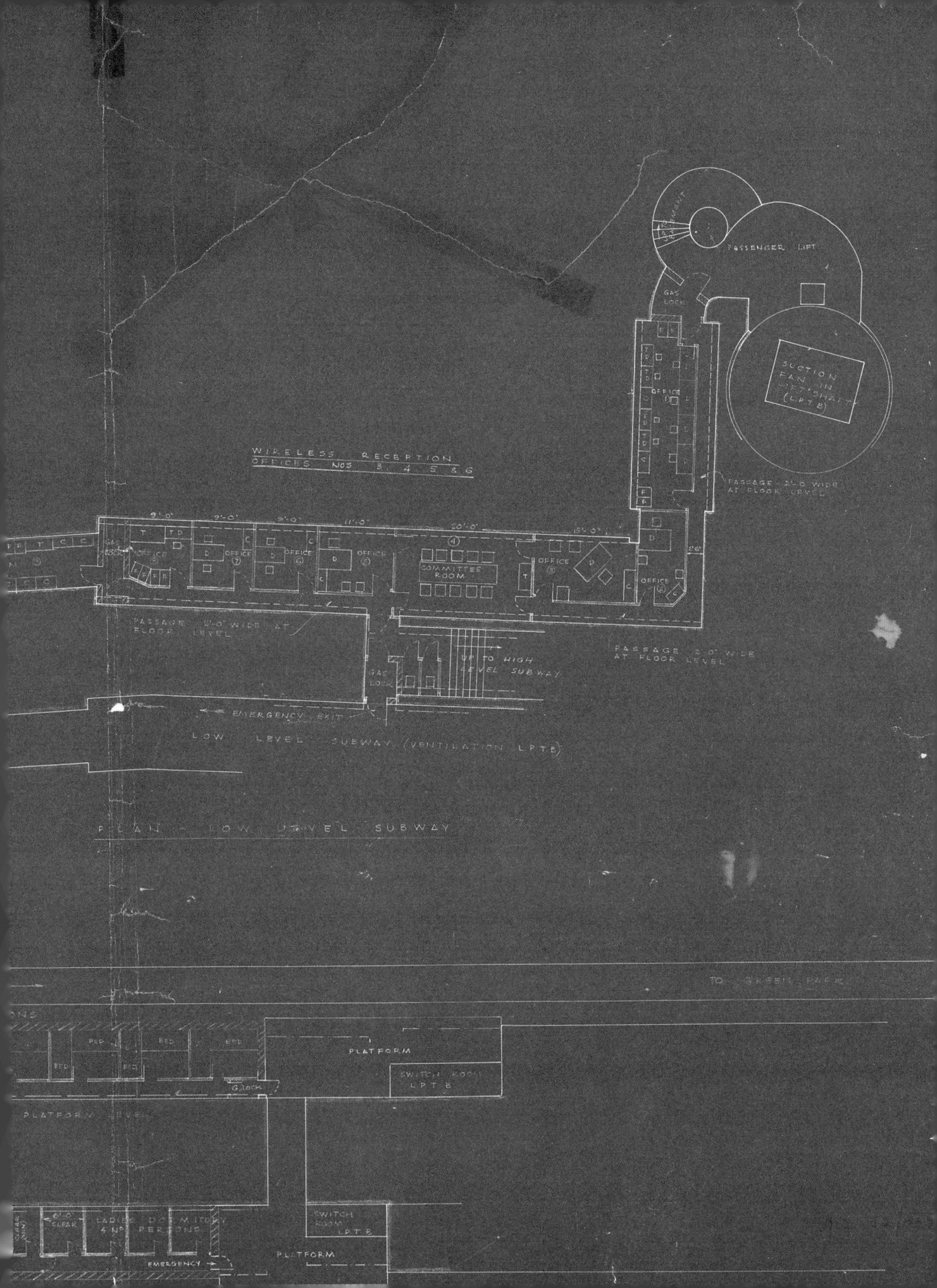

GAS LOCK

SUCTION FAN IN VENT. SHAFT (L.P.T.B.)

PASSAGE 2'-0" WIDE AT FLOOR LEVEL

WIRELESS RECEPTION
OFFICES Nos 3 4 5 & 6

OFFICE 8 | OFFICE 7 | OFFICE 6 | OFFICE 5 | COMMITTEE ROOM (4) | OFFICE 3 | OFFICE 2

PASSAGE 2'-0" WIDE AT FLOOR LEVEL

PASSAGE 2'-0" WIDE AT FLOOR LEVEL

GAS LOCK

UP TO HIGH LEVEL SUBWAY

← EMERGENCY EXIT

LOW LEVEL SUBWAY (VENTILATION L.P.T.B.)

PLAN - LOW LEVEL SUBWAY

TO GREEN PARK

BED | BED | BED | BED | PLATFORM
G. LOCK | SWITCH ROOM L.P.T.B.

PLATFORM LEVEL

LADIES DORMITORY 4 N° PERSONS | SWITCH ROOM L.P.T.B.

EMERGENCY | PLATFORM

London Transport Telephones General.

Emergency Communications.

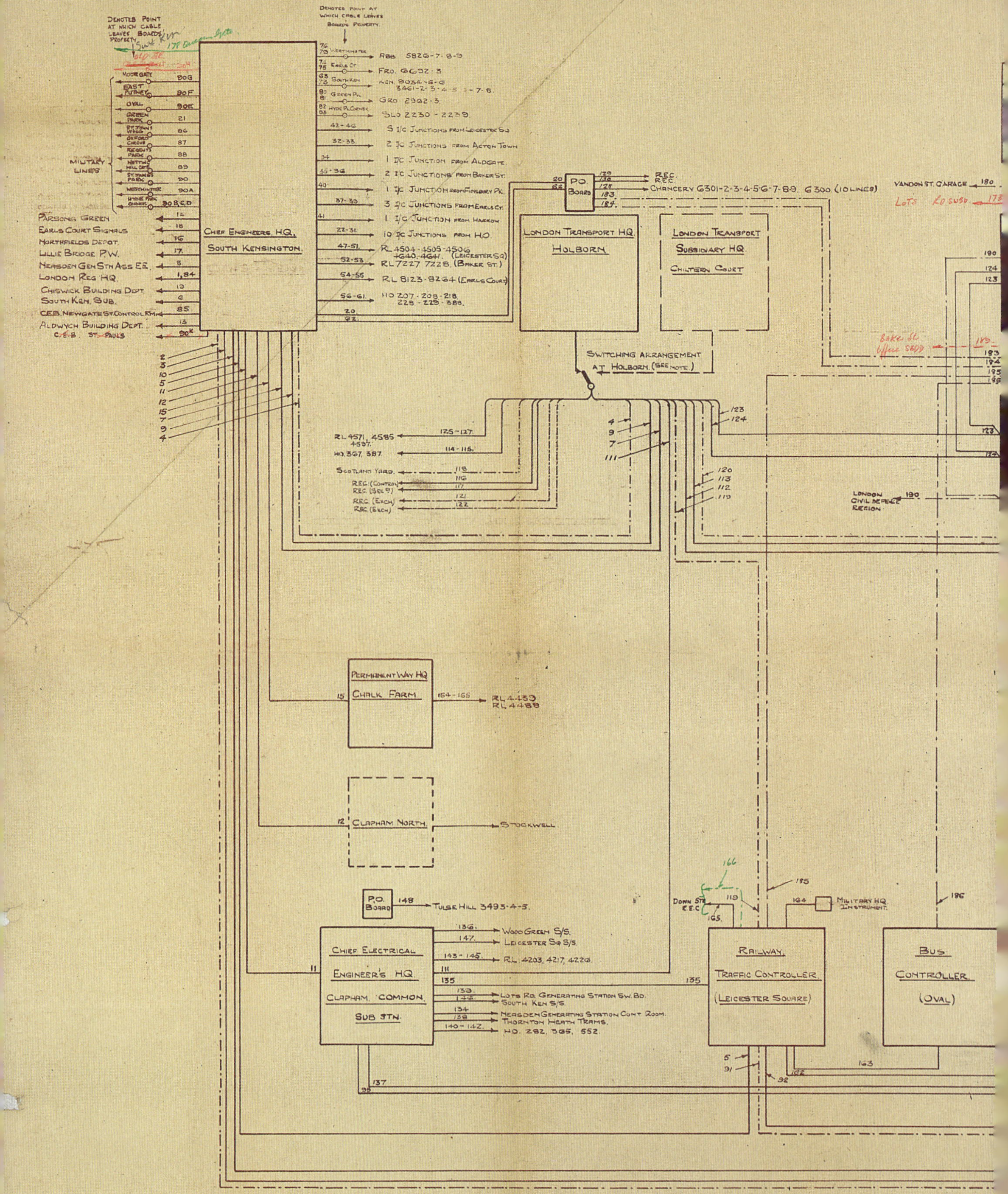

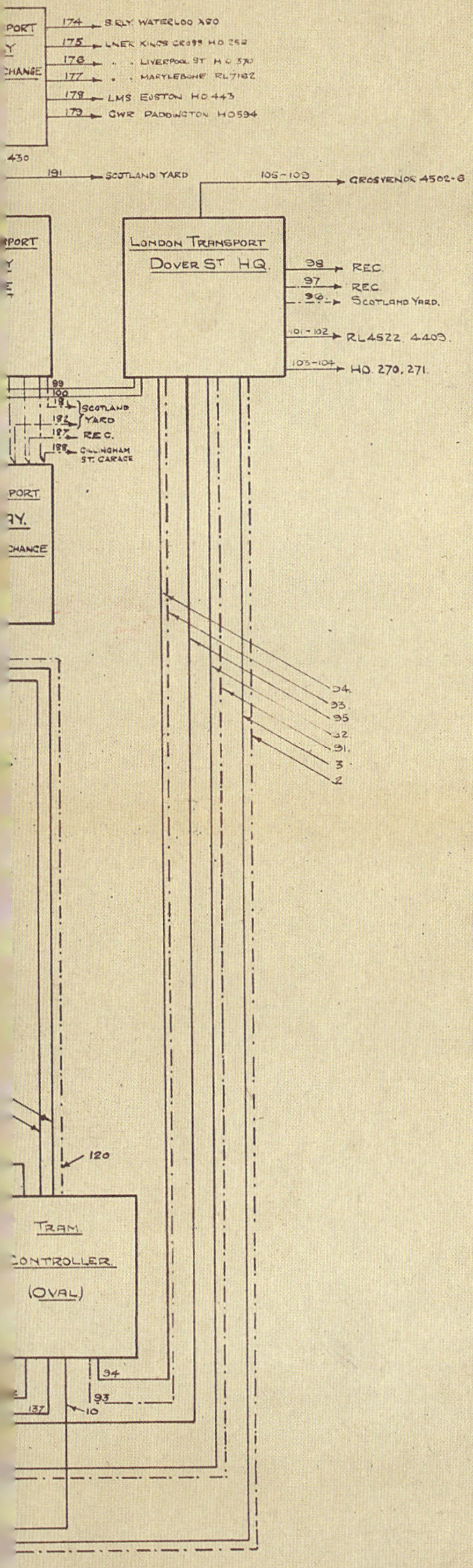

FROM.			TO.		
Location	Ref Nº	Termination.	Location	Termination	Circuit Nº P.O.
South Kensington Chief Engineer's H.Q.	1	Nº 33 Local Bd	London Reg ARP HQ Nº1		
	2	Nº 54 - -	Dover St HQ Nº 1.	Nº 37.	RA 25300 (P/W)
	3	Nº 55 - -	Dover St HQ Nº 2	Nº 38.	
	4	Nº 53 - -	Holborn HQ (LPTB)	Nº 95 (LPTB SWBD)	RA10046 (P/W)
	5	Nº 52 - -	Leicester Sq Cont.	Nº 91 Emer Mag Bd	
	6	Nº 76 - -	South Ken Sub EE HQ	Instrument.	
	7	Nº 75 - -	Holborn HQ Nº 1.	Nº 49	
	8	Nº 74 - -	Neasden P.H. Ass EE	Nº 26	
	9	Nº 73 - -	Holborn HQ Nº 2	Nº 50	
	10	Nº 72 - -	Oval Tram Cont	Nº 5	
	11	Nº 93 - -	Clapham Com Sub EE HQ	Nº 31.	
	12	Nº 98 - -	Stockwell Bld Dept	Instrument.	
	13	Nº 97 - -	Aldwych Bld Dept.	-	
	14	Nº 96 - -	Parsons Gn Bld Dept	Nº 2.	
	15	Nº 95 - -	Chalk Farm P.W. Dept.	Nº 2.	
	16	Nº 93 - -	Northfields PW Dept.	Instrument.	
	17	Nº 94 - -	Lillie Bridge PW Dept	Nº 18.	
	18	Nº 92 - -	Earls Ct Signal Dept	Chief Inspectors Instrument.	
	19	Nº 91 - -	Chiswick Bld Dept.	Instrument.	
	20	Nº 100 Main Bd.	Holborn HQ P.O. Nº 1.	Nº 13	
	21	Nº 80 - -	MILITARY		
	22	Nº 101 - -	HO. I/C Junc Nº 1.	HO. Exchange	
	23	Nº 20 - -	- - - Nº 2	- -	
	24	Nº 102 - -	- - - Nº 3	- -	
	25	Nº 19 - -	- - - Nº 4	- -	
	26	Nº 103 - -	- - - Nº 5	- -	
	27	Nº 18 - -	- - - Nº 6	- -	
	28	Nº 104 - -	- - - Nº 7	- -	
	29	Nº 17 - -	- - - Nº 8	- -	
	30	Nº 105 - -	- - - Nº 9	- -	
	31	Nº 16 - -	- - - Nº 10	- -	
	32	Nº 122 - -	Acton RL I/C Junc 1.	Acton - -	
	33	Nº 40 - -	- - - 2	- -	
	34	Nº 121 - -	Aldgate RL I/C Junc 1.	Aldgate - -	
	35	Nº 123 - -	Baker St RL I/C Junc 1.	Baker St - -	
	36	Nº 39 - -	- - - 2.	- -	
	37	Nº 124 - -	Earls Ct RL I/C Junc 1	Earls Ct - -	
	38	Nº 38 - -	- - - 2	- -	
	39	Nº 125 - -	- - - 3	- -	
	40	Nº 37 - -	Finsbury Pk RL I/C Junc 1.	Finsbury Pk -	
	41	Nº 36 -	Harrow RL I/C Junc 1.	Harrow	
	42	Nº 126 -	Leicester Sq RL I/C Junc 1	Leicester Sq - -	
	43	Nº 35 - -	- - - 2	- -	
	44	Nº 127 - -	- - - 3	- -	
	45	Nº 34 - -	- - - 4.	- -	
	46	Nº 128 -	- - - 5.	- -	
	47	Nº 11 Local Bd.	RL4504	- -	
	48	Nº 12 - -	RL4505	- -	
	49	Nº 13 - -	RL4506	- -	
	50	Nº 142 Main Bd.	RL4640.	- -	
	51	Nº 59 -	RL4641.	- -	
	52	Nº 143 - -	RL7227	Baker St -	
	53	Nº 58 - -	RL7228.	- -	
	54	Nº 141 - -	RL8123	Earls Ct -	
	55	Nº 60 - -	RL8264.	- -	
	56	Nº 56 - -	HO207	H.O. -	
	57	Nº 144 - -	HO208	- -	
	58	Nº 67. - -	HO218	- -	
	59	Nº 145 - -	HO.228.	- -	
	60	Nº 146 - -	HO.229.	- -	
	61	Nº 16 Local Bd.	HO. 388	- -	
	62	Nº 181 Main Bd.	Holborn HQ. PO Nº 2	Nº 14	
	63	Nº 61 - -	Kensington 9034	G.P.O. Exchange	
	64	Nº 62 - -	- 9035	- -	
	65	Nº 63 - -	- 9036	- -	
	66	Nº 166 - -	- 3461	- -	
	67	Nº 75 - -	- 3462	- -	
	68	Nº 167 - -	- 3463	- -	
	69	Nº 74 - -	- 3464	- -	
	70	Nº 168 - -	- 3465	- -	
	71	Nº 73 - -	- 3466	- -	
	72	Nº 169 - -	- 3467	- -	
	73	Nº 72 - -	- 3468	- -	
	74	Nº 76 - -	Frobisher 6692	- -	
	75	Nº 165 - -	- 6693	- -	
	76	Nº 164 - -	Abbey 5826	- -	
	77	Nº 78 - -	- 5827	- -	
	78	Nº 163 - -	- 5828	- -	
	79	Nº 77 - -	- 5829	- -	
	80	Nº 162 - -	Grosvenor 2962	- -	
	81	Nº 79 - -	- 2963	- -	
	82	Nº 80 - -	Sloane 2239	- -	
	83	Nº 161 - -	- 2230	- -	
	84	Nº 34 Local Bd	London Reg. ARP HQ. Nº 2		
	85	Nº 35 " "	CEB. Newgate Str. Control Room		
	86	Nº 82 Main Bd.			
	87	Nº 83 " "			
	88	Nº 84 "			
	89	Nº 85 " "	S.W. Sub Area.	P.O. S.Bd. Wes 1661.	Military [illegible]
	90	Nº 86 "	MILITARY		
	90A	Nº 87 "			
	90B	Nº 88 " "			
	90C	Nº 90 " "			
	90D	Nº 91 " "			
	90E	Nº 81 " "			
	90F	Nº 92 " "			
	90G	Nº 93 " "			
	90H	Nº 94			
	90I	Nº 95			
	90J				
	90K	~~Nº 94~~	~~C.E.B. ST PAULS~~		

FROM.			TO.		
Location.	Ref Nº	Termination	Location.	Termination	Circuit Nº P.O.
Dover St H.Q.	91	Nº 31 Mag Bd.	Leicester Sq Cont 1.	Nº 96 Emer Mg Bd	RA25298. (P/W)
	92	Nº 32 - -	- - - 2	Nº 97 - -	
	93	Nº 34 - -	Oval Tram Cont 1.		RA25301.
	94	Nº 35 - -	- - - 2		
	95	Nº 40 - -	Clapham Com Sub EE HQ.		
	96	Nº 10 -	Scotland Yard.	(WHI 1212 ARP SWBD)	RA25299. (P/W)
	97	Nº 24 - -	Down St Rec Nº 1.	(LMS SWBD WHI 6166)	RA25302. (P/W)
	98	Nº 25 - -	- - - Nº 2		
	99	Nº 21 - -	H.O. P.O. Nº 1.		
	100	Nº 22. - -	- - Nº 2		
	101	Nº 1 - -	RL4409	Leicester Sq Ex	
	102	Nº 2 - -	RL4522	- -	
	103	Nº 6 - -	HO.270	H.O. Exch.	
	104	Nº 7 - -	HO.271.	- -	
	105	Nº 11 - -	Grosvenor 4502	G.P.O. Exchange	
	106	Nº 12 - -	" " 4503	" "	
	107	Nº 13 - -	" " 4504	" "	
	108	Nº 14 - -	" " 4505	" "	
	109	Nº 15 - -	" " 4506	" "	
	110				
Holborn H.Q.	111	Nº 57 Mag Bd	Clapham Com Sub EE HQ.	Nº 34 Mag Bd	
	112	Nº 41 - -	Oval Tram Cont Nº 1	Nº 8 Ann	
	113	Nº 42 - -	- - - Nº 2	Nº 9 Ann.	
	114	Nº 62 - -	HO367	HO. Exch	
	115	Nº 63 - -	HO387	HO. Exch.	
	116	Nº 73 - -	Down St R.E.C.	Operating Control	
	117	Nº 76 - -	- - REC. (Mr Deacon)	Mr Deacons	
	118	~~Nº 94~~	~~Scotland Yard~~	[illegible]	RA100647
	119	Nº 91 - -	Leicester Sq Cont.	Nº 52 Emer Mg Bd	RA30683 (P/W)
	120	Nº 96 - -	Oval Cont. (Tram)	Nº 10 Ann.	RA100645 (P/W)
	121	Nº 97 - -	Down St REC.	LMS SWBD	RA100168?
	122	Nº 98 - -	- - -	" WHI 6166	RA100169?
	123	Nº 67 - -	H.O. PO Nº 1.	Nº 12 Position 2.	
	124	Nº 68 - -	- - Nº 2.	Nº 13 - 2.	
	125		RL4571	Leicester Sq Ex	
	126		RL4585.	- -	
	127		RL4597	- -	
	128	GPO SW Bd	Chancery 6301-9, 6300	GPO Exchange	
	129	" " 21	Down St. REC	Operating Control	LMS Instr.
	130	" " 20	Down St. REC.	Mr Deacons	" "
	131				
	132				
	133				
Clapham Common Sub Stn Chief E.E's H.Q.	134	Nº 33	Neasden S/S Cont	Nº 19 Mag Bd.	
	135	Nº 18	Leicester Sq Cont	Nº 340 Emer Mg Bd	
	136	Nº 40	Wood Green S/S Cont.	Instrument	
	137	Nº 20	Oval Tram Cont.	Nº 6 Ann.	
	138	Nº 21	Thornton Heath Tram	Instrument.	
	139	Nº 37	Lots Rd Gen SW Bd.		
	140		HO.282	HO. Exch	
	141		HO365	- -	
	142		HO. 552	- -	
	143		RL4203	Clapham N. Ex.	
	144		RL4217	- -	
	145		RL4226.	- -	
	146	Nº 24.	South Ken S/S	Instrument.	
	147	Nº 29.	Leicester Sq S/S Room Cont	Nº 2	
	148	GPO. SW Bd.	Tulse Hill 3493-5	GPO. Exchange	
	149				
	150				
	151				
	152				
	153				
Chalk Farm H.Q.	154	Nº 1	RL4439	Leicester Sq Ex.	
	155	Nº 10	RL4488	- -	
	156				
	157				
	158				
	159				
	160				
	161				
Leicester Sq Traffic Controller	162	Nº 260 Emer Mg Bd	Oval Tram Cont.	Nº 1 Ann	
	163	Nº 259 - -	" Bus Cont.	Nº 2 Ann.	
	164	Instrument.	Military HQ.		
	165	Nº 92 Emer Bd	Down Str R.E.C		
	166	Nº 10? "	- -	Instr LMS	RA 23573
	167				
	168				
	169				
	170				
Oval Tram Controller	171	Instrument.	Military HQ.		
	172				
	173	Main Exch	Lots Rd [illegible]	SWBD (LPTB)	
55 Broadway etc.	174	Auto Exchange	S.Rly. Waterloo X30	Private SW Bd.	
	175	" " "	LNER Kings Cross HO 252	" "	
	176	" " "	" " Liv St. HO370	" "	
	177	" " "	" " Marylebone RL7162	" "	
	178	" " "	LMS Euston HO 443	" "	
	179	" " "	GWR Pad HO 594	" "	
	180	Main Exchange	Vandon St Garage	[illegible]	EATN 379
	181	" "	Scotland Yard.	P.O. SWBD WHI 1212	RA100034
	182	Main & Emergency Exchanges	" "	" "	RA100167
	183	" "	Holborn HQ	P.O. SW Bd. Chan 63..	RA100861
	184	" "	" "	" "	RA100862
	185	" "	Leicester Sq	Inf Desk	Extn (M37 E26)
	186	" "	Oval Bus Cont	Inst P.O.	Extn (M7 LE/25)
	187	" "	Down St Rec.	Private SW Bd.	RA100159
	188	" "	Gillingham St Garage	[illegible]	RA100801
	189	" "	Baker St Offices	LPTB SWBD WEL [illegible]	CA41655
	190	Main & Emergency Exchanges	London Reg. ARP HQ	P.O. SWBD KEN 3431	RA100071
	191	Inst Room 430	Scotland Yard	Inst. Mr Tripp	P.W.L.R 237

—·—·—·— Denotes PO Private Wires

— — — — Proposed lines to Chiltern Court (See note)

Note:- It is assumed that the proposed switching arrangement at Holborn is still under consideration.

Signal Engineers Office Earls Court Stn. S.W.5.
Checked by ... Date 10.12.41
Approved ... Date 10-12-41

G Ref 90G 90K + 165 added WNT 7-5-42.

F. Ref 90F added. Ref 189 deleted. Est. office memo 53315/19.6.41 (F1/TS4)

E Refs 99, 100, 123, 124, 190 amended. Est. office

D Refs 90C-90E added. Refs 20 & 190 mod. 1-12-41

C Revised to letter 50382/LU226 16-10-41 from Est. office 6.11.41

B Refs. 84-90B added 24.10.41 HEB

A. Revised

London Passenger Transport Board
Chief Engineer's Dept
Office of Signal Engineer
Earls Court Station S.W.5
Drawn by GBS. Traced by GBS.
Checked by ... 19.6.41
Drg. No ...

Churchill had been dining in the basement behind closed steel shutters at the other end of the house. The following night, another bomb fell in Downing Street yard. F. W. Deakin, Churchill's pre-war researcher, wrote to the prime minister on 18 October, 'Please do take care of yourself in these trying days.'[6]

The Cabinet War Rooms (CWR) were not strong enough to act as a shelter and, while the War Rooms being reinforced and no.10 patched up, the prime minister was temporarily without a protected central London shelter. To the consternation of the War Cabinet, Churchill was a reluctant shelterer and was keen to pursue 'business as usual' as far as possible at Downing Street, to support public morale.[7] On this occasion he allowed himself to be persuaded by his cabinet colleague Josiah Wedgwood (brother of Sir Ralph Wedgwood) to take refuge in the REC headquarters until more suitable accommodation could be provided. Churchill later recalled 'I used to go there to transact my evening business and sleep undisturbed.'[8] But despite the comforts available at the REC, internal memos and oral history accounts suggest that the need for secrecy led to Churchill's camping in Cole Deacon's office at night, rather than sleeping in the staff bedrooms at platform level.[9]

According to the personal diary and oral accounts of Churchill's private secretary, John Colville, the prime minister spent at least eight nights at Down Street station between 23 October and 20 December 1940, by which time the Cabinet War Rooms' reinforcements had been completed.[10] The occasions Colville describes when he himself or the prime minister were present at Down Street show that the REC treated Churchill very well as their guest, with caviar, champagne and vintage brandy on offer, presumably provided from the stores of the railway hotels. The diary suggests that the opulent conditions at Down Street allowed Churchill to conduct business in his favoured manner – over dinner and drinks, with key figures such as Minister of Labour Ernest Bevin – in the same way he had at 10 Downing Street in the months prior. Colville recalls that other members of the War Cabinet and War Office were invited to the REC bunker; a diary entry for the night of 30 October records that Churchill and Bevin dined there, had been well plied with brandy and had great difficulty operating the lift. Once outside, the prime minister was nearly arrested in the street for arguing with a police officer about having car sidelights that were too bright.[11]

Colville described Down Street as 'the safest place', in stark contrast to civilian life on the surface. During the Blitz, Madeleine Henrey lived with her husband Robert and their baby son in a luxury flat in Shepherd's Market, less than 100 metres from Down Street. She published an invaluable account of their village's and neighbours' experience of nightly bombing and fires:

> We became accustomed to the sudden drone of an aeroplane in the middle of the morning, the screech of a bomb, the dull crash of its explosion and the smell of cordite ... Each morning it became a rite to visit neighbouring damage ... the road squads were still sweeping away the shattered glass and the hosepipes of the Auxiliary Fire Brigade lay snakelike from pavement to pavement.[12]

One night in November 1940, a bomb fell several streets away from the flat and shattered the windows in their spare room: 'the glass pounded to shreds and driven like nails into the opposite walls'. For civilians in the Blitz, even a near miss could be deadly. When compared with the experience of life working in heavily protected bunkers, it is easy to see why Churchill wrote of feeling 'a natural compunction at having more safety than most other people'.[13]

During this time, the War Cabinet were in process of commissioning of civilian deep-level shelters, while Churchill was still using Down Street as an occasional bolthole. The REC headquarters clearly left a good impression on the prime minister and his staff. He wrote fondly of his stay at Down Street and, according to Colville, nicknamed the site 'the burrow'. As a parting gift on the 21 December 1940, he sent £10 to the REC for their Christmas fund.[14]

A SECRET WITHIN A SECRET

Churchill adopted a policy of making his movements unpredictable in response to personal danger. His private secretaries rarely knew far in advance where he was going to settle for day or night-time work; they had to be ready at any moment to scuttle after him with the relevant papers. At the end of October 1940, John Colville recalls a colleague, John Peck, writing a spoof memo in the style of Winston Churchill:[15]

ACTION THIS DAY

Pray let six new offices be fitted for my use, in Selfridge's, Lambeth Palace, Stanmore, Tooting Bec, the Palladium and Mile End Road. I will inform you at 6 each evening at which office I shall dine, work and sleep. Accommodation will be required for Mrs Churchill, two shorthand typists, three secretaries and Nelson [black cat resident at 10 Downing St]. There should be shelter for all and a place for me to watch air-raids from the roof. This should be completed by Monday. There is to be no hammering during office hours, that is between 7 a.m. and 3 a.m. W.S.C.
31.10.40.

In January 1941 a genuine request came to the REC from the prime minister, asking for the only remaining empty passageway at Down Street to be converted for his use, 'as speedily as possible'. Churchill's request was enough to overcome London Transport's objection to building a suite of offices and accommodation in the second ventilation passageway [FIG.76].[16] The REC and London Transport delivered this request in less than six weeks, at a cost of more than £7,000 and in great secrecy.[17] Physical evidence survives in this passageway showing that the works were carried out using similar methods as for the rest of the headquarters, while employing techniques also used in conversions elsewhere, at Dover Street, for example.

Most of London Transport's records and plans of this secret project were subsequently destroyed, but a special requisition financial note reveals that the accommodation contained a suite of bedrooms, dining room, conference room and kitchen, and meeting rooms.[18] On 30 August 1941 Churchill wrote to the chairman of the REC to thank him for his hospitality of the previous autumn, and the note reveals that he had yet to return to visit his special premises.[19] Here the trail goes cold – no firm evidence has yet been found of who may have used the conversion from this point onwards.

[FIG.71] ABOVE The Railway Executive meeting in the committee room of Down Street headquarters on 26 April 1940. Seen, from left to right: Sir Eustace J. Missenden (SR); Sir James Milne (GWR); Sir William Wood (LMSR); W.H. Mills (REC Minute Clerk); E.G. Marsden, (REC Assistant to Secretary); Sir Charles H. Newton (LNER); Frank Pick (London Passenger Transport Board); Sir Ralph Wedgwood (first chairman); Gerald Cole Deacon (REC Secretary); and V.M. Barrington Ward (chairman of the Operating Committee).

[FIG.72] OPPOSITE ABOVE Though the original plan drawing numbered E.17478 was destroyed, it has been possible to recreate many of the features of Winston Churchill's special accommodation at Down Street by examining surviving witness marks and services, financial records and comparative studies of bunker modifications at other disused stations built during the same period. Careful examination of the site has determined that two of the rooms, likely to be bedrooms, shared a bathroom.

[FIG.73] OPPOSITE BELOW LEFT The surviving sewage ejector equipment was hidden from view of the REC in the base of the lift shaft, but it did much to maintain dignity and sanitation in the bunker. The alternative would have been the dreaded chemical toilet, which was the more typical solution for lavatories in places below sewer level, but also the cause of unpleasant smells in enclosed shelters.

[FIG.74] OPPOSITE BELOW RIGHT The most important equipment in the complex was the telephone exchange. The remains of the 50-line, two-person switchboard survive in the exchange room in their original position.

[FIG.75] NEXT Down Street's telephone exchange was directly connected to all the British mainline railway company headquarters, as well as strategically important government, military and national services.

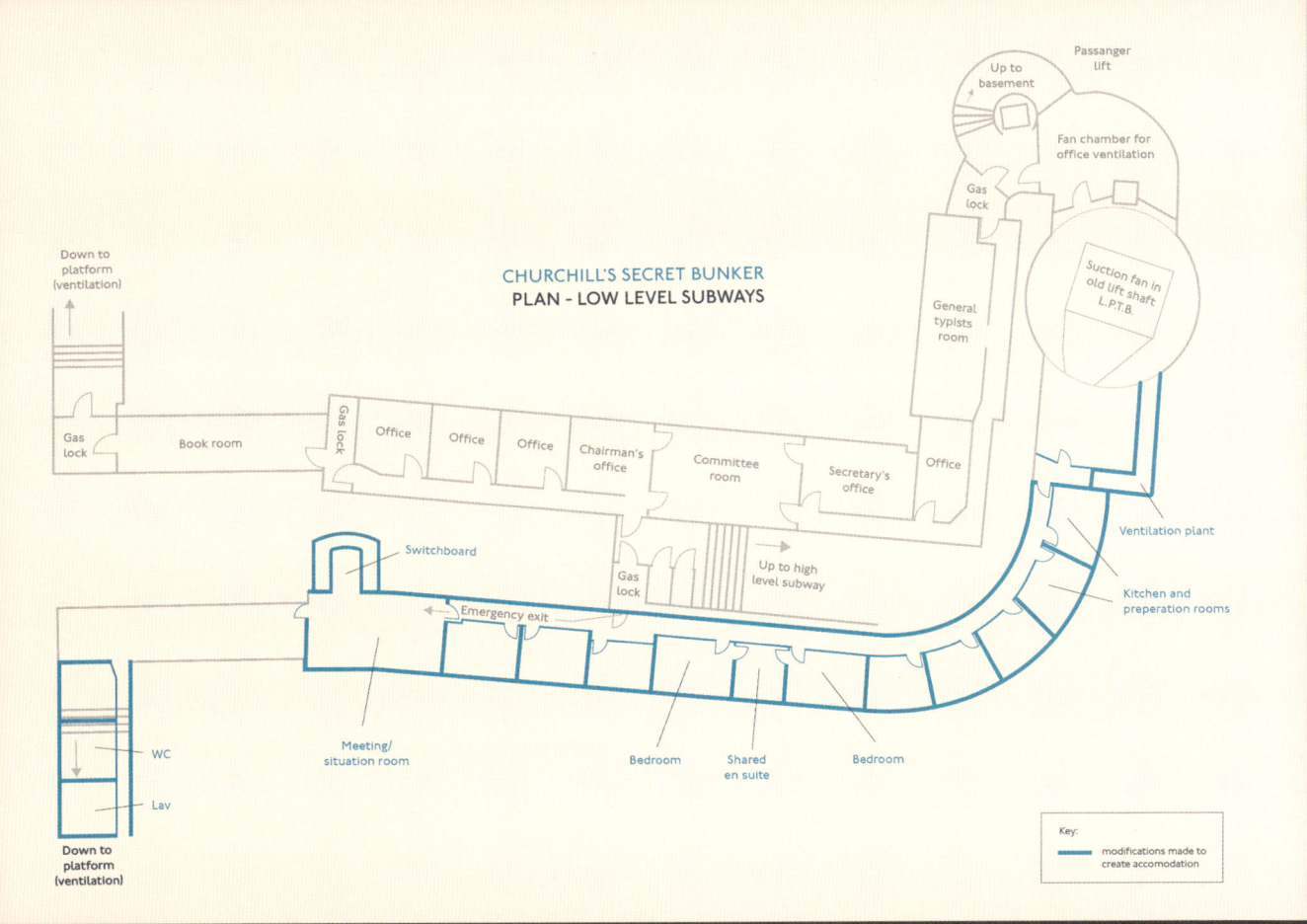

CHURCHILL'S SECRET BUNKER
PLAN - LOW LEVEL SUBWAYS

Down to platform (ventilation)

Gas lock

Book room

Gas lock

Office

Office

Office

Chairman's office

Committee room

Secretary's office

Office

General typists room

Gas lock

Up to basement

Passenger lift

Fan chamber for office ventilation

Suction fan in old lift shaft L.P.T.B.

Ventilation plant

Kitchen and preperation rooms

Switchboard

Emergency exit

Gas lock

Up to high level subway

WC

Lav

Down to platform (ventilation)

Meeting/ situation room

Bedroom

Shared en suite

Bedroom

Key: modifications made to create accomodation

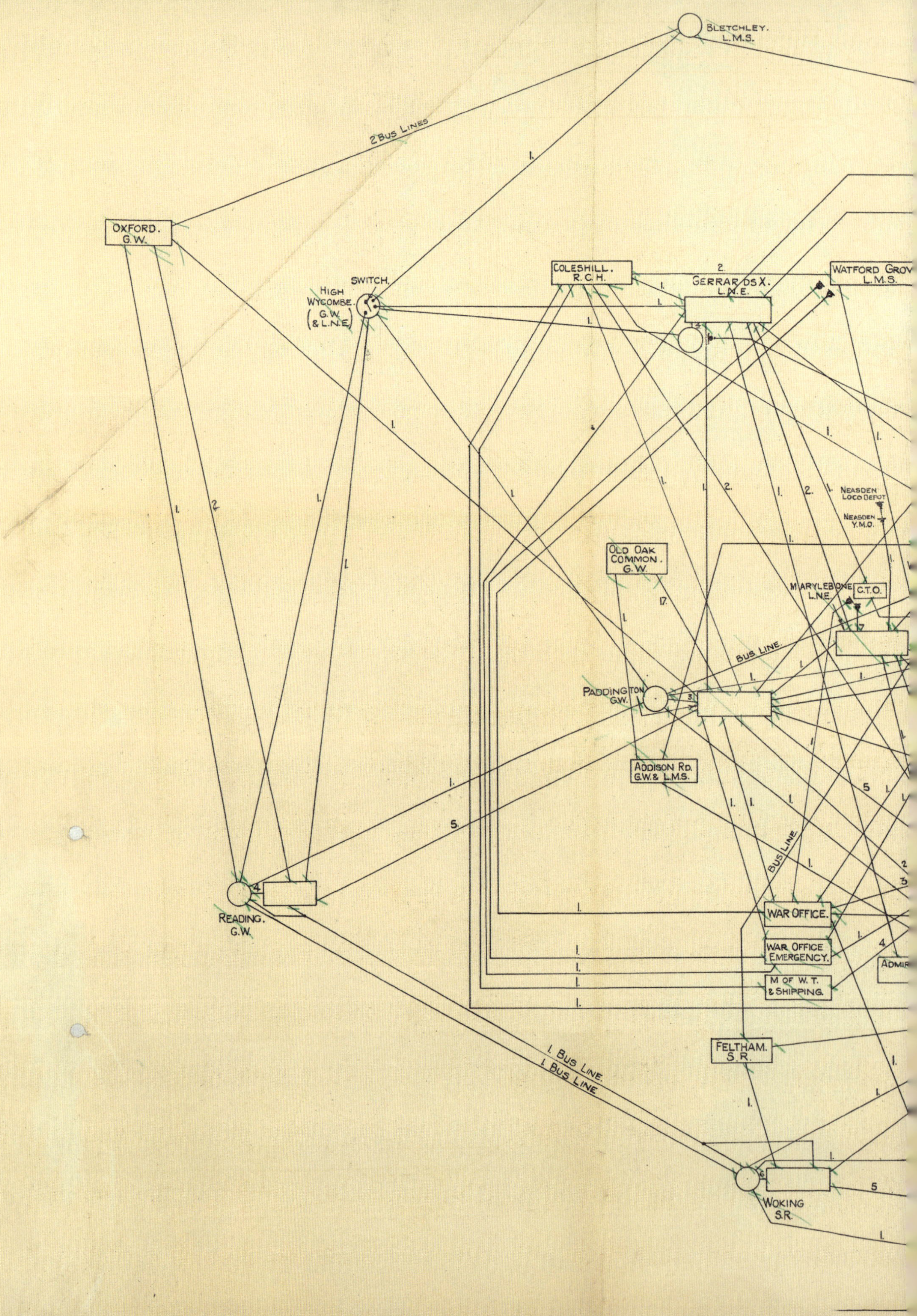
BLETCHLEY. L.M.S.
2 BUS LINES
OXFORD. G.W.
SWITCH.
HIGH WYCOMBE. (G.W. & L.N.E.)
COLESHILL. R.C.H.
GERRARDS X. L.N.E.
WATFORD GROV
L.M.S.
NEASDEN LOCO DEPOT
NEASDEN Y.M.O.
OLD OAK COMMON. G.W.
MARYLEBONE L.N.E.
C.T.O.
BUS LINE.
PADDINGTON G.W.
ADDISON RD. G.W. & L.M.S.
READING. G.W.
BUS LINE.
WAR OFFICE.
WAR OFFICE EMERGENCY.
M OF W.T. & SHIPPING.
FELTHAM. S.R.
1. BUS LINE.
1 BUS LINE
WOKING S.R.

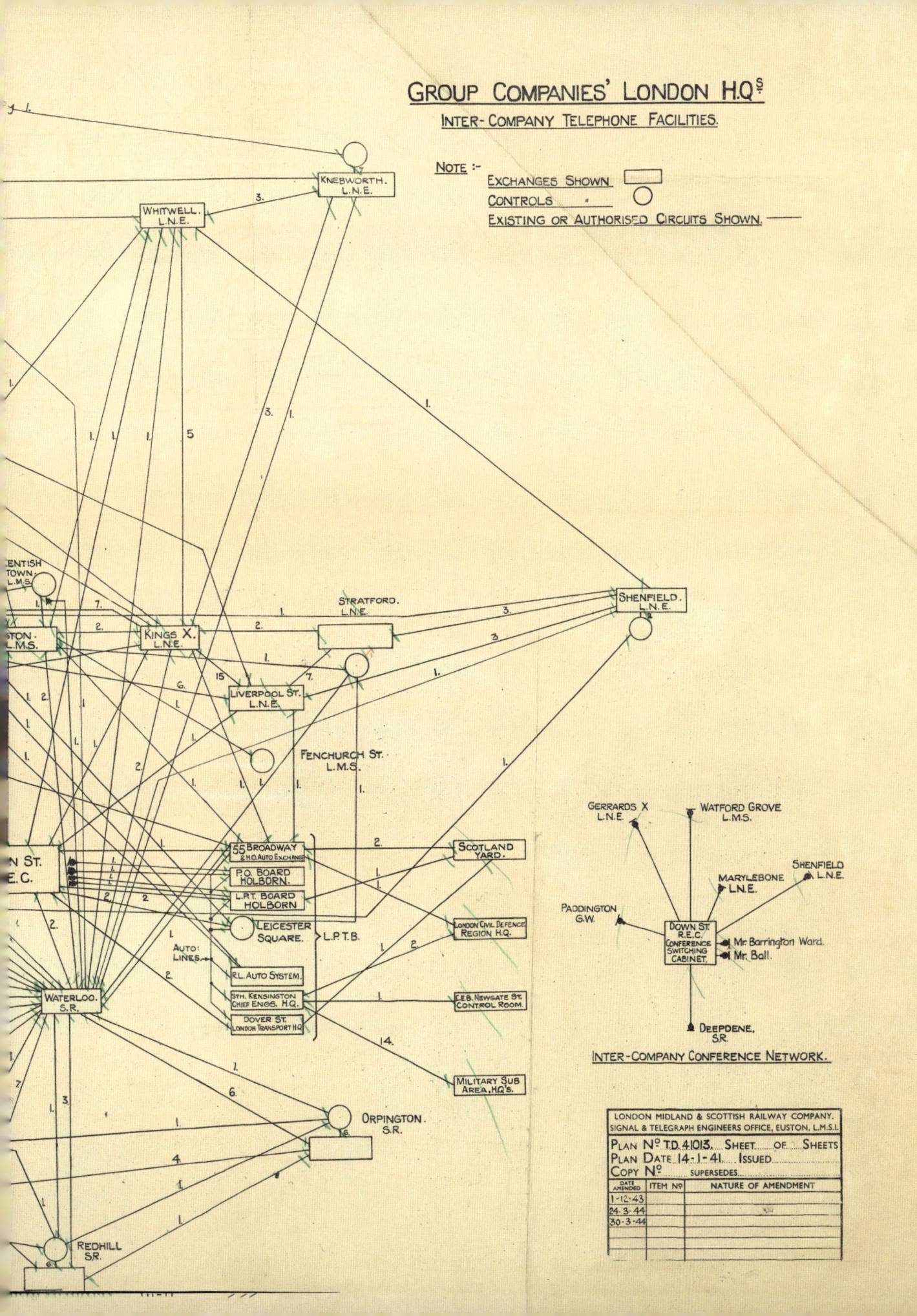

GROUP COMPANIES' LONDON H.Q.ˢ
INTER-COMPANY TELEPHONE FACILITIES.

NOTE:—
- EXCHANGES SHOWN ▭
- CONTROLS " ○
- EXISTING OR AUTHORISED CIRCUITS SHOWN ———

Exchanges/Controls shown on main diagram:
- KNEBWORTH. L.N.E.
- WHITWELL. L.N.E.
- KENTISH TOWN. L.M.S.
- ...STON. L.M.S.
- KINGS X. L.N.E.
- STRATFORD. L.N.E.
- SHENFIELD. L.N.E.
- LIVERPOOL ST. L.N.E.
- FENCHURCH ST. L.M.S.
- ...N ST. E.C.
- 55 BROADWAY & H.O. AUTO EXCHANGE
- P.O. BOARD HOLBORN.
- L.P.T. BOARD HOLBORN.
- LEICESTER SQUARE. } L.P.T.B.
- R.L. AUTO SYSTEM.
- STH. KENSINGTON CHIEF ENGRS. H.Q.
- DOVER ST. LONDON TRANSPORT H.Q.
- SCOTLAND YARD.
- LONDON CIVIL DEFENCE REGION H.Q.
- C.E.B. NEWGATE ST. CONTROL ROOM.
- MILITARY SUB AREA, H.Q.ˢ
- WATERLOO. S.R.
- ORPINGTON. S.R.
- REDHILL. S.R.

INTER-COMPANY CONFERENCE NETWORK.

- GERRARDS X L.N.E.
- WATFORD GROVE L.M.S.
- PADDINGTON G.W.
- MARYLEBONE L.N.E.
- SHENFIELD L.N.E.
- DOWN ST. R.E.C. CONFERENCE SWITCHING CABINET.
- Mr. Barrington Ward.
- Mr. Ball.
- DEEPDENE. S.R.

LONDON MIDLAND & SCOTTISH RAILWAY COMPANY.
SIGNAL & TELEGRAPH ENGINEERS OFFICE, EUSTON, L.M.S.I.

PLAN Nº T.D. 41013. SHEET ___ OF ___ SHEETS
PLAN DATE 14-1-41. ISSUED _____
COPY Nº ___ SUPERSEDES _____

DATE AMENDED	ITEM Nº	NATURE OF AMENDMENT
1-12-43		
24-3-44		
30-3-44		

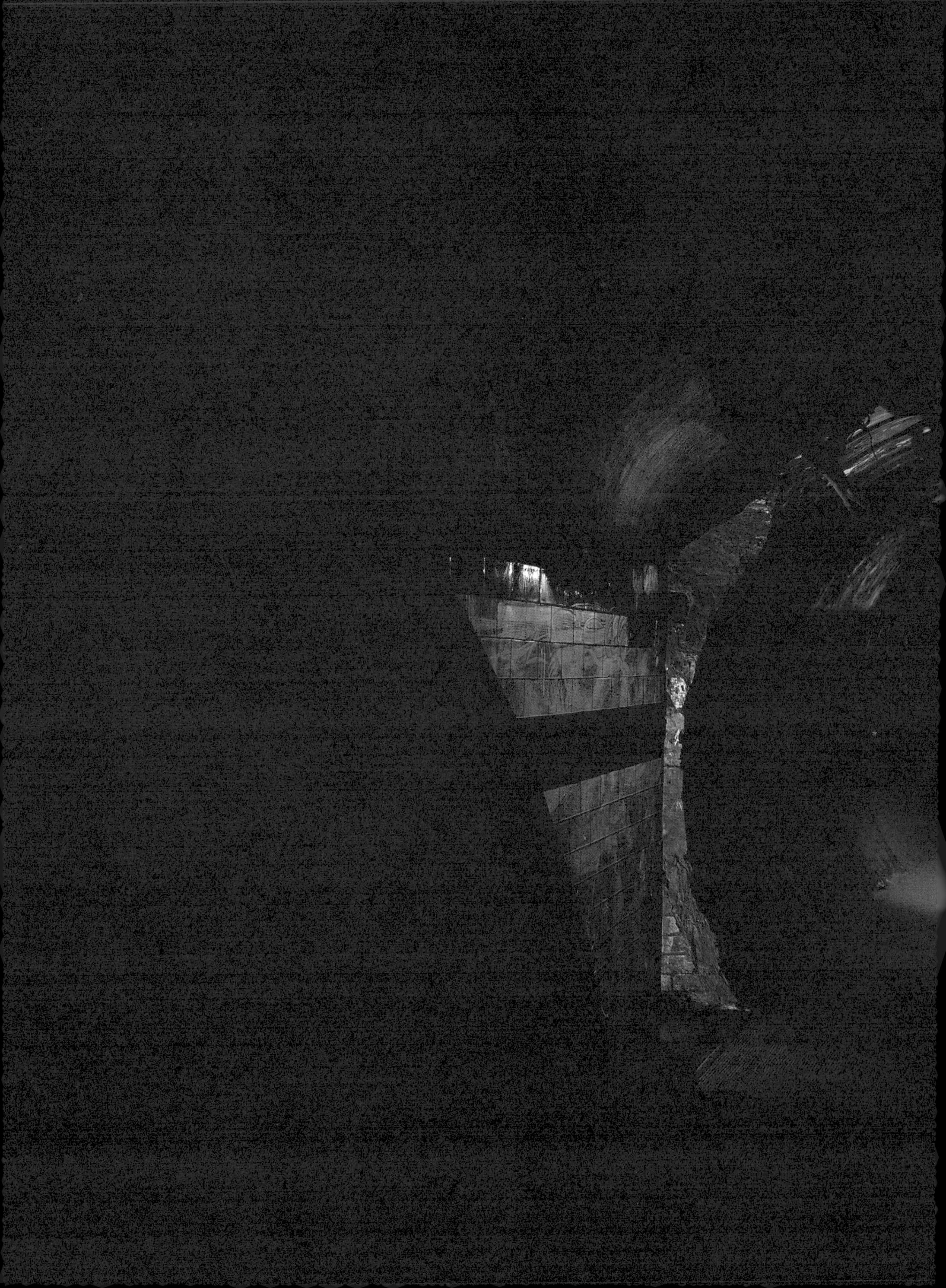

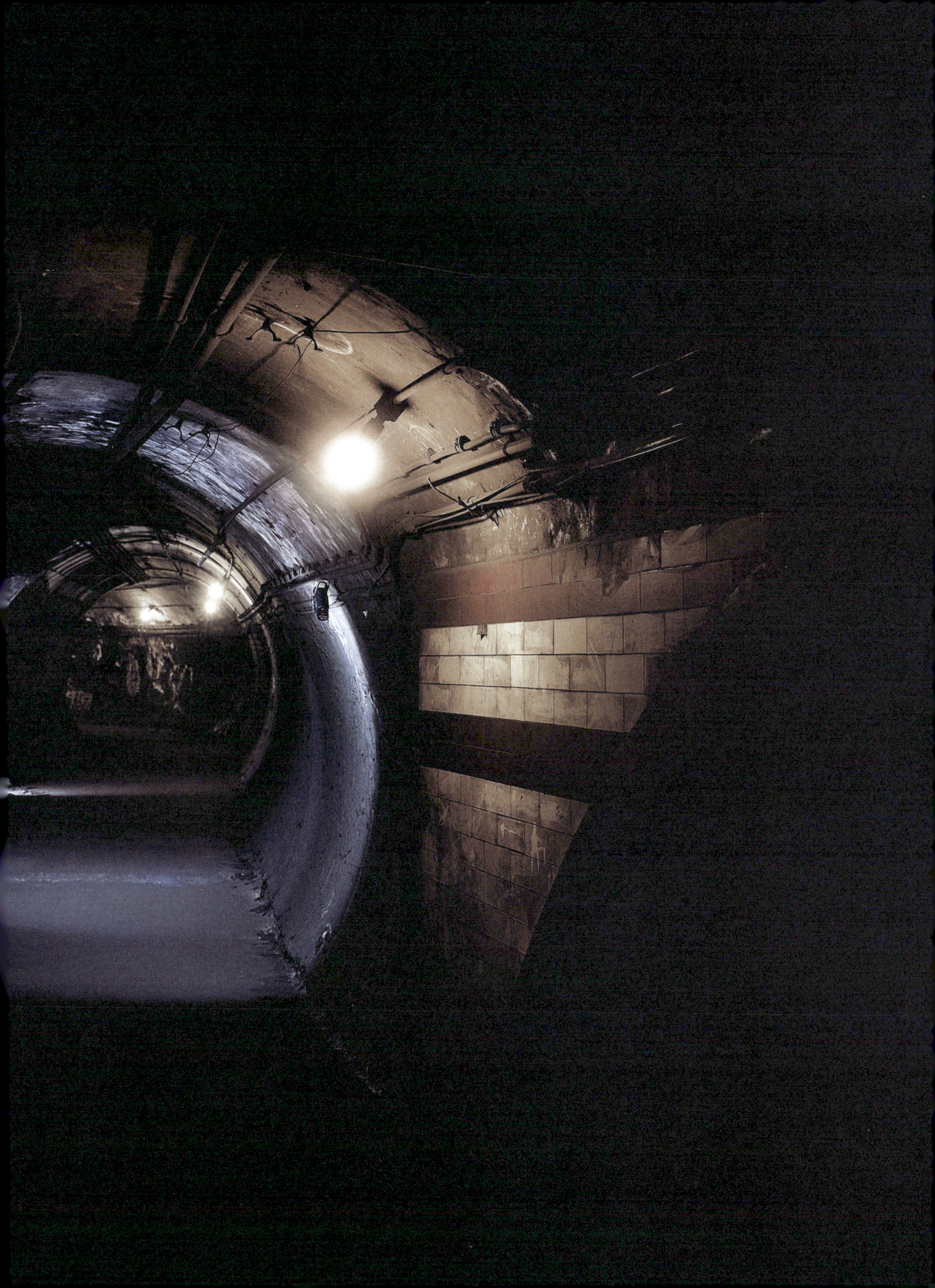

DOWN STREET TODAY

[FIG.76] PREVIOUS The ventilation passage that London Transport finally relinquished at Churchill's request on 22 January 1941, to be converted as a bunker for his use. London Transport maintenance staff cheekily referred to this facility as 'number 10'. The plastered corridor wall, levelled floors and surviving stubs of walls still hint at the purpose of this otherwise ordinary tunnel.

[FIG.77] ABOVE In 2016 the boards covering the station name were removed to inspect the condition of the tiled letters. The tiles for D and T appear to have been removed when a canopy was installed on the station facade in the latter years of its operation. Some of the letters have a little damage but most survive with a little gold leaf still on their surface.

Having performed war service, Down Street continued to host the REC until 31 December 1947, when it was dissolved, as Britain's railways nationalised on 1 January 1948. Afterwards, the station quickly reverted to its former role as a ventilation shaft; some of the modifications made for the REC were removed to allow air to flow through passageways again, but many survive (where they are not in the way, or where equipment is too awkward to be easily removed). Dark corridors, small rooms, the rumble of trains, and gas-lock doors that slam in the breeze created by passing trains — all contribute to the atmosphere of the site. The brickwork around the heavy steel door is the only remaining external evidence of the station's war service [FIG.77].

OTHER WARTIME CONVERSIONS

BROMPTON ROAD

[FIG.78] Brompton Road station opened on 15 December 1906, its entrance close to the Victoria and Albert Museum between Knightsbridge and South Kensington stations. The station met a similar fate to Down Street and closed on 30 July 1934.

Before the outbreak of the Second World War, the War Office bought the surface building, lift shafts and lower passageway of the disused Brompton Road station from London Transport, to be converted and form the central London anti-aircraft operations command centre for the Royal Artillery. The War Office also leased the platforms and a second passageway from London Transport and implemented a remarkable bunker scheme, much of which served as a prototype for the Down Street REC bunker.

[FIG.79] TOP LEFT Constructed in a lift shaft, this space housed the command centre for the 26th London Anti Aircraft Brigade. Works were completed by construction firm McAlpine, who were later awarded the contract to convert Down Street.

[FIGS 80 & 81] TOP RIGHT AND ABOVE A wartime briefing room with projection screen (top) and original platform tiling (above).

HOLBORN

[FIG.82] RIGHT Holborn's disused tunnels were adapted for use as additional headquarters accommodation for London Transport staff. The distinctive tiling pattern served to decorate the walls of the rooms built along a platform.

[FIG.83] BELOW Today, Holborn's platform 5, with its original tiling pattern, serves as valuable accommodation for night-time engineering equipment.

SOUTH KENSINGTON

Engineering was critical to the resilience of the transport network during wartime. Part of South Kensington station was repurposed as the protected headquarters for London Transport's engineering control services during the Second World War.[20] A deep-level tunnel constructed for the District line had been built between Earls Court and Gloucester Road in 1903 but abandoned. In 1927 it was remodelled as a school for signalling engineers but, in 1939, it was repurposed as offices and a plan store for the chief engineering services staff.

[FIGS 84 & 85] ABOVE During the Second World War, disused District line tunnels at South Kensington housed offices and bomb detection equipment linked to hydrophones under the Thames.

[FIG.86] BELOW The lift passageways of South Kensington, with posters and original tiles preserved from 30 September 1974, when escalators replaced the lifts.

YORK ROAD

York Road was a surprisingly large station given its location in what was one of the poorer areas of London when it opened in 1906. When closed on 19 September 1932, it was earmarked as a station with strong potential as a shelter and, in 1939, the site was considered as a location for the protected headquarters for senior London Transport staff. However, staff successfully lobbied Frank Pick to choose a different location, since York Road was far from the city centre, and Dover Street was chosen instead.[21]

[FIG.87] York Road's four lift shafts are brought together in a beautifully engineered vaulted lobby.

DOVER STREET

[FIG.88] BELOW The layout of the telephone exchange for the London Transport headquarters, built in a former lift passageway at Dover Street. This plan corroborates the witness marks at Down Street station, left by wall construction techniques used to build Churchill's bunker.

[FIG.89] NEXT A disused lift passageway at Dover Street bears the witness marks of its conversion to protect the chairman of London Transport and his staff during the Second World War. Marks on the floor and walls show where lavatories and office rooms were constructed. The yellow paint suggests an attempt to brighten the dark passageways.

Dover Street's lift shafts stood empty after the station was remodelled with escalators and renamed Green Park in 1933. Although not as deep as York Road, it was more centrally located. It was also conveniently positioned, just a few minutes' walk from the Mayfair home of London Transport's chairman, Albert Stanley, Lord Ashfield, in South Street. In the spring of 1941, the empty passageways and twin lift shafts were fitted out with impressive facilities, to accommodate 12 people, including Ashfield, his heads of department and a handful of service staff. The bunker included offices, a telephone exchange, bedrooms and plumbed toilets and washing facilities.[22]

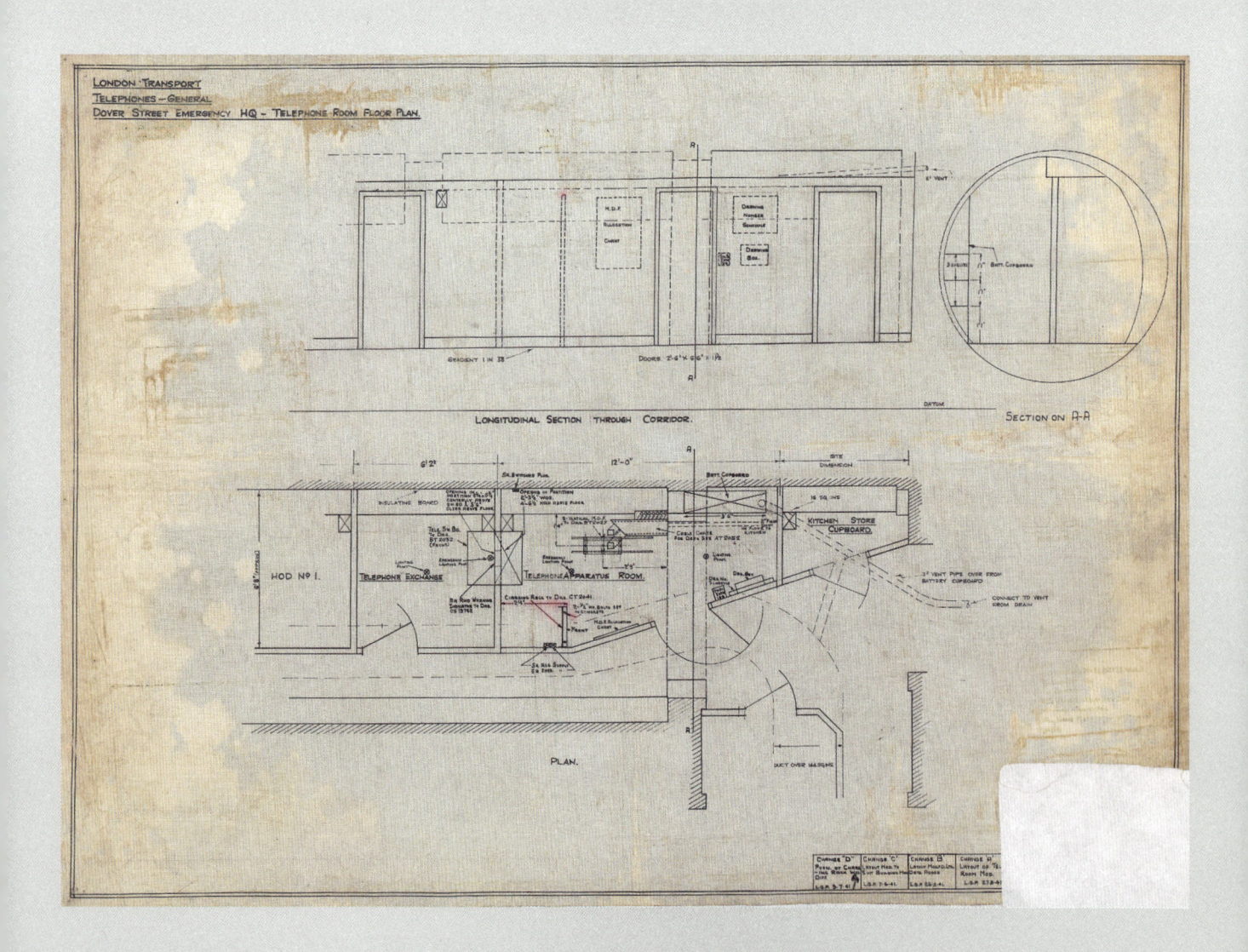

1   For further reading on the Spanish Civil War and its context, see Paul Preston, *The Spanish Civil War: Reaction, Revolution and Revenge* (Collins, 1996).
2   TfL Archive, LT000527/002/002.
3   Memo from Frank Pick to F.C. Buller, Esq., 29 March 1939, TfL Archive, LT509/70124/D.
4.   *Railway Gazette*, 24 November 1944.
5.   Cited in Sir Martin Gilbert, *Winston S. Churchill, Volume 6: Finest Hour, 1939–1941* (Hillsdale College Press, 2011), pp.842–4.
6.   Gilbert 2011, p.852.
7.   Letter from Sir Archibald Sinclair [Secretary of State for Air] to Churchill, chastising him for neglecting to use an air-raid shelter himself while insisting that the rest of the country do so, 15 September 1940, Churchill Archive Centre, CHAR 20/8/12-13.
8   Winston Churchill, *The Second World War 4: The Commonwealth Alone* (Cassell, 1964), p.50.
9   Note to messengers from Gerald Cole Deacon, 28 October 1940, National Archives, 521/4 Pt2.
10   Sir John Colville, oral history, Imperial War Museum, 2717.
11   Sir John Colville, *The Fringes of Power: Downing Street Diaries 1939–1955* (Weidenfeld & Nicolson, 2004), p.236.
12   Robert Henrey, *A Village in Piccadilly* (J.M. Dent, 1942), pp.26–7.
13   Churchill 1964, p.50.
14. Letter from Winston Churchill to Gerald Cole Deacon, December 1940, Churchill Archive Centre, CHAR 20/2B/167 21.
15   Colville 2004, p.237. Nelson was the black cat who lived at 10 Downing Street.
16   'Conversion of the Passage at the above address', 20 January 1941, TfL Archive, LT233/377 E/3/9.
17   'Report no. 441, Special Expenditure Requisition 11/2154', 30 September 1942, TfL Archive, LT233/377 A/41/3.
18   Ibid.
19   Letter from Churchill to Sir Ralph Wedgwood upon his retirement [as chairman of] the Railway Executive Committee, thanking him for his services to Government, 30 August 1941, Churchill Archive Centre, CHAR 20/22A/89.
20   Desmond F. Croome and Alan A. Jackson, *Rails Through the Clay: A History of London's Tube Railways* (Capital Transport, 1993), p.21.
21   York Road Emergency Headquarters, 27 April 1939, TfL Archive, LT000042/023.
22   Accommodation at Dover Street and second floor, 55 Broadway, 7 March 1941, TfL Archives, LT233/377 A/41/3.

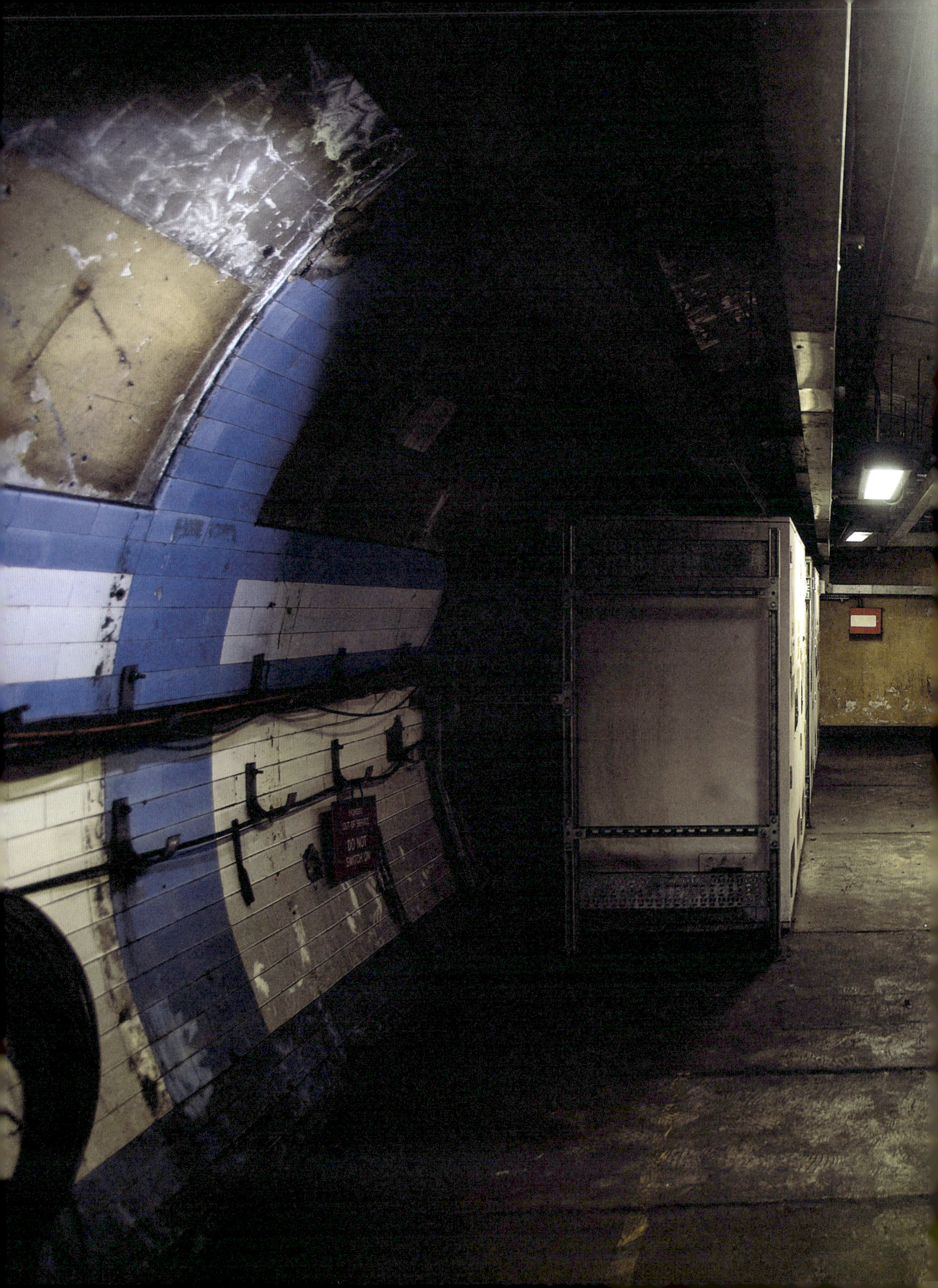
DO NOT
SWITCH ON

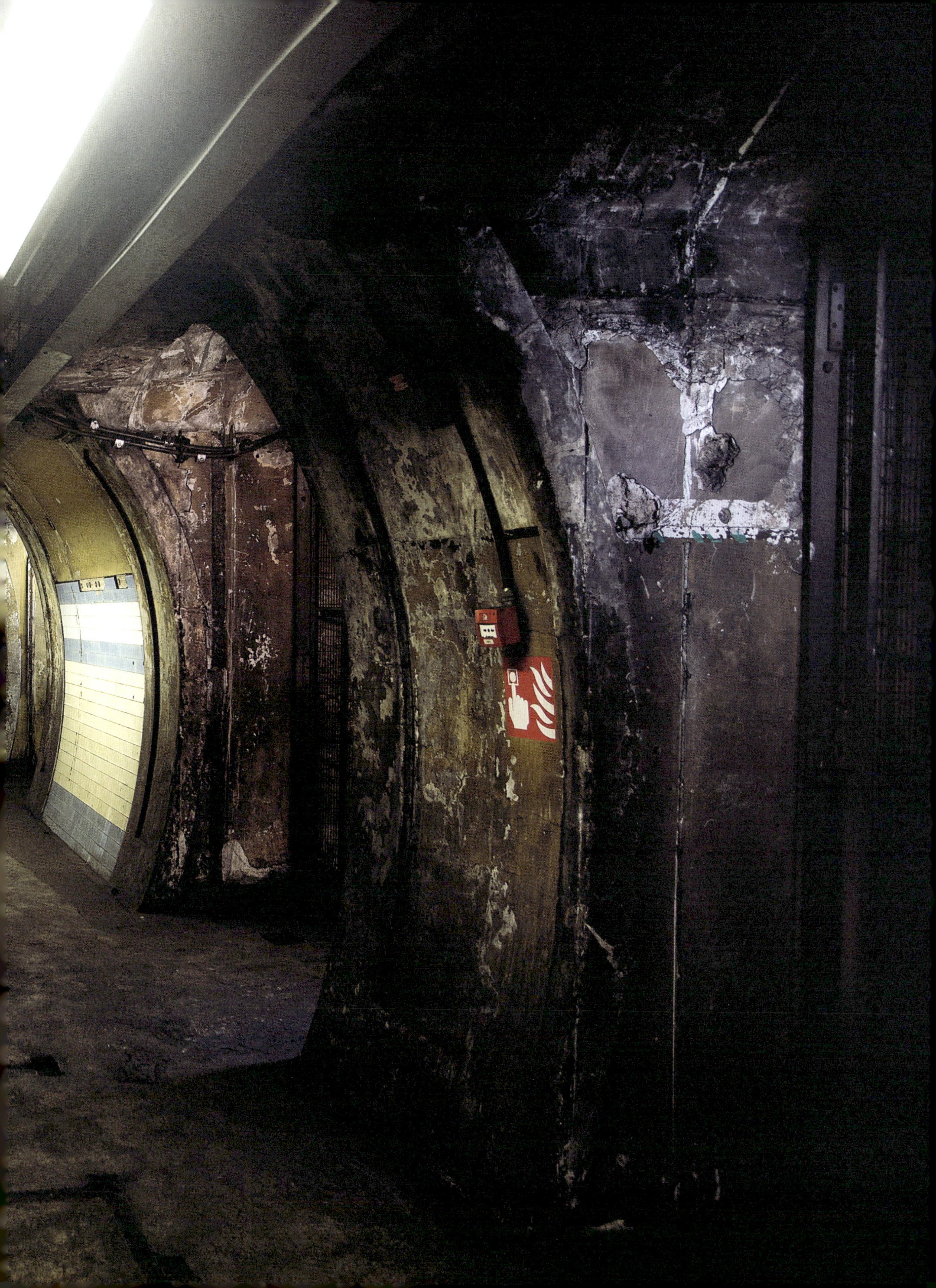

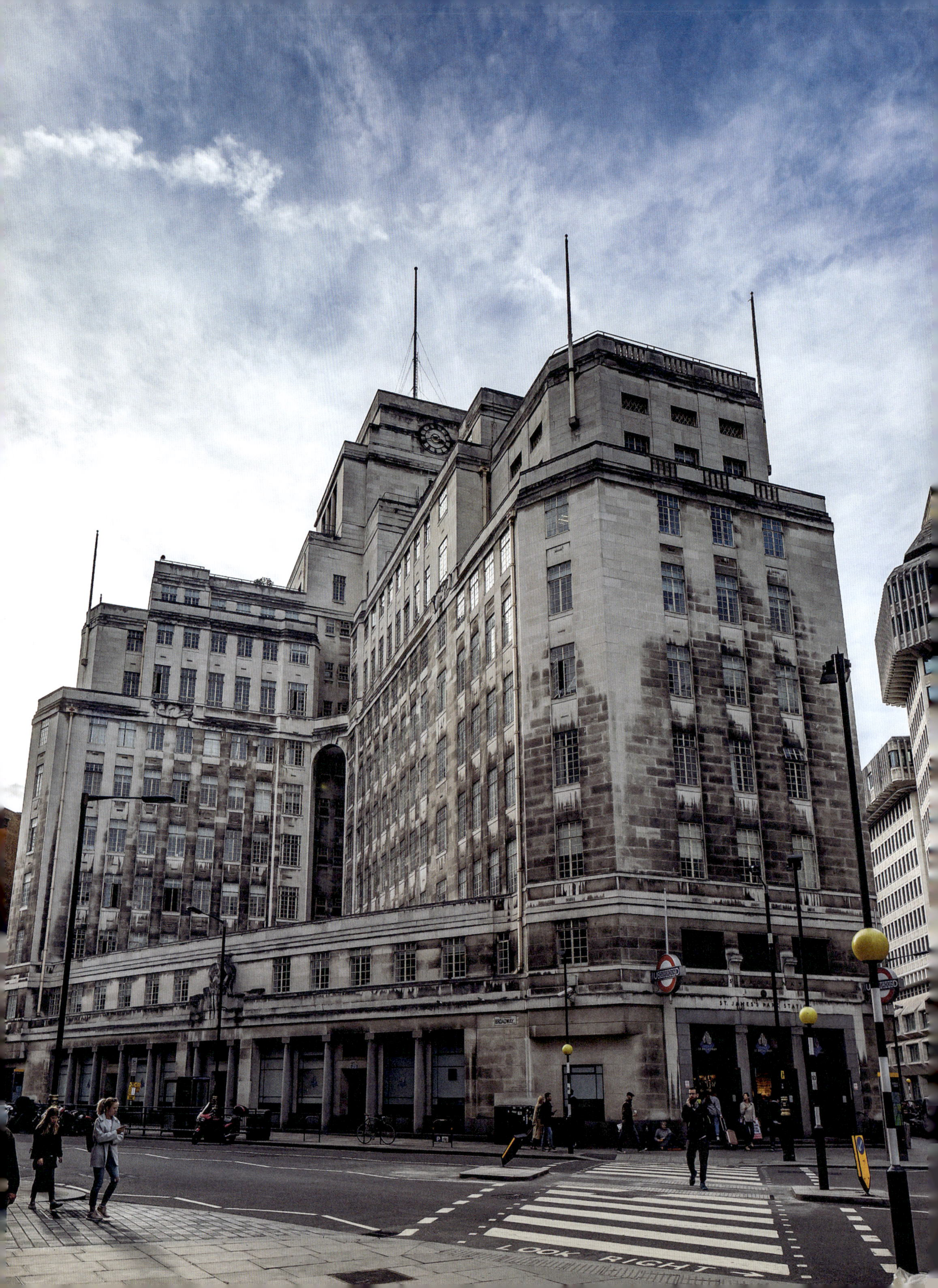
BROADWAY
LOOK RIGHT

55 BROADWAY

A CATHEDRAL OF MODERNITY

Metropolitan District Railway.

Saint James's Park Station

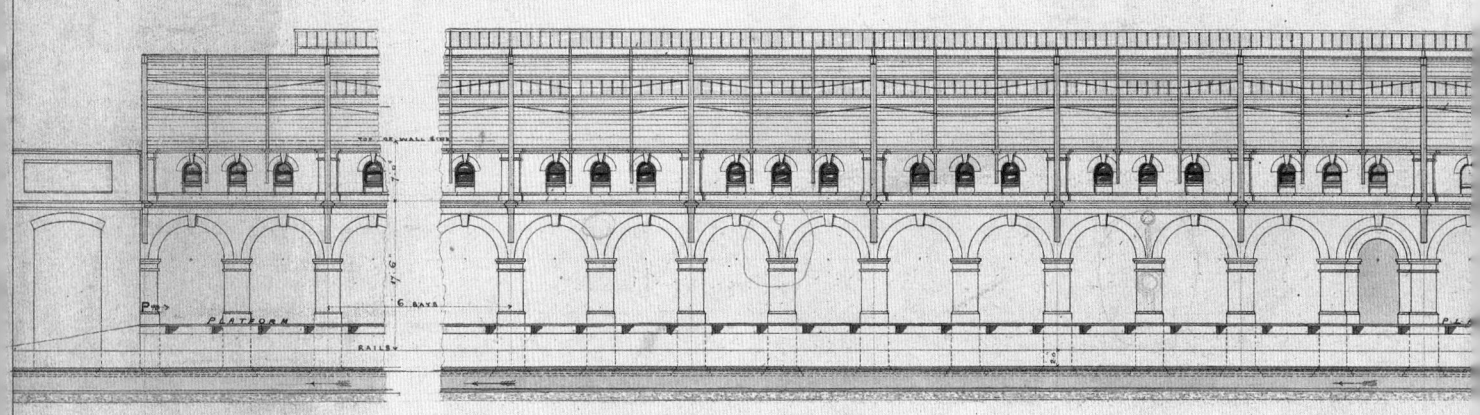

15 BAYS OF ROOF

INCLINATION OF DRAIN 1 IN 132

INCLINATION OF DRAIN 1 IN 1320

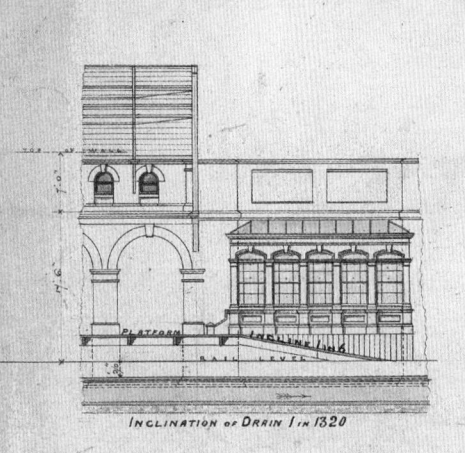

ELEVATION OF SIGNAL BOX.

SEC

DRAWING No 5.

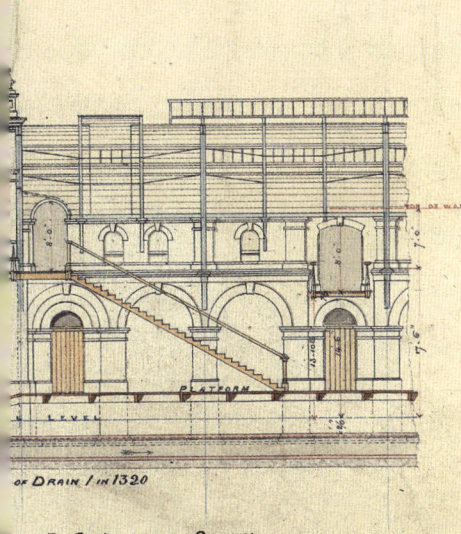

C-D

D-C LOOKING SOUTH

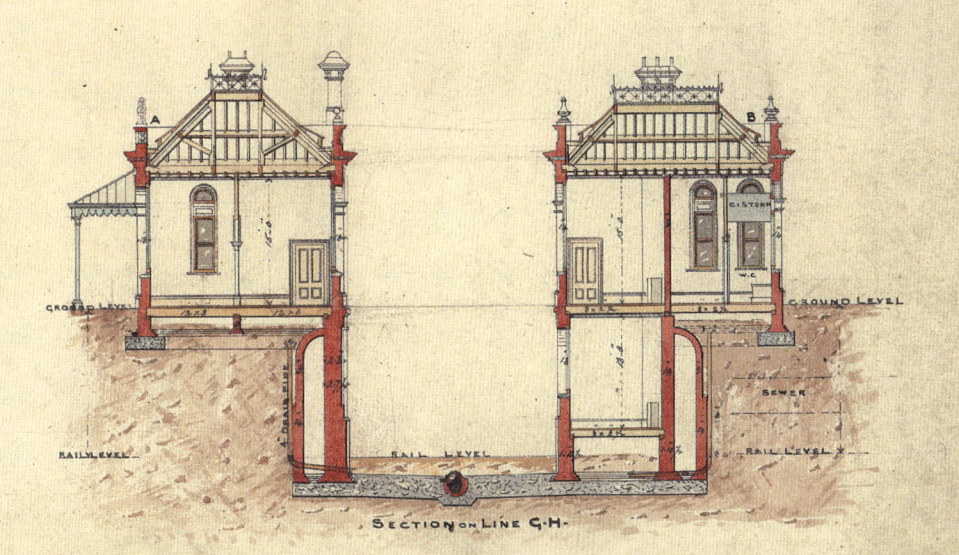

SECTION ON LINE G-H

SCALE OF FEET

52/006

[FIG.90] PAGE 108 55 Broadway – at ten storeys, with an additional central tower rising to 53 metres (175 feet), it was London's tallest office building when built in 1929.

[FIG.91] PREVIOUS 55 Broadway sits above St James's Park Underground station, opened in 1868 as part of what is now the District line. This plan shows the original surface station and platform canopy, which were later demolished to make way for a modest head office known as Electric Railway House, the predecessor of 55 Broadway.[1]

[FIG.92] ABOVE How things might have looked. This early proposal for an enlarged head office was drawn up by the Underground Group's in-house architect, Stanley Heaps, in 1916. Occupying the current site of 55 Broadway, the structure was tentatively, and unimaginatively, named 'Traffic Buildings'. The proposal was probably shelved due to wartime material shortages and later rejected altogether in favour of a more modern design.

For 90 years, the imposing, Portland stone facade of the historic headquarters of Transport for London (previously, London Transport) has dominated the junction of Broadway, Petty France and Tothill Street in the heart of Westminster. Known simply by its postal address of 55 Broadway, this building is a masterpiece of Modernist design. Cleverly symbolising the progressive civic values that the Underground Group advanced from its formation in 1902, the building, commissioned in 1926, placed public transport at the heart of the capital's social and commercial life.

The headquarters of the Underground Electric Railways of London, Underground Group (as the building was originally) was intended to be both a striking architectural statement and the realisation of the 'fitness for purpose' philosophy advocated by the Group's managing director Frank Pick and the building's chief architect, Charles Holden. The result was London's first American-style skyscraper, featuring many innovative design solutions, including a cruciform plan and tapering, stepped form, which maximised admittance of natural light to the open-plan office spaces. Every detail, from light fittings and office furniture through to the famous exterior sculptures, was carefully considered to create a unified whole. Described as 'a cathedral of modernity' in one source, 55 Broadway was awarded the London Architectural Medal by the Royal Institute of British Architects (RIBA) in 1929 and the building has since received Grade I Listed status, placing it among the nation's most important historic structures.[2]

Yet 55 Broadway is relatively little-celebrated today. Few Londoners rushing though the ground-floor arcades to St James's Park station below are aware of the building's historic significance. Fewer still have had an opportunity to access the working spaces that are hidden from public view.

[FIGS 93 & 94] The realisation of 55 Broadway was down to the vision of two exceptional men: Frank Pick (left), the managing director of the Underground Group, and Charles Holden (right), a lead architect of the firm Adams, Holden and Pearson. As founding members of the Design & Industries Association (DIA), both men were committed to the highest standards of architectural design, placing equal emphasis on the look and usability of modern buildings. In choosing Holden, Pick was consciously rejecting the conservative style of the Underground in favour of a distinctive new identity for public transport – one that was 'fit for purpose'.[3]

[FIGS 95 & 96] 55 Broadway is located on an awkward, diamond-shaped site. Charles Holden's inspired solution was to build a cruciform structure, with four wings radiating from a central tower: 'I do not think I was ever more excited than when I realised the possibilities of the cross-shaped plan – good light, short corridors, and a compact core containing all services, complete with lifts and staircases communicating directly with all four ways.'[4] Work began in 1927 (right), with the building structured around a steel-framed skeleton of the type pioneered for American skyscrapers. The sparse exterior was clad in Portland stone from Broadcroft in Dorset, with granite piers and black marble capitals on the ground floor. As can be seen from a plan of the ground floor (below), a key consideration for Holden was ease of public access from street level to St James's Park station.

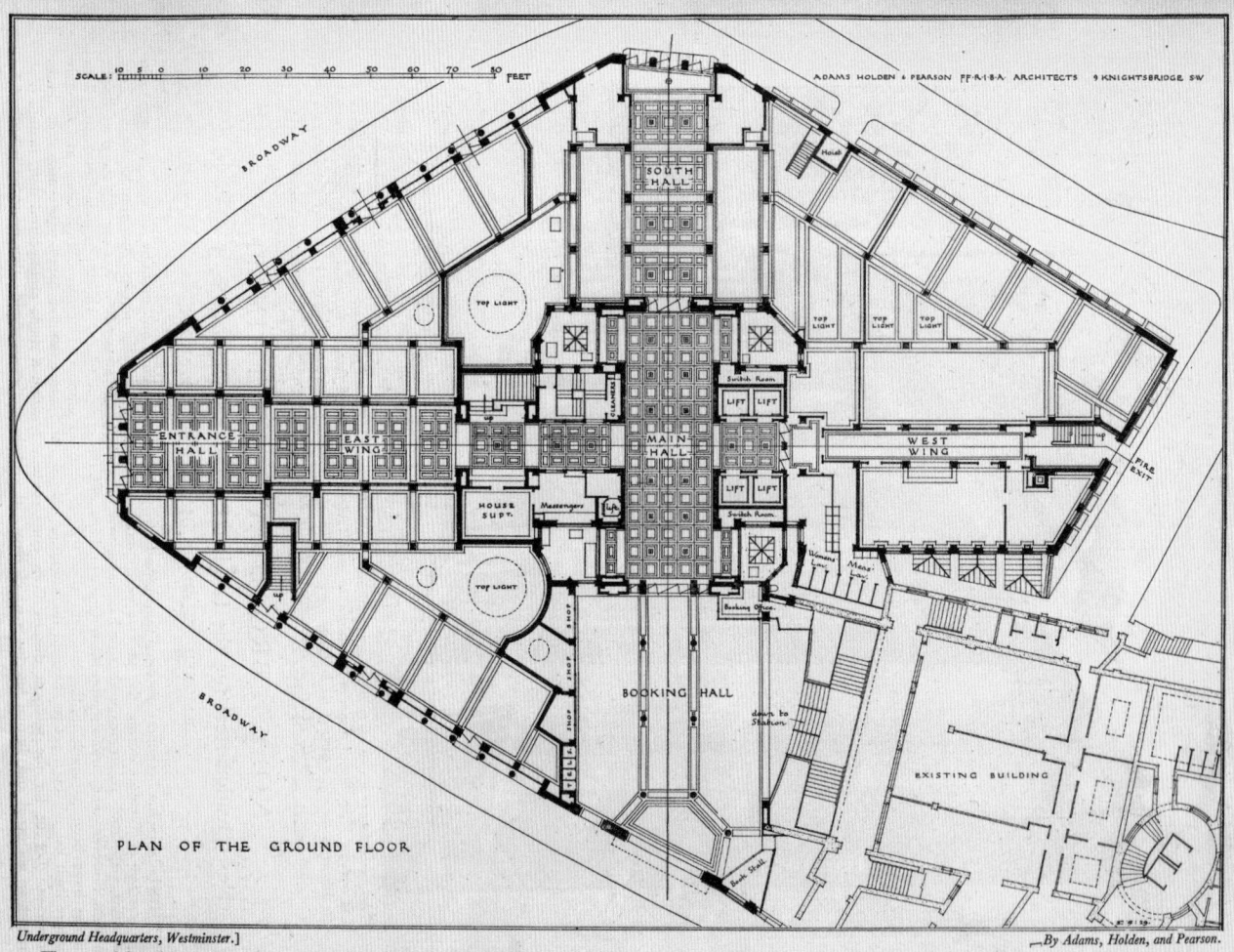

PLAN OF THE GROUND FLOOR

Underground Headquarters, Westminster.] — *By Adams, Holden, and Pearson.*

The ground-floor plan. The site is traversed by the Underground Railway, which lies just below ground level, and St. James's Park Station had to be incorporated into the plan. The office bays are set out in the form of a cross. In the centre, under the tower, is the vertical circulation of lifts and the main staircase. This type of plan is eminently suitable for the site, and gives maximum light and air. The north entrance to the building is also that to St. James's Park Station.

[FIG.97] ABOVE The 'cathedral of modernity', photographed by Aerofilms in 1929. At this time, the gleaming white facade of 55 Broadway dominates the low-rise Westminster skyline. Holden's later buildings would be more starkly Modernist, using brick and raw concrete rather than Portland stone as a finish.

[FIG.98] RIGHT Also designed by Charles Holden, the ground-floor concourse and interior corridors were lavishly treated in Italian travertine marble, with bronze doors, shutters and windows. This drawing shows the modern-day staff entrance, originally a public thoroughfare for passengers approaching St James's Park station from Broadway.

[FIG.99] RIGHT The top two floors of the central tower at 55 Broadway contain the winding mechanism for the roundel-inspired clock face, seen here in a dramatic night-time photograph from 1951.

[FIG.100] BELOW Charles Holden commissioned some of the most famous sculptors of the day to carve large figurative reliefs directly onto the exterior stonework.[5] The most controversial were two groups created by the avant-garde artist Jacob Epstein. Entitled *Day* and *Night*, they were attacked in the popular press as being vulgar and primitive, but the designs generated considerable public interest, as this contemporary commercial postcard testifies. Epstein was unmoved by the criticism: 'The man on the street is a fool, and I don't care a whit about his opinion. I should be a fool, too, if I were in the least influenced by him.'[6] Holden and Frank Pick also stood by the work, the latter offering to resign in support of Epstein. The resignation was not accepted and the sculptures can be seen today above the original entrances on Broadway and Petty France.

[FIGS 101, 102, 103, 104] Behind the grand exterior and away from the public areas, the true purpose of 55 Broadway is revealed.

While many office blocks of the period contained a maze of small, disconnected rooms, 55 Broadway adopted American-style, open-plan spaces, which could be subdivided by glass partitions as necessary. It was all part of Charles Holden's plan to create a flexible working environment, fit for purpose. The various departments of the organisation, such as those focusing on railways, buses and public relations, were concentrated on separate floors, but with a strong sense of interconnectedness, reinforced by centralised and shared facilities. The building also reflected the social hierarchy of the early days, with palatial board room facilities and an 'officers' dining room'. The chairman's office (top left), photographed in 1931, has a suitably impressive and austere feel, with walnut panelling to dado height, a moulded ceiling and French windows leading to a stone balcony.

Some of these social distinctions survived into the 1970s. Nick Agnew, a trainee with Central Road Services in 1969, and later general manager of the District line, remembers the strict dress codes enforced at the time (suits and ties for men), and the feeling of 'an unchanging environment', oblivious to wider social trends.[7] Staff were addressed as 'Sir' or 'Mister', depending on their rank (there were few senior women), while uniformed lift attendants formally greeted employees on their arrival. In another throwback to the past, all correspondence was dealt with by a central typing pool of female secretaries (top right), with messengers delivering notes between offices.

While most women employed at Broadway before the war had secretarial jobs, it is noticeable that all the 'draughtsmen' shown in the 1938 drawing office are women (below right), underlining London Transport's more progressive, if ultimately limited, approach to recruitment. The photograph (below left) shows a meeting of the Public Relations Committee, with the publicity officer, Harold Hutchinson, reviewing the latest poster design by the artist David Lewis in 1951.

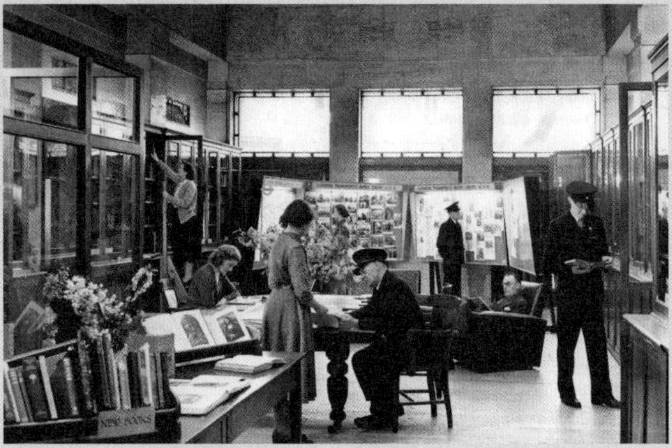
NEW BOOKS

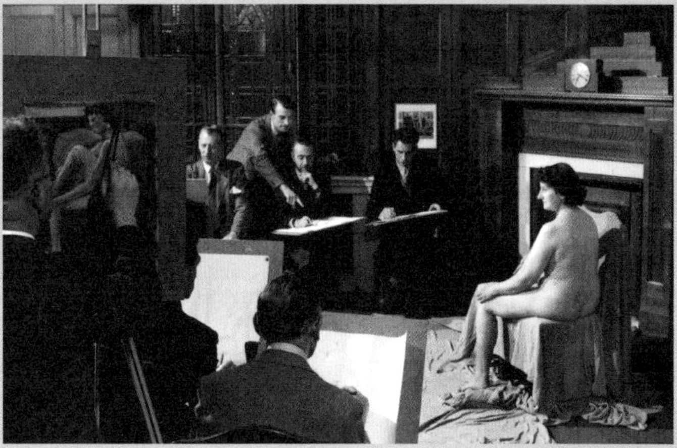

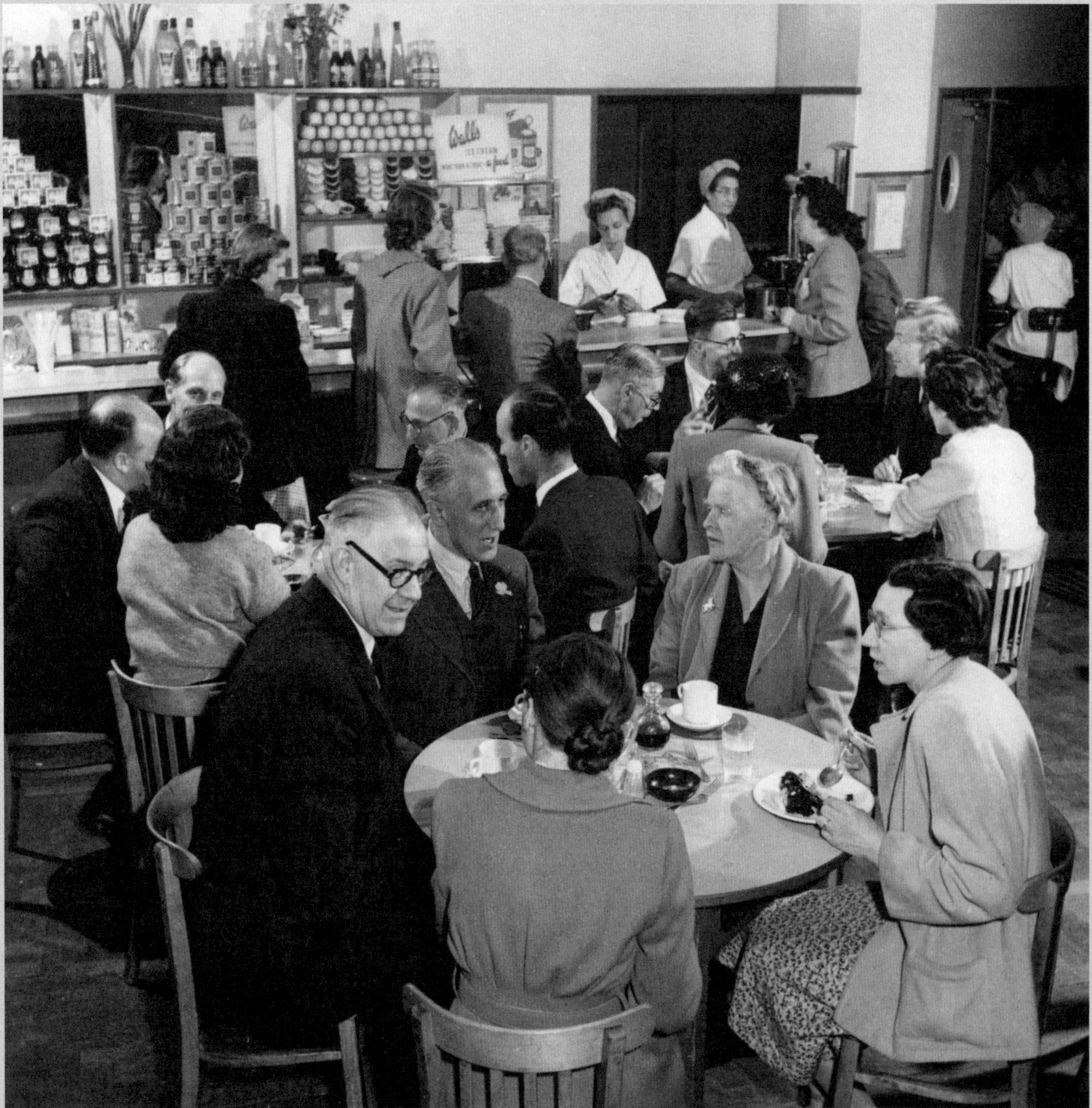
Wall's

[FIGS 105, 106, 107] OPPOSITE Working for London Transport was more than just a day job. Staff were actively encouraged to socialise together, with 55 Broadway providing facilities for a range of after-work activities; these included art classes (above right), a music society and clubs for photography, sports and industrial archaeology. In keeping with the progressive views of senior management, Broadway also boasted a well-stocked library for the educational welfare of the staff (above left). Eating together was similarly regarded as an important way of encouraging *esprit de corps*, although the first staff dining rooms introduced in the 1950s (left) separated middle managers from lower ranking workers, who had their own canteen on the ground floor. These distinctions were finally abolished in the 1980s with the creation of a single, shared, staff restaurant.

[FIG.108] ABOVE As the strategic headquarters of the capital's transport network, 55 Broadway took precautions against air raids as the likelihood of conflict increased in the years leading up to the Second World War. These included relocating the telephone exchange to the newly bombproofed basement to secure communications. Broadway was hit by a high explosive bomb on 14 October 1940, damaging several floors of the west wing.[8] Although quickly repaired internally, the exterior cladding was not replaced until 1963 due to shortages of Portland stone.

[FIG.109] ABOVE From the 14th floor, a rooftop viewing area and garden offer incredible panoramic views of London. Like the city it serves, the role of Broadway has changed in recent years. Considered modern and revolutionary in 1929, the 90-year-old building is less 'fit for purpose' than once it was. Many of its functions have moved to more high-tech office premises elsewhere, such as Palestra in Southwark and Endeavour Square at Stratford. In 2013 plans were announced to convert the building into luxury apartments, although these have yet to come to fruition.[9] For now, 55 Broadway remains in use with Transport for London, standing as a monumental link between the present day and the visionary pioneers who created the capital's transport network.

[FIG.110] RIGHT In the 1980s the ground floor of 55 Broadway was redesigned to create a more secure reception area for the London Transport offices and a street-level shopping mall, as this poster advertises. As part of the refurbishment, 50 years' worth of grime was cleaned off the exterior stonework and improvements were made to internal facilities, including the lifts and staff restaurant.

1   *London Underground Headquarters including St James's Park Underground Station* (1219790), Historic England, https://historicengland.org.uk/listing/the-list/list-entry/1219790, accessed 4 September 2018.
2   From 1898, the District Railway had offices at St James's Park station; these were subsequently enlarged to create Electric Railway House in 1909, as the headquarters of the recently formed United Electric Railways of London Ltd (UERL; otherwise known as the Underground Group, see p.33). Desmond F. Croome and Alan A. Jackson, *Rails Through the Clay: A History of London's Tube Railways* (Capital Transport, 1993), p.211.
3   For the best accounts of Frank Pick's wider interests in industrial design, see Christian Barman, *The Man Who Built London Transport* (David & Charles, 1979) and Oliver Green, *Frank Pick's London* (V&A Publishing, 2013). For more on Holden, see Eitan Karol, *Charles Holden: Architect* (Shaun Tyas, 2007).
4   David Bownes, Oliver Green and Sam Mullins, *Underground: How the Tube Shaped London* (Penguin, 2012), p.128.
5   Eight sculptures representing the four directions of the winds were commissioned for the upper storeys, from artists including Eric Gill, Henry Moore, Eric Aumonier, Samuel Rabinovitch, Allan Wyon and Alfred Gerrard. Two larger sculptures were commissioned from Jacob Epstein for the main entrances.
6   The controversy was surprisingly widely reported, with this quote from Epstein appearing on the front page of the *Midland Daily Telegraph*, 15 October 1929. For a summary of the public furore, and Pick's response, see Green 2013, p.85.
7   Interview with Nick Agnew, 17 July 2014, London Transport Museum, LTM 2015/6031.
8   London Passenger Transport Board Meeting Minute 2295, Appendix 19, 7 November 1940. Further information about the role and history of the building during the Second World War can be found at the TfL Archives, especially documents LT000107, LT000131, LT000172, LT000347, LT000341, LT000501 and LT0001862.
9   'Tube's historic HQ to be turned into high-price flats', *Evening Standard*, 15 May 2013.

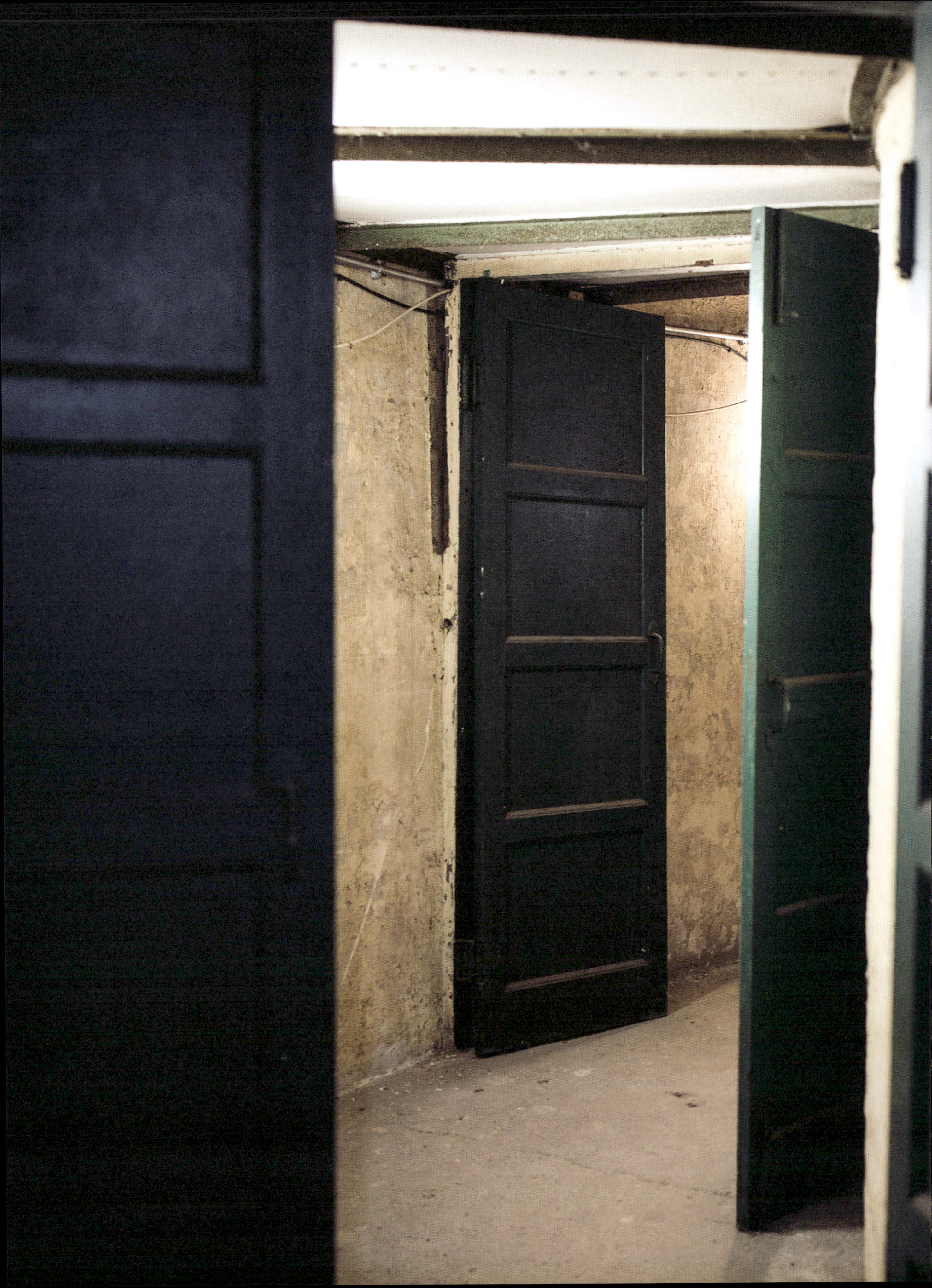

CLAPHAM SOUTH

DEEP-LEVEL SHELTER
BENEATH THE COMMON

[FIG.111] PREVIOUS Original doors leading to Grade II Listed air raid shelter at Clapham South, now open for public tours.

[FIG.112] TOP The crater at Balham the day after the bombing disaster, 15 October 1940. The bus fell into the crater moments after the bomb fell. Remarkably, the bus driver, who was hurrying home to Merton bus garage, survived.

[FIG.113] ABOVE The northbound platform at Balham station in the aftermath of bomb damage. The platform quickly filled with a landslide of water, earth and sewage, causing the death of more than 60 civilians sheltering there for the night.

In 1944 a Pathé newsreel hailed the deep-level civilian bomb shelter at Clapham South as luxury tunnels. The state-of-the-art shelter was one of eight deep-level shelters planned by the government at the height of the Blitz in 1940. London Transport was commissioned to build the shelters, being the only organisation experienced enough in deep tunnelling and in a position to undertake the job and complete the task quickly, and, indeed, the shelter under the Common was ready by the summer of 1942. All the planned shelters were of a similar design. At Clapham South, two tunnels over 400 metres (1,312 feet) in length lay beneath the station – more than 36 metres (118 feet) below ground and beyond the reach of the most powerful German bomb – and they were capable of accommodating 8,000 people within one hour [FIG.122]. This shelter at Clapham South, originally named Nightingale Lane, and the other seven that were built undoubtedly saved lives during the war, and in peacetime many took on new and varied roles, now largely forgotten. Today, their simple surface buildings barely hint at the scale of what lies beneath.

The Blitz had hit London and its people hard from September 1940. All the 'phoney war' preparations up to this point – Anderson shelters in back gardens or Morrison table shelters inside houses, people carrying gas masks at all times, brick shelters appearing on street corners – had seemed unreal.[1] Then the war came to London, and for four months from the night of 7 September 1940, the city was subjected to nightly bombing raids. Theoretically targeted, but in effect indiscriminate, bombs hit homes, schools, shops, docks, offices and factories, killing 20,000 people and making many more homeless or 'bombed out'. Underground stations were sought out as places of safety, as they had been during the previous conflict, but sheltering in the Underground night after night was not pleasant. Platforms quickly became unsanitary, with few or no facilities and hundreds of bodies crammed on cold, dirty, poorly lit platforms. Because of this, many Londoners actively chose not to shelter in the Tube, preferring to take the risk of sleeping at home or in their home-made shelters. One such was Norman Atkinson, who was a teenage Air Raid Precautions (ARP) warden, and lived in Balham, south London, at the time:

> I didn't like sheltering in the Underground, they weren't very pleasant you know, just imagine there would be two to three hundred people down there and the place didn't smell very nice. People were living under awful conditions and would go down there at night-time around six o'clock and stay there until the raid was over about 6 in the morning. They probably slept better than we did but it was awful for them really, like refugees.[2]

Public concern regarding the inadequacy of public shelters began to grow with the severity and persistence of the bombing. Thousands wrote to members of parliament (MPs) and members of the War Cabinet to express their discomfort and displeasure as the casualties mounted. One person who received countless letters on sheltering was Clementine Churchill, wife of the prime minister, Winston Churchill. She championed the shelter issue on behalf of Londoners, using her influence to lobby government officials to improve the shelters. After she started visiting Underground stations in 1940, the conditions started to improve. (One such visit was made to Euston station; see p.214.)

Alongside the lobbying undertaken by Mrs Churchill, debates continued in the House of Commons regarding provision of shelters and the possibility of creating deep shelters. On 10 October 1940, Home Secretary Herbert Morrison fervently reminded MPs that they shouldn't discourage home sheltering and that deep shelters would take a very long time to build.[3]

Then, on the night of 14 October 1940, an enormous bomb penetrated the High Street above Balham Tube station, blasting a huge crater and rupturing the water and sewer mains as well as the top of the Underground tunnel and flooding the platform level where people were sheltering [FIG.112]. The bomb killed at least 60 shelterers and was one of the worst single domestic incidents of the war [FIG.113]. The platforms had been sealed off with watertight doors to prevent flooding from above, thus trapping shelterers when the bomb struck. Norman Atkinson lived just off the High Street and, on the night in question, he was sheltering with his family in their Anderson shelter in the back garden. He remembered that when the bomb hit, 'There was a tremendous whack and the Anderson Shelter lifted a couple of feet off the ground.'[4]

The devastation at Balham and across the capital led to members of the public feeling increasingly vulnerable, with a growing sense of unease about the limitations and squalor of existing public shelters. It was time for the Government to guarantee the safety of its people by providing purpose-built shelters.

PUBLIC DEMAND FOR PURPOSE-BUILT SHELTERS

The day after the Balham disaster, Herbert Morrison met with David Anderson of consulting engineers Mott, Hay and Anderson to consider options for the provision of deep-level shelters for 100,000 people.[5] Four ways of building shelters were discussed: driving tunnels into hills; driving tunnels radiating out from existing deep-level Tube railway stations; constructing portions of Tube railways that might be required by traffic in the future; and constructing comparatively shallow (semi-surface) shelters protected by alternate layers of earth and concrete.

Anderson set out some guiding principles regarding the most efficient way to build shelters to accommodate a total target of 100,000 persons. He recommended constructing tunnels 5 metres (16 feet and 6 inches) in diameter, using concrete linings rather than cast iron, and cautioned that worksites would need to protect against the escape of light, lest they become a target for night bombing [FIG.116]. Those involved quickly realised that the most practical option would be to focus on building shelters connected to the Underground, and Albert Stanley, Lord Ashfield, chairman of London Transport, was approached to recommend suitable locations and manage the construction of ten deep-level shelters.

Within a month, London Transport had rapidly evolved plans with Morrison. On 14 November 1940, London Transport's chief engineer, V.A.M. Robertson, advised that accommodation for up to 100,000 people could be provided across ten sites: St Paul's, Chancery Lane, Mornington Crescent, Warren Street, Goodge Street, Oval, Stockwell, Clapham North, Clapham Common and Clapham South [FIG.114].[6] In Lord Ashfield's view, 'it would be the quickest and cheapest way of providing shelters at a suitable depth.'[7] When the sites were surveyed,

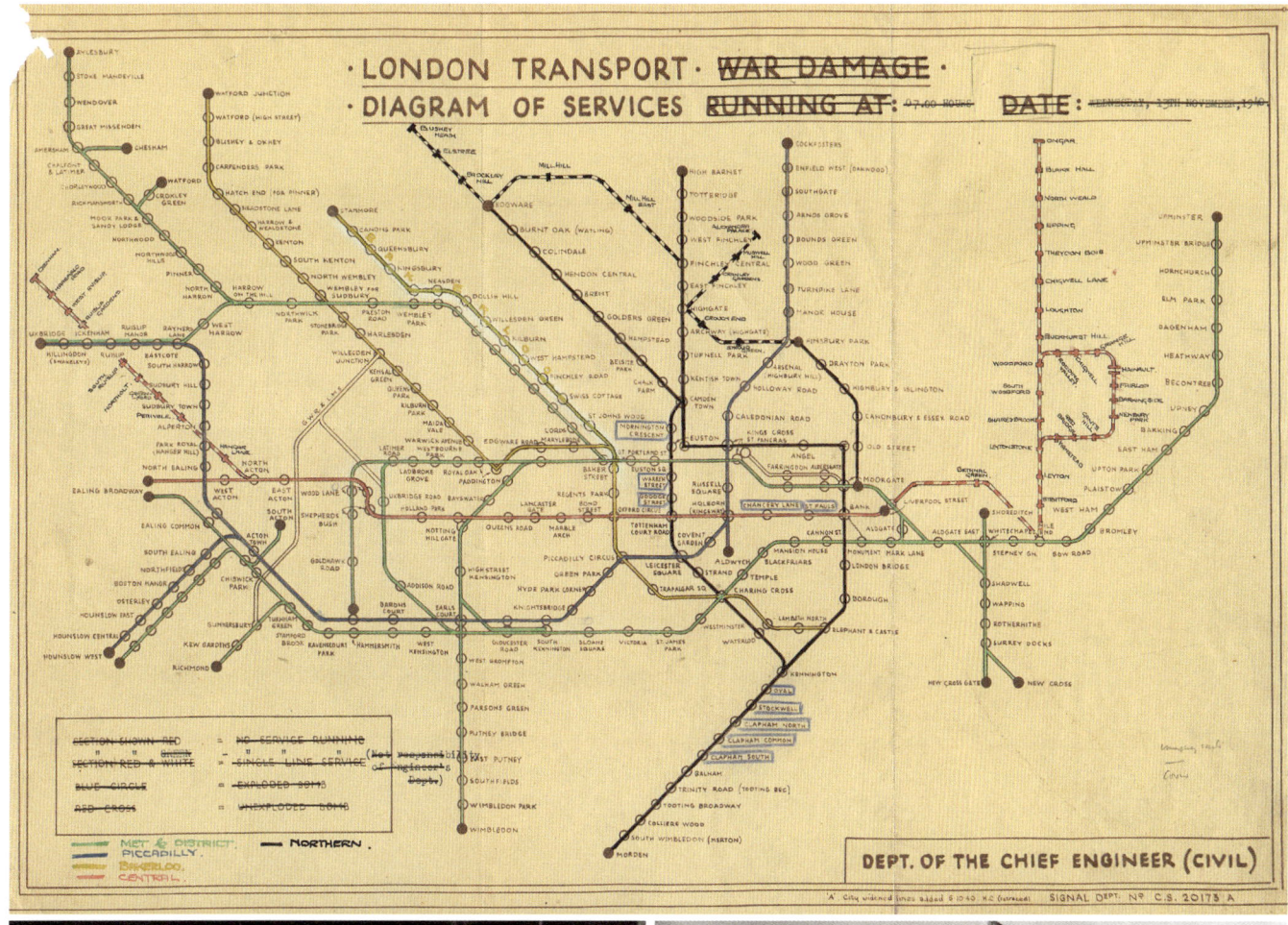

[FIG.114] TOP A map from 1940, showing the intended locations for ten purpose-built, deep-level civilian shelters under Tube stations.

[FIG.115] ABOVE LEFT In November 1940, London Transport constructed a number of models of bunks and passageways at its works department in Parsons Green to test possible layouts for deep-level shelters.

[FIG.116] ABOVE RIGHT The deep-level shelters were built while the raids of the Blitz continued. Camouflaged hoardings were used to disguise the construction site of this shelter near Belsize Park, on the Northern line, in 1941. Such measures also helped to prevent light escaping from the worksite during blackout conditions.

Mornington Crescent and Warren Street were found to be unsuitable, and Belsize Park and Camden Town were selected instead.

Anderson's suggestion that the shelters might be used as part of future tube railways was reflected in the selection of the locations. London Transport's 1935 New Works Programme had considered the possibility of building express, deep-level Tube lines alongside existing sections of the Underground. However, Ashfield was keen to stress that these were notional plans and London Transport was in no way committed to these developments, stating, 'At this moment the Board could not contribute any co-ordinated plans in this matter. The deep level shelters might be a portion of some co-ordinated plan.'[8] The important issue of the legal right to build the tunnels was resolved by locating the shelters underneath existing Tube railway tunnels, which already had 'wayleave' or rights of way. This avoided the need to seek new planning permission. Meanwhile, London Transport began the design of the shelters [FIG.115] and the appointment of construction companies.

At a meeting with Lord Ashfield at the Ministry of Home Security on 20 November, Herbert Morrison described the proposed locations as 'excellent' and the practicalities of the scheme were discussed. Ashfield agreed that travel to the shelters would be free to those with a shelter ticket and offered to help provide a fleet of 100 lorries to transport the spoil away from the tunnel works.[9] London Transport agreed to sell its spare stock of cast-iron lining rings to the project to allow construction to begin immediately [FIG.117], while concrete lining segments were ordered to complete the remaining two-thirds of each shelter. Use of these spare parts led to the shelters having unusual tunnel designs and a mix of cast-iron and concrete lining rings. Although the shelters were built to a common design principle, each one was also slightly different, to accommodate the unique ground conditions around its parent station [FIGS 118 & 119].

LUXURY TUNNELS OPEN IN LONDON

The shelters were built with extraordinary speed and completed by mid-1942, but at great expense. The estimated cost of the shelters was £1.5 million in 1940, but by the time of their completion two years later, that cost had risen to over £3 million – an enormous sum of money for a cash-strapped government.[10] During construction, the need for civilian shelters had lessened as nightly raids on London subsided, so the new deep-level shelters were not opened to the public. Instead, civilians continued to shelter at operational stations, and the deep-level shelters that represented such a huge investment in safe and secure spaces were given over to accommodate various branches of government services. Goodge Street was partly allocated to the US military, Chancery Lane was assigned to the Ministry of Information, and the remaining deep-level shelters housed military and civil service personnel.

In February 1944 London was once again subjected to a series of short, sharp air raids and Herbert Morrison was questioned in the House of Commons about the availability of the deep-shelters. He responded by saying that there were sufficient shelter facilities already and that the deep shelters were 'equipped and reserved for the accommodation of vital war services'.[11] As the year progressed, London found itself again in the firing line, but this time from the

[FIG.117] LEFT The shelter tunnels were dug by hand in dangerous conditions. In the background of this photograph, a miner pushes a muck truck through an unusually shaped 'figure-of-eight' tunnel.

[FIG.118] BELOW This undated schematic drawing shows the principles of deep-level shelter layout. The arrangement of the toilet blocks to one side of the cross passage indicates that this drawing is based on the shelters in the north of London, as those in the south had toilet blocks on both sides of the passageway.

[FIG.119] NEXT A diagram of Clapham Common deep-level shelter shows a layout typical of the shelters: parallel twin tunnels beneath the Tube, following the shape of the road above.

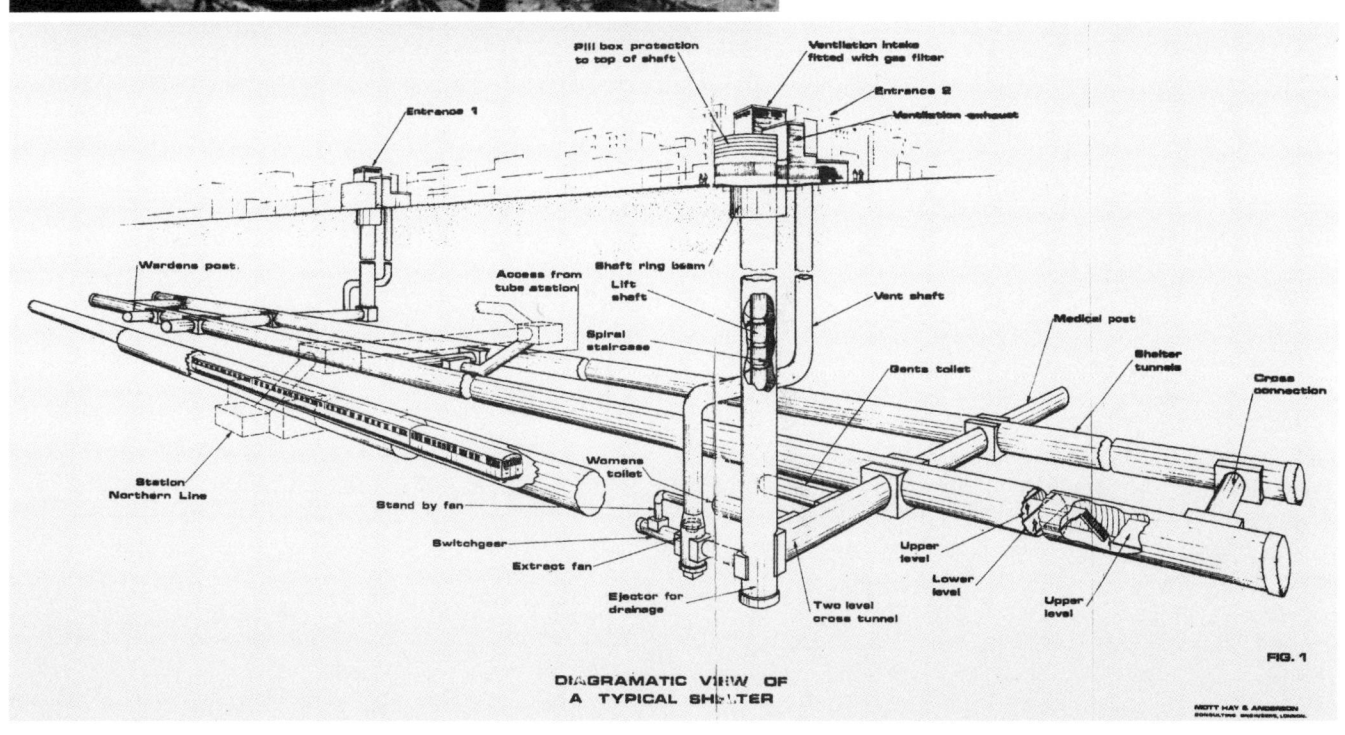

CLAPHAM COMMON

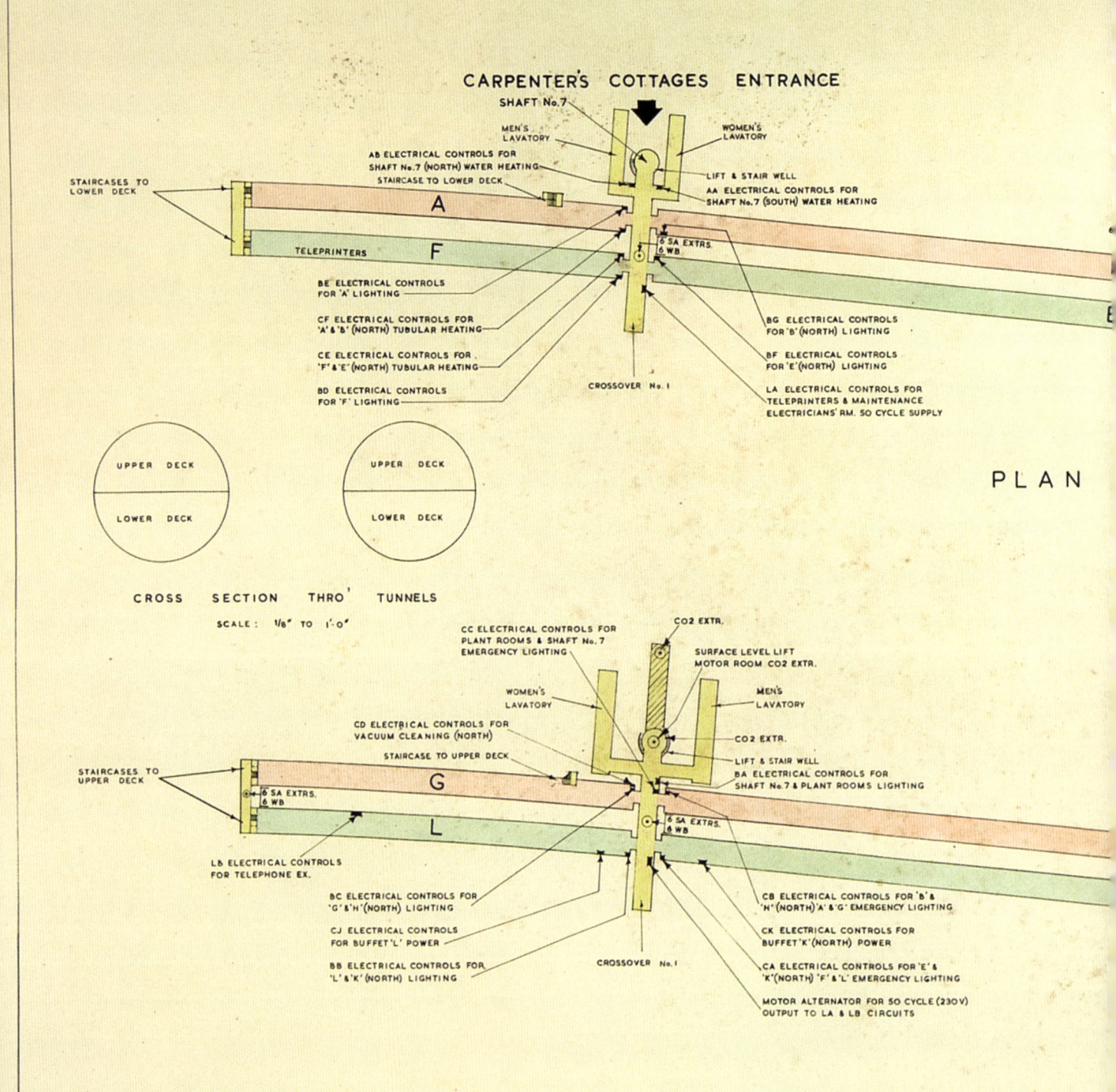

CARPENTER'S COTTAGES ENTRANCE
SHAFT No.7
MEN'S LAVATORY
WOMEN'S LAVATORY
AB ELECTRICAL CONTROLS FOR SHAFT No.7 (NORTH) WATER HEATING
LIFT & STAIR WELL
STAIRCASES TO LOWER DECK
STAIRCASE TO LOWER DECK
AA ELECTRICAL CONTROLS FOR SHAFT No.7 (SOUTH) WATER HEATING
A
TELEPRINTERS
F
6 SA EXTRS.
6 WB
BE ELECTRICAL CONTROLS FOR 'A' LIGHTING
CF ELECTRICAL CONTROLS FOR 'A' & 'B' (NORTH) TUBULAR HEATING
BG ELECTRICAL CONTROLS FOR 'B' (NORTH) LIGHTING
CE ELECTRICAL CONTROLS FOR 'F' & 'E' (NORTH) TUBULAR HEATING
BF ELECTRICAL CONTROLS FOR 'E' (NORTH) LIGHTING
BD ELECTRICAL CONTROLS FOR 'F' LIGHTING
CROSSOVER No. 1
LA ELECTRICAL CONTROLS FOR TELEPRINTERS & MAINTENANCE ELECTRICIANS' RM. 50 CYCLE SUPPLY

PLAN

UPPER DECK / LOWER DECK
UPPER DECK / LOWER DECK

CROSS SECTION THRO' TUNNELS
SCALE: 1/8" TO 1'-0"

CC ELECTRICAL CONTROLS FOR PLANT ROOMS & SHAFT No.7 EMERGENCY LIGHTING
CO2 EXTR.
SURFACE LEVEL LIFT MOTOR ROOM CO2 EXTR.
WOMEN'S LAVATORY
MEN'S LAVATORY
CD ELECTRICAL CONTROLS FOR VACUUM CLEANING (NORTH)
CO2 EXTR.
STAIRCASE TO UPPER DECK
LIFT & STAIR WELL
STAIRCASES TO UPPER DECK
6 SA EXTRS.
6 WB
G
BA ELECTRICAL CONTROLS FOR SHAFT No.7 & PLANT ROOMS LIGHTING
L
6 SA EXTRS.
6 WB
LB ELECTRICAL CONTROLS FOR TELEPHONE EX.
BC ELECTRICAL CONTROLS FOR 'G' & 'H' (NORTH) LIGHTING
CB ELECTRICAL CONTROLS FOR 'B' & 'H' (NORTH) 'A' & 'G' EMERGENCY LIGHTING
CJ ELECTRICAL CONTROLS FOR BUFFET 'L' POWER
CK ELECTRICAL CONTROLS FOR BUFFET 'K' (NORTH) POWER
BB ELECTRICAL CONTROLS FOR 'L' & 'K' (NORTH) LIGHTING
CROSSOVER No. 1
CA ELECTRICAL CONTROLS FOR 'E' & 'K' (NORTH) 'F' & 'L' EMERGENCY LIGHTING
MOTOR ALTERNATOR FOR 50 CYCLE (230V) OUTPUT TO LA & LB CIRCUITS

PLAN

FIRE SYMBOLS	
SA EXTR.	2 GAL. SODA ACID EXTINGUISHER
CO2 EXTR.	CARBON DIOXIDE EXTINGUISHER
WB	WATER BUCKETS

100 50 0

TUNNEL SHELTER

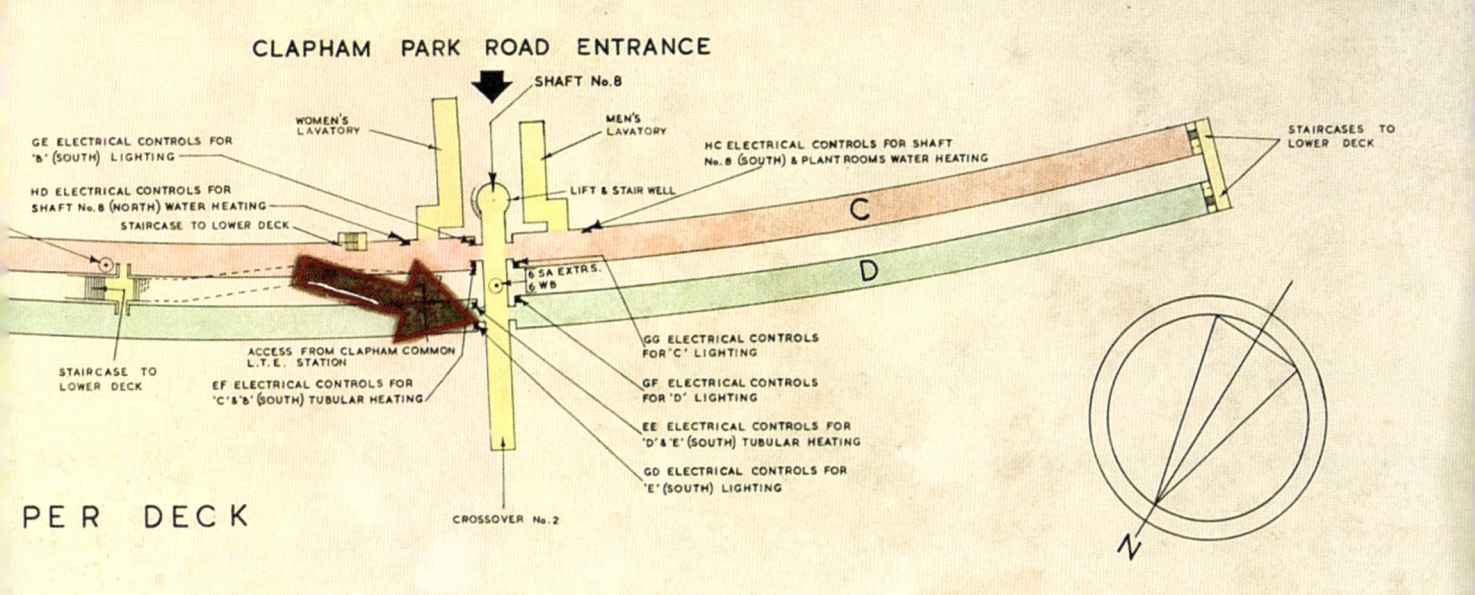

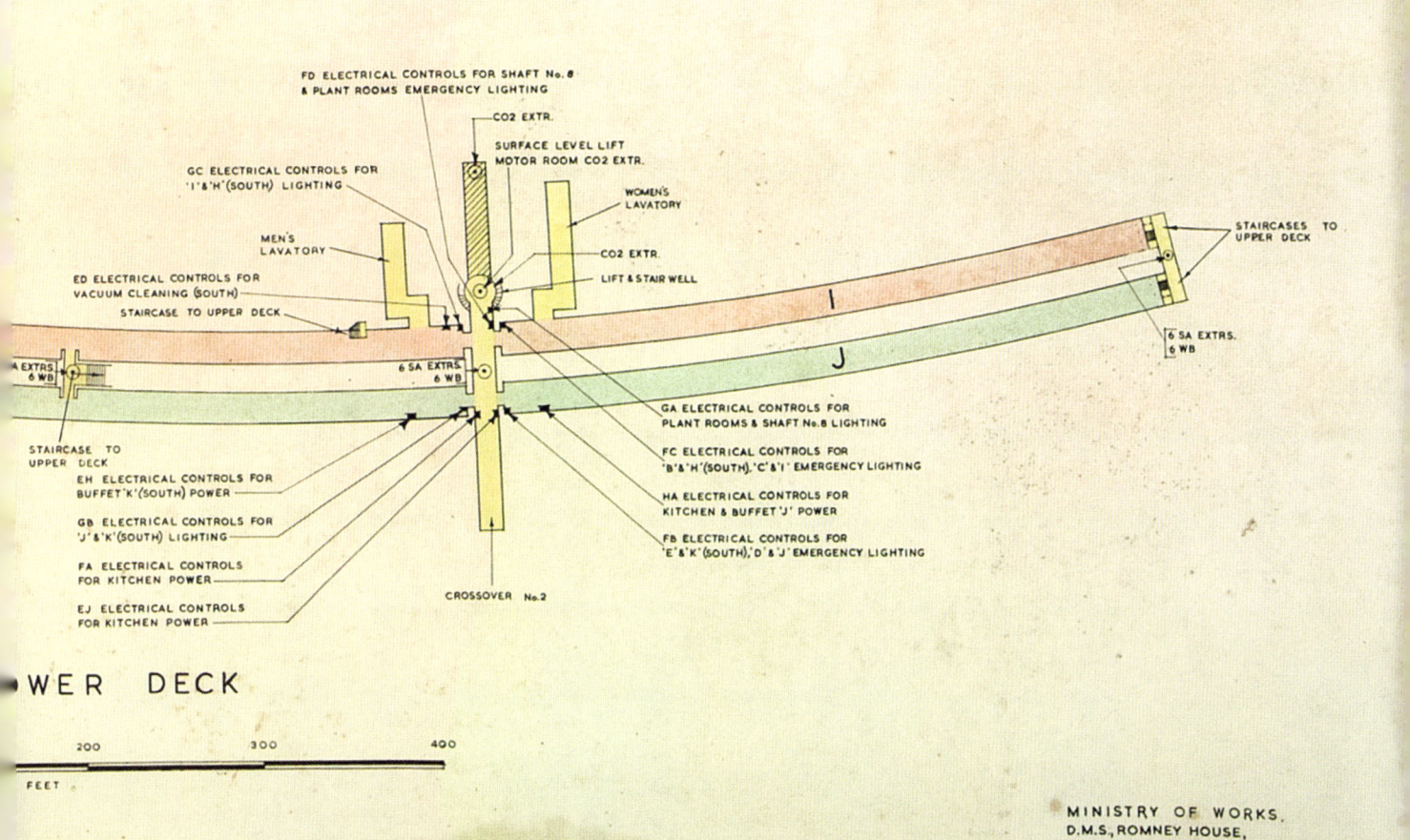

Ministry of Works
D.M.S., Romney House,
Marsham Street, London, S.W.1.
May 1962.

UPPER DECK

CLAPHAM PARK ROAD ENTRANCE — SHAFT No. 8

- GE ELECTRICAL CONTROLS FOR 'B' (SOUTH) LIGHTING
- HD ELECTRICAL CONTROLS FOR SHAFT No.8 (NORTH) WATER HEATING
- STAIRCASE TO LOWER DECK
- WOMEN'S LAVATORY
- MEN'S LAVATORY
- HC ELECTRICAL CONTROLS FOR SHAFT No.8 (SOUTH) & PLANT ROOMS WATER HEATING
- LIFT & STAIR WELL
- STAIRCASES TO LOWER DECK
- STAIRCASE TO LOWER DECK
- ACCESS FROM CLAPHAM COMMON L.T.E. STATION
- EF ELECTRICAL CONTROLS FOR 'C' & 'B' (SOUTH) TUBULAR HEATING
- 6 SA EXTRS. 6 WB
- GG ELECTRICAL CONTROLS FOR 'C' LIGHTING
- GF ELECTRICAL CONTROLS FOR 'D' LIGHTING
- EE ELECTRICAL CONTROLS FOR 'D' & 'E' (SOUTH) TUBULAR HEATING
- GD ELECTRICAL CONTROLS FOR 'E' (SOUTH) LIGHTING
- CROSSOVER No. 2

Tunnels C, D

LOWER DECK

- FD ELECTRICAL CONTROLS FOR SHAFT No. 8 & PLANT ROOMS EMERGENCY LIGHTING
- CO2 EXTR.
- SURFACE LEVEL LIFT MOTOR ROOM CO2 EXTR.
- GC ELECTRICAL CONTROLS FOR 'I' & 'H' (SOUTH) LIGHTING
- WOMEN'S LAVATORY
- MEN'S LAVATORY
- CO2 EXTR.
- LIFT & STAIR WELL
- ED ELECTRICAL CONTROLS FOR VACUUM CLEANING (SOUTH)
- STAIRCASE TO UPPER DECK
- STAIRCASES TO UPPER DECK
- 6 SA EXTRS. 6 WB
- 6 SA EXTRS. 6 WB
- 6 SA EXTRS. 6 WB
- STAIRCASE TO UPPER DECK
- EH ELECTRICAL CONTROLS FOR BUFFET 'K' (SOUTH) POWER
- GB ELECTRICAL CONTROLS FOR 'J' & 'K' (SOUTH) LIGHTING
- FA ELECTRICAL CONTROLS FOR KITCHEN POWER
- EJ ELECTRICAL CONTROLS FOR KITCHEN POWER
- GA ELECTRICAL CONTROLS FOR PLANT ROOMS & SHAFT No.8 LIGHTING
- FC ELECTRICAL CONTROLS FOR 'B' & 'H' (SOUTH), 'C' & 'I' EMERGENCY LIGHTING
- HA ELECTRICAL CONTROLS FOR KITCHEN & BUFFET 'J' POWER
- FB ELECTRICAL CONTROLS FOR 'E' & 'K' (SOUTH), 'D' & 'J' EMERGENCY LIGHTING
- CROSSOVER No. 2

Tunnels I, J

Scale: 200 300 400 FEET

[FIG.120] TOP LEFT By July 1942, Clapham South deep-level shelter was almost completed. This photograph shows the bombproof rotunda entrance just off Nightingale Lane, before works were completed. A spoil heap from the works rises on the common behind.

[FIG.121] TOP RIGHT The Clapham Common rotunda entrance positioned discreetly on the edge of the Common. Its former purpose as an entrance to a shelter is unknown to most of those who pass it today.

[FIG.122] ABOVE LEFT Protected inside the core of the rotunda at Clapham South are a pair of staircases, arranged in a double helix around a service lift. The two entrances allowed a steady flow of up to 8,000 people to enter the building in less than an hour.

[FIG.123] ABOVE RIGHT Civilians bed down for the night in a deep-level shelter in 1944. Images such as these were broadcast widely as propaganda.

persistent V-weapon terror campaign of V-1 'Doodlebugs' and V-2 rockets. The devastation began in June 1944 and, in the space of just one month, the 'flying bombs' had killed over 2,700 civilians in London.[12] Questioned again on 20 July 1944 about whether he would have all of the deep-level shelters opened, Morrison replied, 'Yes, as soon as I can.'[13]

Only five shelters out of the eight built were opened to the public, and these were never full to their capacity of 8,000 people. They were well fitted out, with lavatories, canteens, medical-aid posts and civil-defence posts. Families were allocated bunks together in cubicles, and wider berth longitudinal bunks were provided for mothers with small children – a specific request of Clementine Churchill.[14] Clementine herself visited Clapham South, along with Henry Morgenthau, the United States Secretary of the Treasury, on 15 August 1944, to inspect the medical-aid posts and the conditions of the shelter.[15]

Ticket priority was given to those who had been bombed out and the shelter became home to many families for years.[16] The reality of living in these 'luxury tunnels' every night was hardly palatial [FIG.123]. Most importantly, though, the deep shelters were beyond the reach of the most powerful bombs of the time, giving Londoners a most welcome respite after five years of warfare. Margaret Barford, whose family lived in Clapham South station every night for almost two years from August 1944, after being bombed out of their house, remembers the chemical toilets being rather foul-smelling and the ventilation system so efficient that the shelters often became very cold at night. Margaret was ten years old at the time and remembers having a wonderful time – exploring the tunnels, being given food from the canteens, and enjoying dances and entertainment during her stay:

> People were all in the same boat down there, it was a great leveller. Whether you were rich, poor or what you were, you were homeless really and people were very kind to each other, much more than they are now. It's funny isn't it, it takes a war to do that.[17]

POST-WAR USE OF THE SHELTERS

After the war ended in May 1945, the shelter at Clapham South continued to house hundreds of Londoners, until the government issued compensation in 1946, allowing bombed-out families to purchase new homes. The government needed to find a peacetime role for the shelters. London Transport quickly ruled out the option of acquiring them for integration into the Tube network. Post-war transport priorities had changed and the parts of the ambitious pre-war New Works Programme not yet completed had to be modified in line with revised plans for London and a limited budget.

The shelter at Clapham South was run by the War Department, which converted it into a hostel; the capacity of the shelter was reduced to 2,500 men and 500 women by spacing out the bunks and then using only the top and middle bunks, with the canteens still serving tea and light refreshments. The shelter continued to be well used as a hostel for the next seven years, compensating for the profound lack of such accommodation in war-ravaged London. Through 1947, an estimated 18,000 young visitors from Holland,

[FIG.124] ABOVE Some of the passengers from HMT *Empire Windrush*, photographed in Clapham South shelter shortly after their arrival in the UK in 1948. John Richards (on the right) lived in the shelter for several weeks. He remembered the Northern line trains rumbling overhead and acting as his alarm clock for the duration of his stay.

[FIG.125] RIGHT The canteen of Drake ward at Clapham South was converted into an improvised labour exchange for the passengers of the *Windrush*.

[FIG.126] BELOW This visitor from Germany was one of many who left a record of their visit to Clapham South hostel on the ceiling above their bunk, during the Festival of Britain in September 1951.

[FIG.127] BOTTOM Graffiti on the ceiling of Goodge Street deep-level shelter during its use as a transit camp suggests it was not well regarded by the troops living there, with many of the soldiers nicknaming it 'The Hole'.

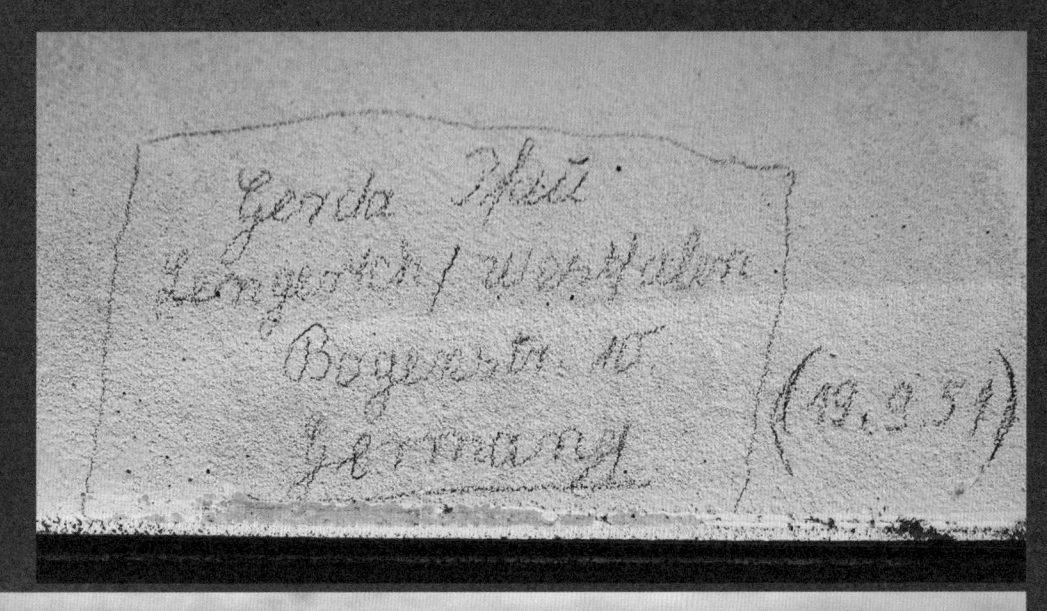

Denmark, Norway, Belgium, Switzerland and France sailed into Tilbury and travelled to Clapham shelter, a reception point from which these young people went to stay with host families across Britain.[18] In 1948, the site accommodated 300 visiting American students; by this point the charge for an overnight stay was a budget-conscious one shilling per night.[19] Later that year, in June, Clapham South hosted over 200 migrants from Jamaica, who had arrived by invitation of the government on HMT *Empire Windrush* [FIG.124]. The migrants who had not prearranged accommodation in the UK were invited to lodge in Clapham South until suitable employment or accommodation could be found. A temporary labour exchange (job centre) was set up in one of the canteens below ground to aid in this search [FIG.125]. For most, this meant only a few weeks. Many of the migrants who lodged in Clapham South found homes and work nearby in south London, particularly in the Brixton area; they helped to establish the West Indian communities thriving in the area today.

Margaret Barford's observation that the shelter was 'a great leveller' extended to peacetime; in post-war Britain many visitors were welcomed to London at Clapham South deep-level shelter. In 1950 the *Daily Mirror* reported that accommodation in London was so hard to find that 'rich Americans have sometimes had to doss down for a night in the Clapham shelter because they simply couldn't find anywhere else to stay.'[20] In 1951 the shelter was used during the Festival of Britain to provide moderately priced hostel accommodation for organised parties of young people and schoolchildren coming to visit the festivities, particularly from overseas [FIG.126]. The *Northern Daily Mail* then described it as 'the cheapest hotel in London … at a rate of 3s a head'.[21] In 1952, the *Evening News* reported on 130 Jamaicans spending the night at Clapham after landing in Southampton and travelling to London in search of work.[22]

GOODGE STREET

Goodge Street also continued to be used for accommodation, though for very different reasons. In December 1941 America had entered the war and sent military personnel to Britain to support the war effort. In 1943, the British government converted part of Goodge Street deep-level shelter for their new allies' use as an intelligence headquarters commanded by Major General Dwight D. Eisenhower.[23] The site came to be known as the Eisenhower Centre and was upgraded to support its new role with an express lift and state-of-the-art communications equipment, including a Lamson tube – a pneumatic message transportation system. The British military also used Goodge Street as a communications centre. After the war, the shelter continued to be used by the military as a transit camp for British troops, though this was unpopular [FIG.127]. Corporal Fraser Pakes recalled staying there briefly en route to a posting in Bermuda:

> We crowded in and out of the [T]ube trains until we reached Goodge Street. The place we have to stay at is the most awful place I've been in the Army. It's an old tube line. We had to walk down hundreds of feet of stone spiral steps. The sleeping quarters are along the sides of the old tube walls.[24]

[FIG.128] TOP RIGHT
The vacuum pump used to power the Lamson tube pneumatic system installed at Goodge Street, which quickly transported messages around the deep-level shelter for American forces.

[FIG.129] TOP LEFT Each shelter was divided into 16 themed wards, alphabetised from A to P, to help shelterers find their way to their bunks. At Clapham South the theme was naval commanders, although 'Oldham' in this tunnel sign is thought to be a reference to a naval architect.

[FIG.130] ABOVE The entrance to Goodge Street shelter as seen today. Behind it is the housing for the express lift installed on site for the US military.

[FIG.131] TOP LEFT In recent years, a mural painted on the Stockwell rotunda has aligned the building more sympathetically with the neighbouring war memorial.

[FIG.132] ABOVE LEFT Some of the shelters retain their original features. Each shelter had two large electrical plant rooms powering the site. A mercury-arc rectifier glows in the corner at Belsize Park – a unique survivor.

[FIG.133] TOP RIGHT Perhaps the most unexpected use of a deep-level shelter can be found at Clapham Common, where Growing Underground has built a low-carbon-footprint farm. Hydroponic growing under LED lights in a quarantined environment requires no pesticides.

[FIG.134] ABOVE RIGHT Seen in the shadows to the left of the streetlight, Chancery Lane deep-level shelter was in an area of high-intensity bombing during the Second World War, surviving near misses from V-1 and V-2 rockets.

With the start of the Cold War and its escalation in the early 1950s, the threat of a nuclear war caused the deep shelters to be considered once more for sheltering in the event of a nuclear attack. However, by the mid-1950s, the invention of the hydrogen bomb made even the deep shelters inadequate; they would not sustain a direct hit from such a weapon. After a large fire in the Goodge Street deep-level shelter, an in-depth inquiry by the London Fire Brigade concluded – just 14 years after their construction had been completed – that the deep-shelters were unsuitable to house people.[25] Their role as hostels and barracks came to end from 1956.

FUTURE AND GROWING THE LEGACY

In March 1956 the deep-level shelters were under discussion once again in the House of Commons. The Brutalist entrance perched on the southern edge of Clapham Common [FIG.121] was described by the MP for Clapham, C.W. Gibson, as 'a most ugly structure and I should have thought that at least something could have been done to cover it up so that the people using the common are not offended every time they look at it.' Although critical of the appearance of the shelters, Gibson had lived through the war and seen how effective they were in soothing the failing morale of Londoners during a time of great distress, so he added, 'They were built at a time of very great stress, and there is not the slightest doubt that they were a godsend to thousands of people during the air raids.'[26] The shelter at Stockwell was subject to particularly scathing criticism from G.R. Strauss, MP for Vauxhall:

> It is a really ghastly sight, but the borough council cannot do anything about it at all. There is the war memorial, this hideous structure and a few square yards of grass around them where, according to my observation, the mangiest cats in the neighborhood [sic] foregather. Not even a decent cat will go there, so depressing is the area.'[27]

The matter of reusing the shelters was discussed at length, with Harry Randall, MP for Gateshead West, observing that 'where there is use there is less deterioration' and suggesting 'there should be an imaginative approach to the way in which we use these shelters in the future.'[28]

Since the 1950s a number of interesting possibilities for the shelters have been explored. Many of the sites were considered for archival and museum storage and Clapham South was used for government archival storage purposes until the 1970s, when it was leased to a private security company. In 1998, seven of the eight shelters were sold to London Transport, as they are costly to maintain and London Transport was the organisation best placed to manage their long-term maintenance. Belsize Park, Camden Town, Goodge Street and Stockwell deep-level shelters continue to be used, successfully, as commercial archives. The proximity of the shelters to their parent stations may also lead them to play a useful role in the future upgrade of stations. Part of the shelter at Camden Town is earmarked for a planned station upgrade.

Chancery Lane deep-level shelter [FIG.134] was never used to protect civilians. Instead, it was modified for use by government civil defence personnel,

[FIG.135] ABOVE Surviving original features in the Grade II Listed shelter at Clapham South, now open for public tours.

[FIG.136] NEXT Clapham North deep-level shelter exemplifies the principle that dereliction will follow if uses for shelters cannot be found. Finding a commercial use for this shelter proved impossible once its lifts failed and the site has been stripped of fittings.

notably the Special Operations Executive in 1944. The secret use of the site was developed further when, in 1954, the General Post Office expanded and converted the site into the secure Kingsway telephone exchange, constructing another four large tunnels and additional access shafts. The exchange had its own generators, which powered a 5,000-line telephone exchange and provided staff accommodation for its operatives. The facilities were decommissioned in 1996 and remain in the ownership of British Telecom.

Clapham South remained a commercial archive until 2008, when the archive company moved operations to an alternative site. The land around the southern rotunda entrance was sold for housing development. In the same year, the shelter beneath was granted a Grade II listing. In 2015 London Transport Museum took over tenancy of the shelter and has been operating tours there since [FIG.135]. The Museum has been gathering original surviving artefacts from the other shelters and personal accounts from those who have stayed there, with the aim of making the history of this remarkable structure accessible.

1   The phrase 'phoney war' refers to an eight-month period at the start of the Second World War – between 3 September 1939 and 10 May 1940 – during which there was only one, limited, military land operation.
2   Norman Atkinson, interview by Beth Atkinson, November 2018, London Transport Museum, unaccessioned.
3   Hansard HC, 10 October 1940, vol. 365, cc515. Herbert Morrison was Home Secretary in the United Kingdom from 4 October 1940 to 23 May 1945.
4   Atkinson, 2018.
5   The Anderson shelter was designed by William Paterson and Oscar Kerrison and named after Sir John Anderson (Lord Privy Seal, 1938–9). Coincidentally, the David Anderson mentioned here evaluated the design before approval.
6   National Archives, MT6/2728.
7   Office of the Engineer in Chief – ref E400, 16 November 1940, National Archives, MT6/2728.
8   Ibid.
9   Office of the Engineer in Chief, 20 November 1940, National Archives, MT6/2728.
10   Wartime Deep Tunnel Shelters 1942–1949, London Transport Museum, LTM 1999/22854.
11   Hansard HC Deb, 29 February 1944, vol. 397, cc1249–51.
12   *Evening News*, 6 July 1944, p.1.
13   Hansard HC, 20 July 1944, vol. 402, cc20.
14   Sonia Purnell, *First Lady: The Life and Wars of Clementine Churchill* (Aurum Press, 2015), p.246.
15   Clementine Churchill papers, 1940, Churchill Archive Centre, CSCT 3/33.
16   Hansard HC, 13 July 1944, vol. 404, cc1873.
17   Interview with Margaret Barford, November 2016, London Transport Museum.
18   'Hundreds say children can stay with us', *Daily Herald Saturday*, 26 July 1947, p.1.
19   'From U.S to Stay in Raid shelter', *Daily Mirror Saturday*, 26 March 1949, p.1. Hansard HC, 5 March 1948, vol. 488, cc97.
20   'Under the Counter', *Daily Mirror*, 9 September 1950, p.6.
21   'Shelter', *Northern Daily Mail*, 30 July 1951, p.2.
22   '130 Jamaicans start Job Search', *Evening News Saturday*, 10 May 1952, p.1.
23   Desmond F. Croome and Alan A. Jackson, *Rails Through the Clay: A History of London's Tube Railways* (Capital Transport, 1993), p.274.
24   'Military Memoirs of (Cpl) Fraser Pakes: "A" Company IDCLI 1955–1957', https://sites.google.com/site/djkl57dcliextension/home, accessed 4 January 2019.
25   Fire Brigade Committee report on Fire at Goodge Street Deep Shelter, 30 May 1956, National Archives, CM 37/214.
26   Hansard HC, 27 March 1956, vol. 550, cc1989.
27   Hansard HC, 27 March 1956, vol. 550, cc1996.
28   Hansard HC, 27 March 1956, vol. 550, cc1993.

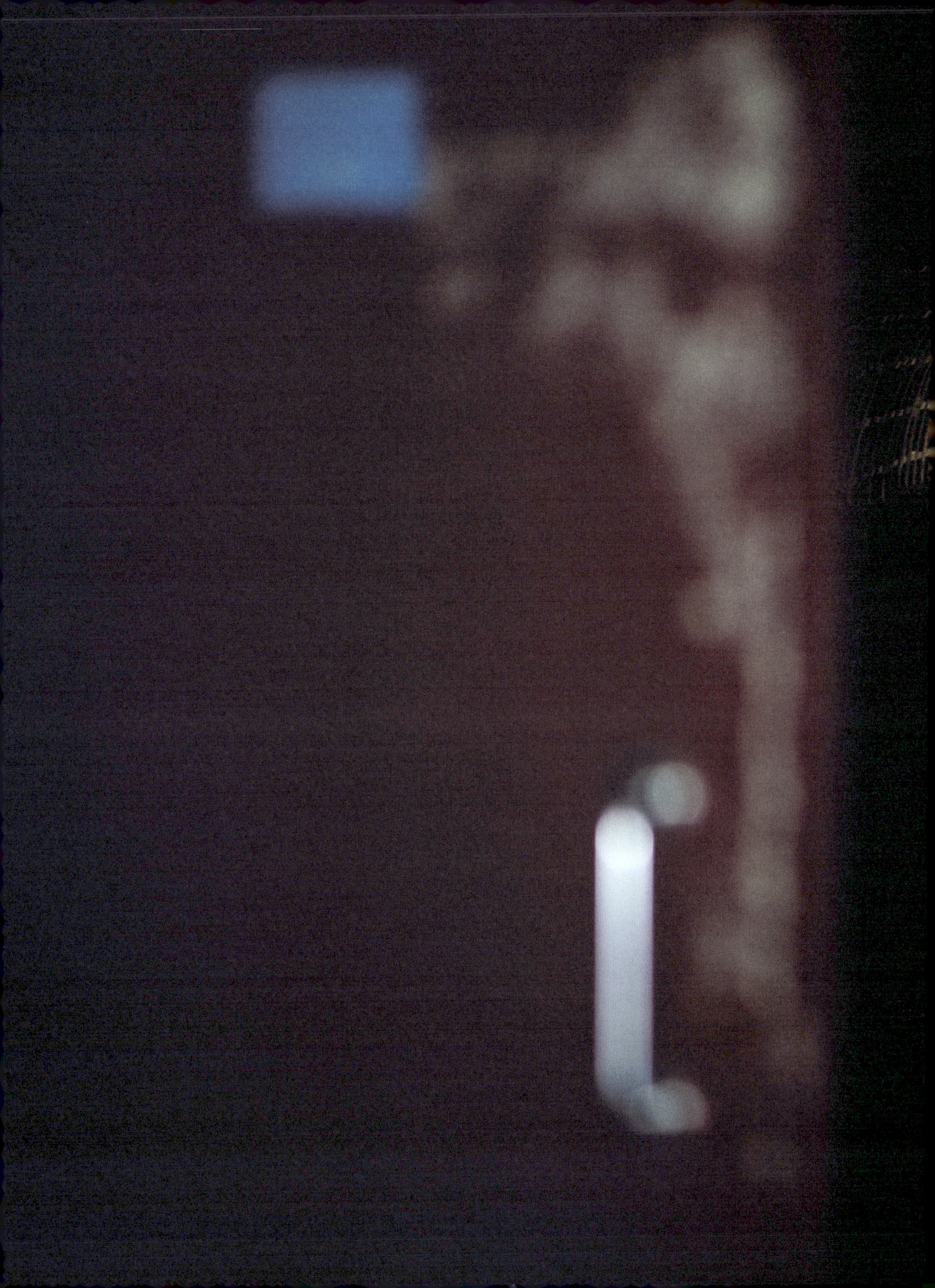

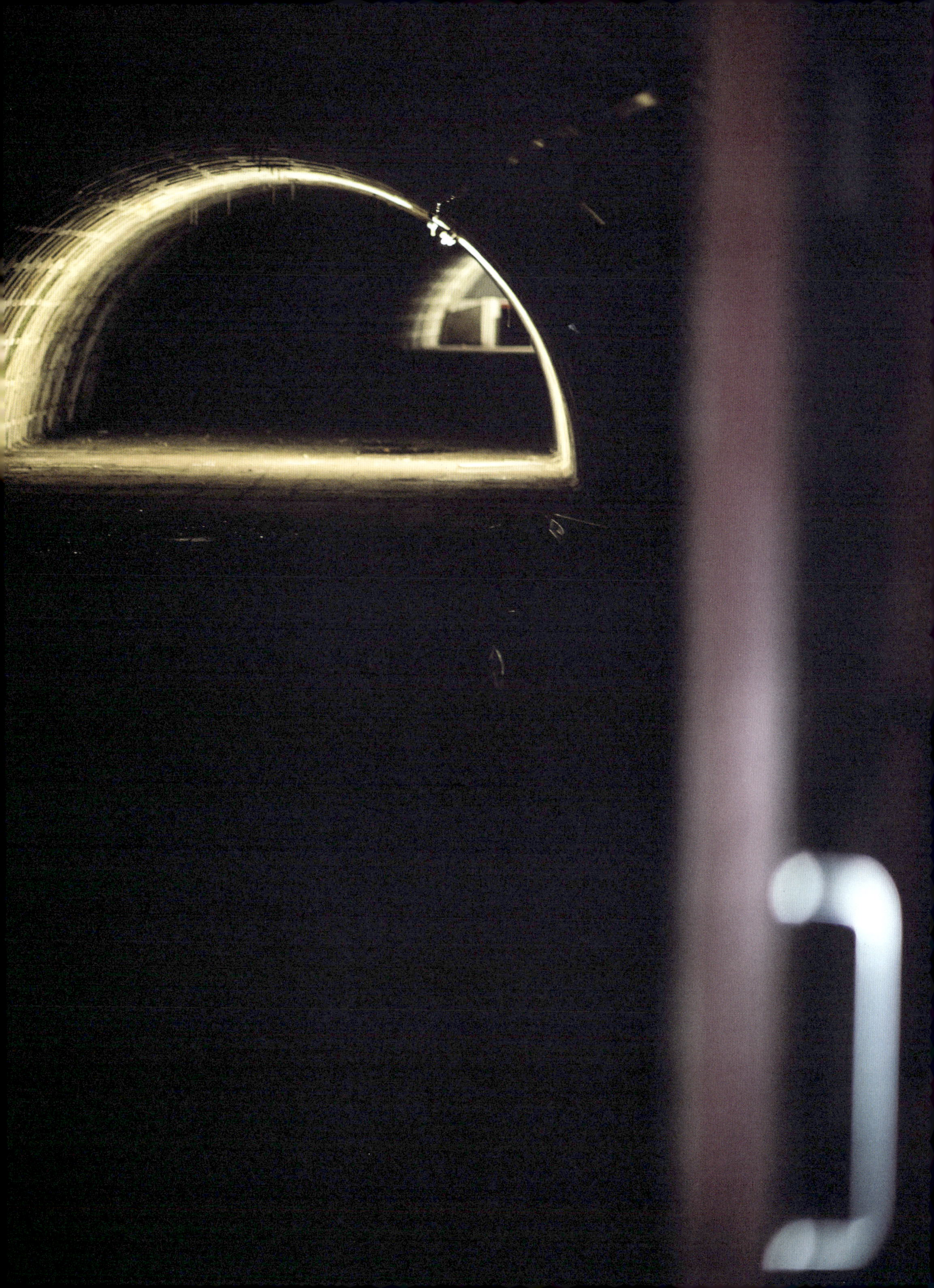

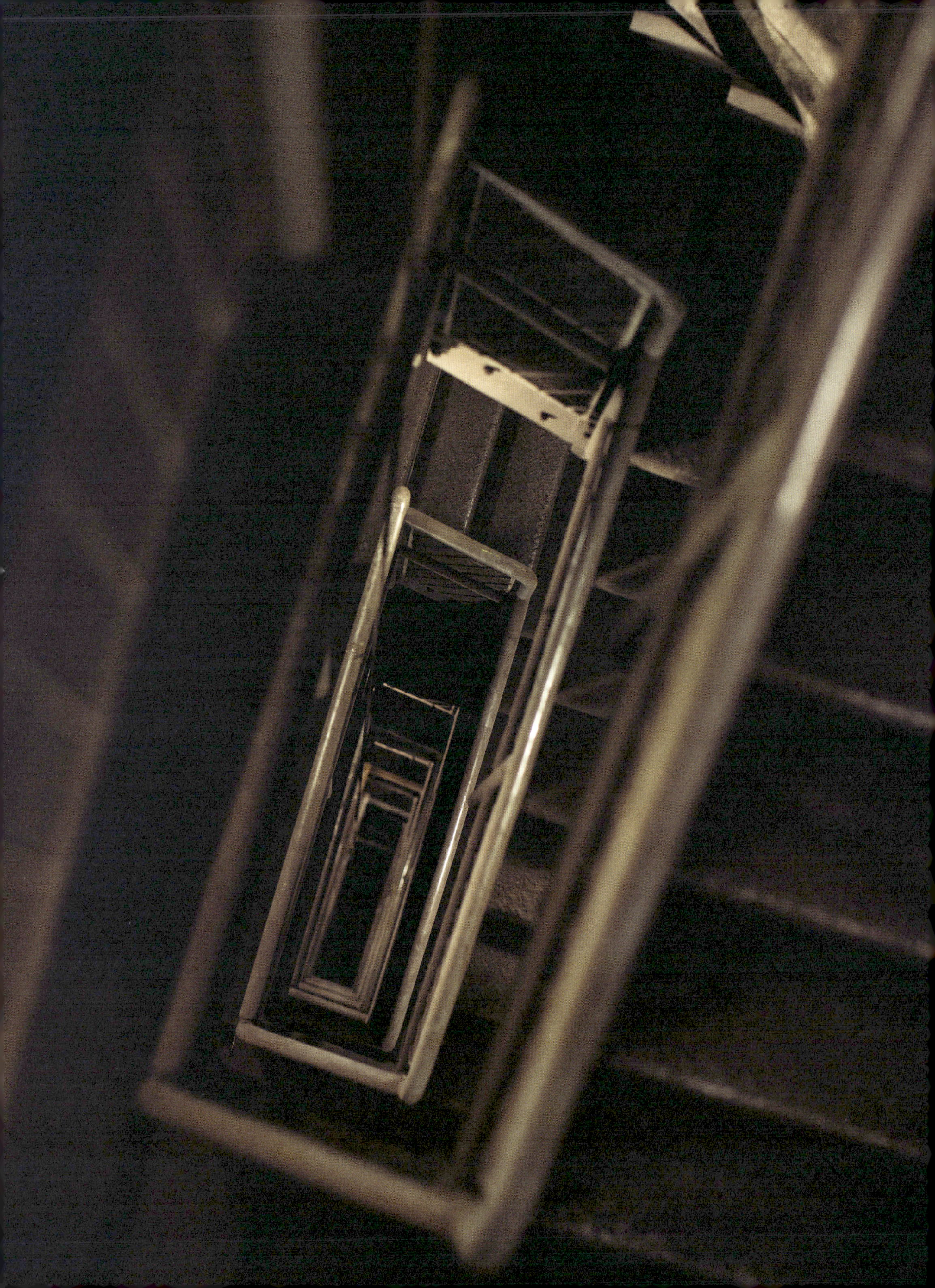

NORTH END

UNOPENED STATION AND
SECRET BUNKER

TUBE STATION

The Fields that might be added to the Heath

THE TUBE Cos OPEN CUTTING

Bishops Wood

TUBE STATION

[FIG.137] PREVIOUS The view down the deep emergency stairway at North End, installed in the 1950s as part of the flood defence conversion works.

[FIG.138] A map showing the location of the proposed Tube stations at Hampstead and North End, prepared by the Hampstead Heath Extension Committee in about 1903. The area highlighted in green shows the 32.4 hectares (80 acres) of Wyldes Farm then earmarked for housing but later preserved as a public space.

Incongruous among the Arts and Crafts houses of Hampstead Way in north-west London is a small, windowless, concrete building, guarded by a metal fence and entered through a reinforced steel door. Everything about the structure is anonymous. On the door, an enamel notice mysteriously instructs that 'All [indecipherable word] staff and contractors are to avoid making unnecessary noise', but otherwise there is no hint as to what might lie beyond. The clue to ownership lies in the choice of Johnston font, the characteristic lettering used by London Transport. Look more closely and you can just make out that the blanked-out word once read 'Underground'. This is, in fact, the surface entrance to one of the capital's least known and most secret Tube stations.

Abandoned during construction over one hundred years ago, North End station sits between Hampstead and Golders Green on the modern-day Northern line. Its origins lie in the thwarted ambitions of an American businessman to develop the surrounding countryside into a Tube-fed suburb. Although never opened to passengers, construction of the station was to have unforeseen consequences for the local area, including the extension of Hampstead Heath as a public space and the subsequent creation of Hampstead Garden Suburb. Deep underground, the refurbished tunnels and passageways were also to play a highly secret and important role in Britain's Cold War defences.

CONSTRUCTION BEGINS

At the turn of the twentieth century, the hamlet of North End on the edge of Hampstead Heath was probably best known for its local pub, the Bull and Bush – soon to be immortalised in the music-hall song of the same name.[1] It was also the location of the picturesque Wyldes Farm (granted to Eton College by King Henry VIII), which had become a favoured haunt of artists, writers and well-to-do day trippers from nearby Hampstead. The farm's many famous tenants and visitors included John Millais, William Blake, John Constable, John Keats and Charles Dickens [FIG.140]. From 1884, it had been the headquarters of the free-thinking Fabian Society.[2] But all this looked set to change when the farmhouse was scheduled to be demolished to make way for a new Tube station, and the fields turned over to rows of high-density housing.

The architect of this scheme was Charles Tyson Yerkes, a transport mogul and businessman from Chicago. Together with a syndicate of American financiers, Yerkes arrived in London to buy up several authorised, but as yet unbuilt, Tube railways. All had stalled due to lack of funds and Yerkes now planned to unite them as a single 'combine' called the Underground Group, which he would operate with the aim of obtaining maximum profit. One of the unbuilt lines was the Charing Cross, Euston & Hampstead Railway (CCE&HR), which the Yerkes syndicate purchased in 1900. Almost immediately, Yerkes began plans to extend the line northwards from Hampstead to rural Golders Green. His experience in Chicago had taught him that money was to be made by developing new transport-enabled suburbs on what had hitherto been greenfield sites. In this instance, Yerkes was to be proved right, as Golders Green grew rapidly into a large residential area – the first Tube suburb – making a fortune for some of his co-investors, who had bought land adjacent to the new station.[3]

All this was in the future. For now, Yerkes needed to get his plans through parliament; these included an intermediate station at North End, which seemed to offer similar scope for residential building. The proposals, however, met with strong opposition from well-connected local residents who feared (somewhat implausibly) that the construction of the Tube under Hampstead Heath would upset the local ecology. An informal committee, headed by Lord Mansfield and the local MP, wrote to householders warning that it was 'imperative that at all hazards [connected with] the erection of a station . . . at North End and the possibility of actual damage to the Heath, should be prevented'.[4] Their agitation ensured that the new Tube under Hampstead Heath would be dug far deeper than at any other point on the network, leaving North End deep below ground.[5]

With parliamentary approval for the extension achieved in 1903, the company purchased 1 hectare (2½ acres) of land (including Wyldes farmhouse and outbuildings) to make the surface-level station building.[6] Deep below the ground, work began on the station tunnels, platforms and low-level subways, which were to be connected to the surface via three passenger lifts and an emergency stairway – a testimony to how busy the planners hoped the station would be [FIG.141]. But, away from the building site, a new movement was gathering momentum that would ultimately halt construction in its tracks.

THE END FOR NORTH END

The agent for this change was the energetic social reformer Henrietta Barnett, who owned a cottage on the Heath. She was a frequent visitor to Wyldes Farm and the surrounding area.[7] Although not opposed to the idea of a station at North End, which she welcomed as offering access to the Heath for the labouring poor, Barnett was concerned that large crowds of day trippers would trample to oblivion the relatively small section of publicly accessible heathland nearby. Her concerns were echoed by the *Hampstead and Highgate Express*, which said that 'the projected station . . . at North End will probably outstrip all other means of approach [to the Heath] in popularity, thereby placing an intolerable strain on the wilderness beyond.'[8]

Barnett's solution was to set up a public fund, administered by the Hampstead Heath Extension Council, to buy 32.4 hectares (80 acres) of the Wyldes estate adjacent to the station, which would be preserved for 'the recreation . . . and the general health of the community' [FIG.138].[9] This land had already been earmarked for cheap housing, but the owners, the Eton College Trust, were prepared to sell to the Committee at a discounted rate, providing the funds could be raised quickly.

This would have been unwelcome news for Yerkes and his associates. They had little interest in opening a station primarily for infrequent holidaymakers. The business model for North End depended on the success of speculative residential building in creating a new suburb populated by regular commuters around the station. Their options were limited, however, as Wyldes Farm represented by far the largest tract of available land. To the south, the preserved status of the Heath made building impossible, while, to the west, a recent preservation scheme protected the extensive Golders Hill estate from developers' clutches.[10] Even so, Yerkes felt confident enough in his plans to reject a Committee proposal to reroute the Tube further west, avoiding the Heath altogether.[11] Instead, he pushed on with the construction of the underground station and a new approach road, which the railway hoped would open up further farm land for building.

Meanwhile, support for the Hampstead Heath Extension project had outstripped expectation. Even the Princess of Wales was said to be a subscriber to the fund, and by September 1904, enough money had been raised to secure the land for public use. Barnett was delighted. In a letter to the *Standard* she rejoiced that 'the far-reaching view is saved, the sylvan beauty around the Tube station preserved, new walks and roads with broad outlooks made possible, and some 50 acres of playing fields added for the benefit of London youth.'[12]

With success achieved, Barnett had already begun to turn her attention to a more ambitious scheme: the creation of a 'garden suburb' on the remaining 98 hectares (243 acres) of Wyldes Farm. Inspired by the garden city philosophy espoused by Ebenezer Howard, Hampstead Garden Suburb would be managed by a trust and provide high-quality, environmentally sympathetic housing for rich and poor.[13] Undoubtedly motivated by genuine reforming zeal, Barnett was also responding to what she referred to as the 'small streets of small houses' planned by the speculative builders at North End. By contrast, her vision for a low-density suburb of architect-designed homes would stand as a protest against the unruly expansion of London, which recent developments in public transport had done so much to enable.

It would be a mistake though to conclude that Barnett was opposed to the Tube as such. The 1906 prospectus for Hampstead Garden Suburb explicitly drew attention to the proximity of both Golders Green and North End stations which, it claimed, 'will give admirable facilities of access' to the new estate.[14] In setting forth her case for a mixed-class suburb, Barnett had previously argued that working-class residents would be within 'a two-penny tube touch with all parts of London by the Electric Railway' – a reference to the cheap standard fares offered at that time.[15] Wealthier residents, too, would be attracted by good transport connections, and the first luxury homes were planned for Hampstead Way, next to the proposed station. Consequently, North End station appeared on all of the early plans for the suburb and was frequently mentioned in supporting literature [FIG.139].

This may explain why the railway company carried on with its preparations for a new station, even after it became apparent that the hoped-for mass housing was not going to materialise. Three passenger lifts were ordered for North End from the Otis Elevator Company in March 1906, though this was soon modified to two lifts occupying one shaft as a cost-saving measure [FIG.141] – the first sign that the railway was beginning to lose confidence in the venture. As work on the rest of the line accelerated towards completion, progress slowed to a halt at North End. Neither the lift shaft nor any part of the surface building was constructed and, within a few months, the company had decided to abandon the station for good. In some respects, it was an odd decision, given the investment that had already been made in the site and the fact that some new housing was on the way. The abandonment shows that Tube investors were fully prepared to cut their losses if a return on their investment was in doubt.[16]

The rest of the CCE&HR opened to passengers on 22 June 1907, with trains running through the unused North End station [FIG.141]. Most of the surface plot

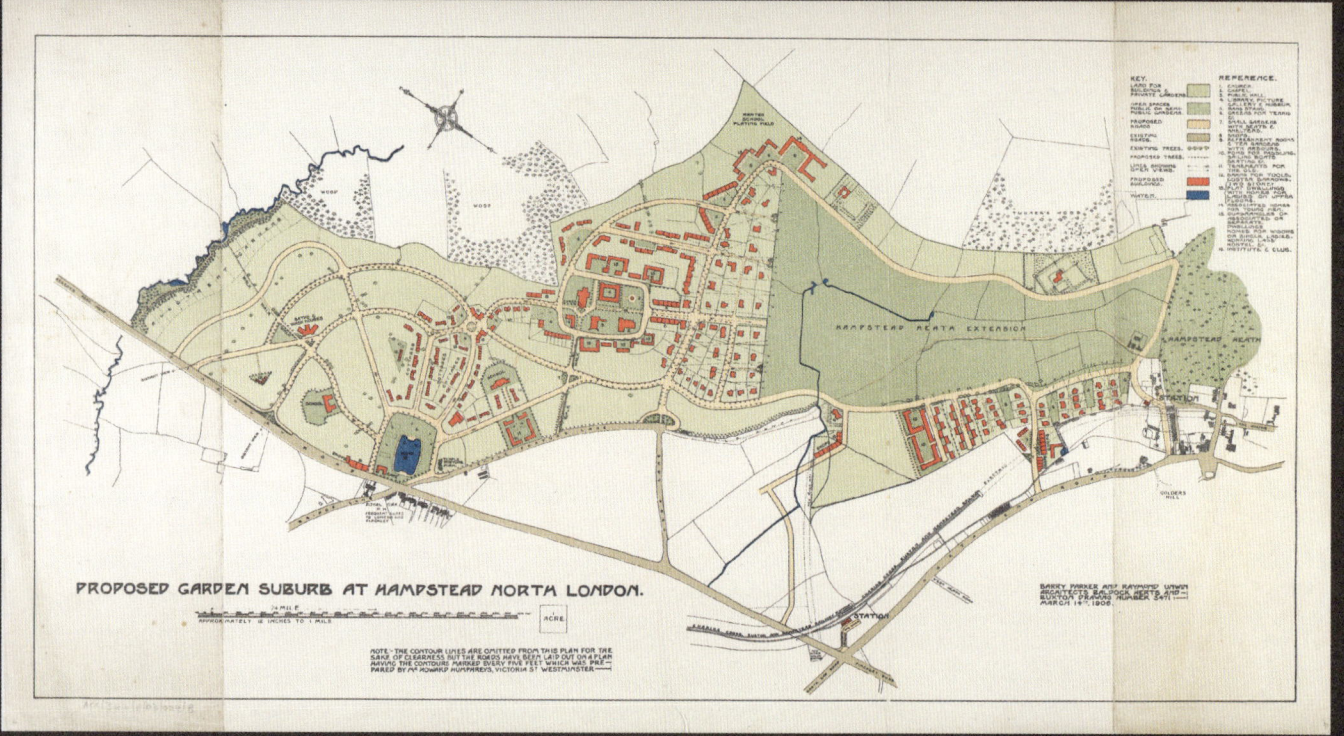

[FIG.139] TOP The proposed Hampstead Garden Suburb in a plan from 14 March 1906. At this date, North End station is prominently shown at the bottom of the image, together with the new approach road built by the railway.

[FIG.140] ABOVE Wyldes Farm, painted by the artist John Everett Millais in 1848. The house had been the centre of a working farm since the 1600s. By the nineteenth century it had become a fashionable retreat for artists, writers and political thinkers.

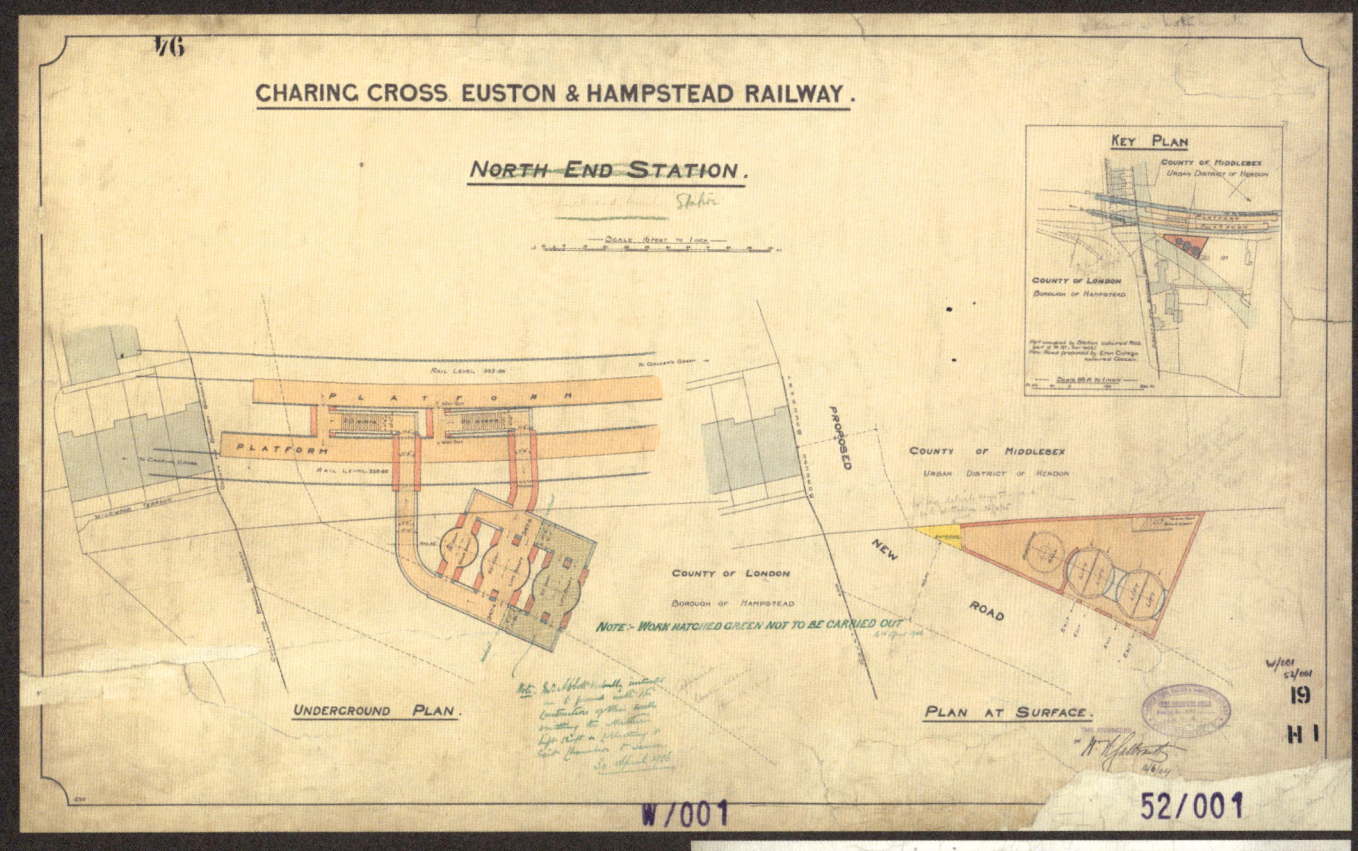

[FIG.141] ABOVE The original plans for North End, from June 1904, show the location of the surface station on present-day Hampstead Way and access to the underground platforms. A handwritten annotation from April 1906 records the cancellation of the second lift shaft. In the event, no connection was made with the surface until the 1950s.

[FIG.142] RIGHT Charles Tyson Yerkes hoped that the Charing Cross, Euston & Hampstead Railway (usually known as the 'Hampstead Tube') would unlock new residential districts for development. This official guidebook from 1910 shows the route of the new Tube and features homes at Hampstead Garden Suburb on the cover.

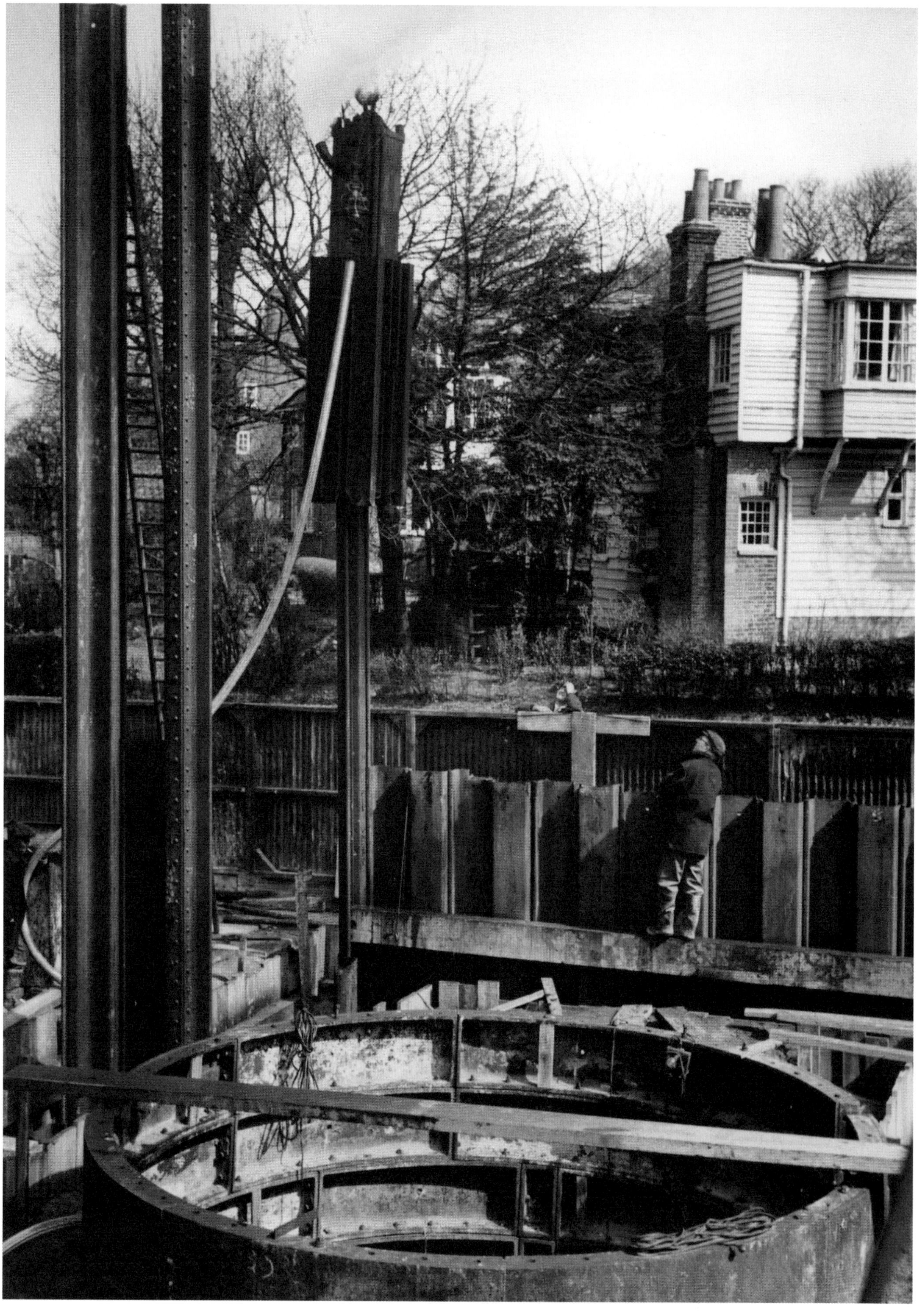

[FIG.143] Construction of the Bull and Bush Emergency Control Headquarters access shaft at North End in April 1956, with Wylde's Farm in the background. Everything about the new facility was secret. Even this London Transport record photograph, taken for archival purposes, was anonymously captioned 'special tunnel work, Bull & Bush'.

was subsequently sold off, including the historic Wyldes farmhouse, which became the estate office for the Hampstead Garden Suburb Company; this survives today.[17] Physically unconnected with the surface, the abandoned station tunnels were largely forgotten over the next 50 years.[18] The station name slowly disappeared from memory, with Underground staff referring to the disused space as 'Bull and Bush' after the nearby hostelry. Yet there can be few unbuilt stations that have had such an impact on their locality. Without the proposal to develop North End it is doubtful whether the Heath Extension or the Garden Suburb would exist today.

THE NORTH END BUNKER

North End could easily have remained a footnote in the history of the Northern line, but its location deep under Hampstead Heath meant that it was uniquely placed to be repurposed as a civil defence flood-control bunker during the early years of the Cold War. The origins of this extraordinary, and hitherto secret, reuse are to be found during the Second World War, when London Transport had taken positive steps to counter the threat of flooding posed by aerial bombing.

If the Underground's tunnels under the Thames had been breached during the war, flooding could have inundated the central London Tube network, bringing the system to a standstill for months and causing innumerable deaths. At first, the Underground was, understandably, ill-prepared for such an eventuality. During the dark days of the Munich Crisis in 1938, the potential threat of aerial bombardment by the Luftwaffe caused London Transport to hastily fit crude concrete plugs to the Thames tunnel sections of the Bakerloo and Northern lines to prevent flooding in the event of a direct hit.[19] This was, however, only a temporary solution. Within a year, the plugs had been replaced at Embankment, and at other vulnerable stations, with purpose-built, hydraulically powered watertight doors operated from a central control room at Leicester Square. The system enabled tunnels to be sealed to protect the network in the event of an air raid, and then opened again to allow normal service to resume once the threat had passed.

In post-war Britain, the threat of nuclear attack meant that such safety measures were retained, but, with a much shorter warning period and far greater potential for devastation, the advent of nuclear bombs meant that a revised system was required, which could close all flood doors simultaneously from one location. The abandoned remains of North End station were a good choice for such a control facility: lying forgotten, deep below ground level, the site was naturally protected from potential attack and easily connected by cables to other Underground stations. In 1956 construction began to repurpose the platforms and cross passages to make a control room, staff facilities and storage space [FIG.143]. These were connected to the surface for the first time by a heavily fortified access shaft, equipped with stairs and a lift [FIG.137], and entered from Hampstead Way via an anonymous building that could easily have been mistaken for a small-scale telephone exchange or electricity substation.

The new facility was known within the Underground and government circles as The Bull and Bush Emergency Control Headquarters. As with other government bunkers, it seems that use of the name 'Bull and Bush' followed

[FIG.144] One of the original, subterranean passenger walkways at North End, built in the 1900s but never used, seen here with later flood defence modifications, including a reinforced steel door.

the practice of finding a name that originates reasonably close to the actual site but usefully distracts all but the determined searcher from the real location. Protected and hidden, the headquarters took control of the entire network of London Transport floodgates in November 1958 and was able to monitor and operate gates remotely in the case of emergency. The site was linked to the Metropolitan Police's civil defence warning system at Scotland Yard, allowing the Tube network to be quickly sealed up in the event of a suspected nuclear attack. The control room systems were routinely tested to ensure reliability, with each set of floodgates opened and closed on a ten-week cycle and the signal from Scotland Yard tested several times each year.[20]

In common with many early Cold War facilities, the defences of Bull and Bush were rapidly overtaken by the development of nuclear weapons. Only four years after the site was commissioned, new enemy bombs were in use, capable of blasting a crater in the ground far deeper than the bunker itself.[21] The usefulness of the site was diminishing and by the beginning of the 1970s, Bull and Bush was no longer routinely staffed and had fallen into disrepair. A scathing report from the headquarters controller in June 1981 records that neither the lift nor basic communication equipment were working. It was, he concluded, an 'establishment [that] breaks all of the Health & Safety rules' and one that was 'highly unsafe' to visit alone.[22]

In testimony to its declining importance, by the early 1980s Bull and Bush was also being used to store archival film on behalf of London Transport. This rather incongruous dual use could lead to some strange experiences for anyone wishing to retrieve an appropriate reel, as the then-assistant curator at London Transport Museum, Rob Lansdown, discovered:

> I was packed into the tiny lift by a Group or Area Manager, descended for ages to platform level, accompanied by the ever louder and more ominous beeping of the four-minute warning system that echoed through the place. On arrival, I was walked . . . through the dimly lit, dirty, dystopian and unfinished station structure, to a platform end control room, with a large telephone switchboard and a speaker – the source of the beep. We were just in time as it crackled into life with a test message and the code word 'Winchester', which was repeated. This was immediately followed by the reassuring return of the beep and the manager phoned someone to acknowledge the test.[23]

It was all a far cry from the efficient secrecy and preparedness of the facility's early years. As the Cold War drew to a close in the 1980s, the floodgate network was gradually decommissioned. In addition, the completion of the Thames Barrier in 1984 eliminated the immediate threat of a tidal surge flooding London; after that date, Bull and Bush no longer appears to have been regularly maintained. Today, only the remains of the control room and the platform floodgates at Embankment survive as a reminder of the part played by London Transport in national defence during that period.

[FIG.145] BELOW The remains of the flood control office at North End.

[FIG.146] NEXT An engineering drawing reveals the extent of the comprehensive conversion of the disused lift shafts and passageways at St Paul's station, to create a bombproof bunker for the Central Electricity Board control room during the Second World War.

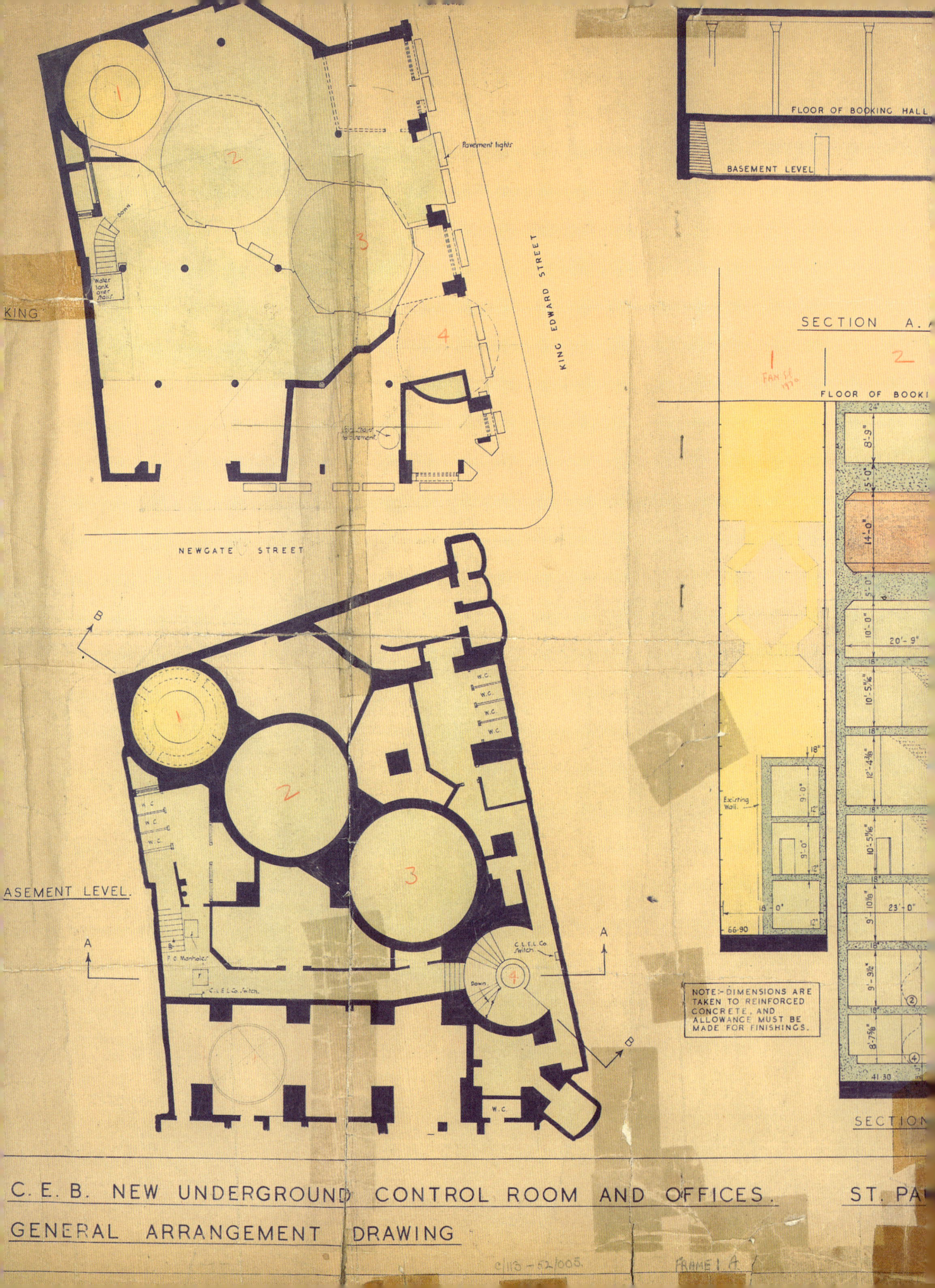

C.E.B. NEW UNDERGROUND CONTROL ROOM AND OFFICES. ST. PA
GENERAL ARRANGEMENT DRAWING

EXISTING STAIR SHAFT

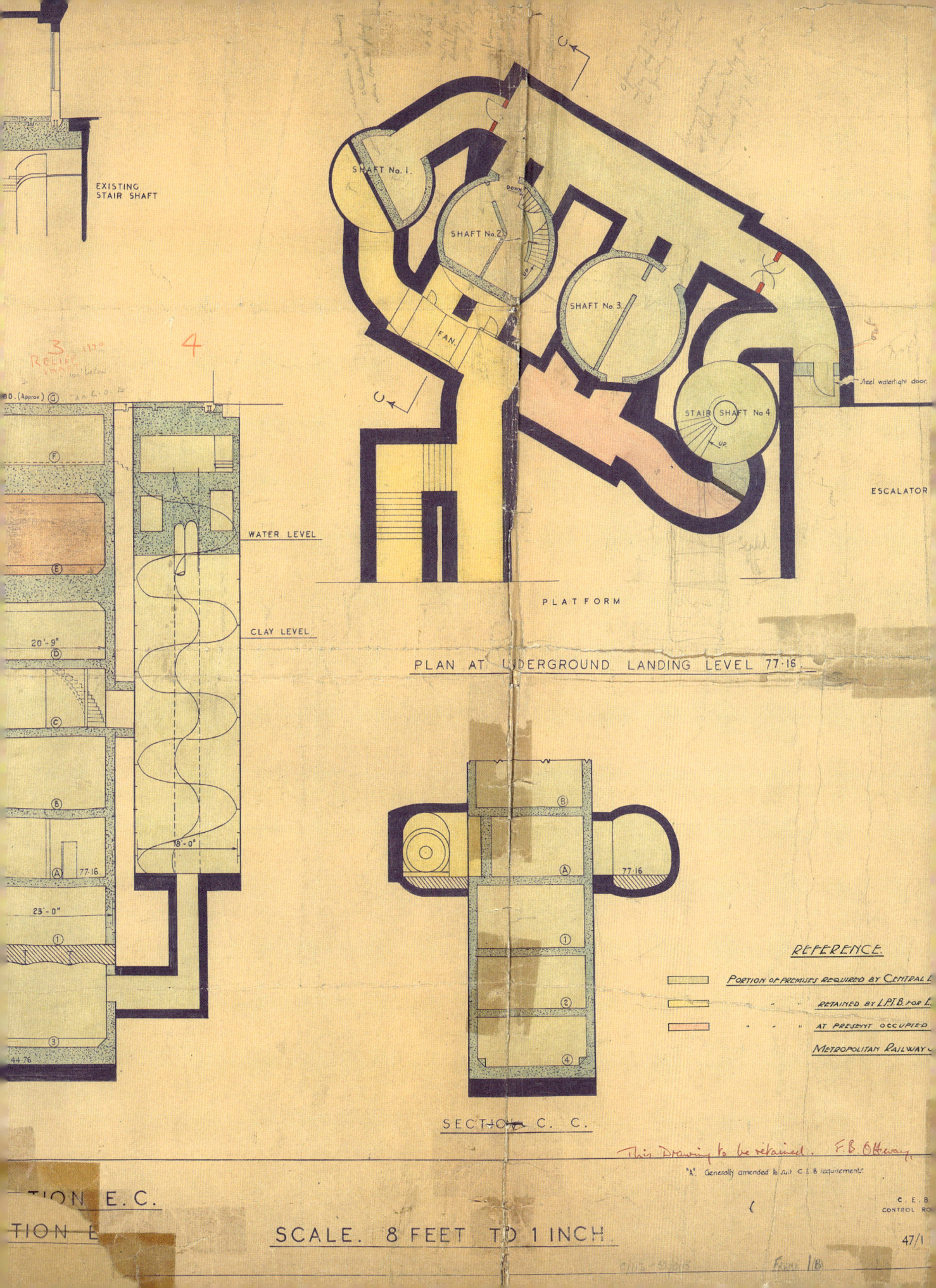

SHAFT No. 1
SHAFT No. 2
SHAFT No. 3
FAN
STAIR SHAFT No. 4
ESCALATOR
PLATFORM

PLAN AT UNDERGROUND LANDING LEVEL 77·16

WATER LEVEL
CLAY LEVEL

20'-9"
18'-0"
77·16
23'-0"
44·76

SECTION C.C.

REFERENCE.
Portion of premises required by Central L
Retained by L.P.T.B. for L
At present occupied
Metropolitan Railway

This Drawing to be retained. F.B. Ottway
"A" Generally amended to suit C.E.B requirements.

TION E.C.
SCALE. 8 FEET TO 1 INCH

C.E.B
CONTROL RO

47/1

ST PAUL'S STATION BUNKER

This remarkable repurposing of an abandoned Tube station as a control bunker was not without precedent. London Transport had experience of doing just the same at St Paul's station (formerly known as Post Office), where the abandoned lift shafts of the station on the Central line, between Chancery Lane and Bank, were transformed into an extensive, bombproof control headquarters for the Central Electricity Board during the Second World War [FIGS 146 & 147]. The transformation began in November 1940 in response to the Blitz and saw the two large lift shafts, as well as emergency staircases and passageways, converted to form a heavily defended suite of offices with staff accommodation and control rooms, which, from August 1941, managed electricity supplies for the National Grid. The control room was conveniently located in central London, near to power stations at Bankside and Battersea, and remained in use until 1957, since which time all of the wartime equipment has been completely stripped out. The empty space left behind continues to serve as a service route for major works on the Central line.

[FIG.147] ABOVE LEFT In 1937, Post Office station was renamed St Paul's and on 1 January 1939, this original ticket hall was replaced by a new hall with two entrances and with new escalators to the platforms, leaving the original lift shafts and passageways available for reuse as a secure control room.

[FIG.148] ABOVE RIGHT Despite the drastic changes to St Paul's station, a relief tile designed by Harold Stabler from around 1938 survives in situ in a disused passageway.

1   A public house since at least 1721, the Bull and Bush obtained a music licence in the 1860s and became a popular destination for day trippers. The music hall song *Down at the Old Bull and Bush* was adapted from a German-language version written in 1903 and popularised by the singer Florrie Ford.

2   (Mrs) Arthur Wilson, 'Wyldes and Its Story', *Transactions of the Hampstead Antiquarian and Literary Society* (1902–3).

3   For a discussion of Yerkes's business methods, see Tim Sherwood, *Charles Tyson Yerkes: Railway Tycoon* (The History Press, 2009). For the development of Golders Green, see Alan A. Jackson, *Semi-Detached London: Suburban Development, Life and Transport, 1900–39* (Wild Swan Publications, 1991), especially pp.37–56.

4   *Pall Mall Gazette*, 4 January 1901, p.5.

5   North End remains the deepest station to have been excavated in London. The deepest operational station is Hampstead Heath, immediately to the south-east of North End, which is 58.5 metres (192 feet) below ground.

6   Desmond F. Croome and Alan A. Jackson, *Rails Through the Clay: A History of London's Tube Railways* (Capital Transport, 1993), p.509.

7   Dame Henrietta Barnett DBE was a notable social reformer, educationist and author, known for her work in London's East End. With her husband, Samuel Augustus Barnett, she founded Toynbee Hall charitable institution and helped establish the Whitechapel Art Gallery (ODNB, 2004).

8   *Hampstead and Highgate Express*, 8 August 1903, p.5.

9   Minutes of Hampstead Heath Extension Council, 1903, London Metropolitan Archives, LMA ACC/3816/01/02/001.

10 Situated a short walk from the proposed North End station, Golders Hill manor house and grounds had been purchased by the London County Council in 1898 for use as a public park.

11 Representatives of the Hampstead Heath Extension Council met with the railway company on at least two occasions, once with Yerkes himself. See Minutes of the Hampstead Heath Extension Committee, 8 October 1903 and 3 March 1904, London Metropolitan Archives, LMA ACC/3816/01/02/007.

12 *Standard*, 3 September 1904, p.2.

13 For an overview of the origins and history of Hampstead Garden Suburb, see Mervyn Miller, *Hampstead Garden Suburb: Arts and Crafts Utopia* (The History Press, 2006).

14 In writing the prospectus, which also served as a manifesto for the garden suburb concept, Barnett employed the estate agents Farebrother, Ellis & Co. to assess the value of the Tube stations to the new development (London Metropolitan Archives, LMA ACC/3816/02/01/006).

15 From an article first published in the *Contemporary Review*, February 1905, and later reissued as a pamphlet entitled *A Garden Suburb at Hampstead* (London Metropolitan Archives, LMA ACC/3816/02/01/006).

16 Jackson 1991, pp.46–8, and Croome and Jackson 1993, pp.509–10. Curiously, in November 1907, the CCE&HR Board agreed that 'provision must be made for completing (North End) station when required', and received cost estimates to that effect, although no further work was undertaken. See Nick Catford and Peter Kay, 'North End (Bull & Bush)', *London Railway Record* (January 2013), p.175.

17 The plot earmarked for the station building is now No.1 Hampstead Way, originally the home of architect Charles Holloway James and artist-calligrapher Margaret Calkin James, who also designed several posters for London Underground.

18 The unused platforms were removed in 1935, and the space used for storing maintenance materials. See TfL Archives, LT 482/010 (083).

19 The Munich Crisis lasted from 27 September to 8 October 1938. For details of floodgate installation, see Croome and Jackson 1993, pp.267–8.

20 TfL Archives, LT001055/010.

21 Peter Laurie, *Beneath the City Streets* (Harper Collins, 1979), p.66.

22 TfL Archives, LT00 1055/010. Similar reports were submitted in 1982, suggesting that by this time the facility was in terminal decline.

23 Interview with Rob Lansdown, 16 November 2018.

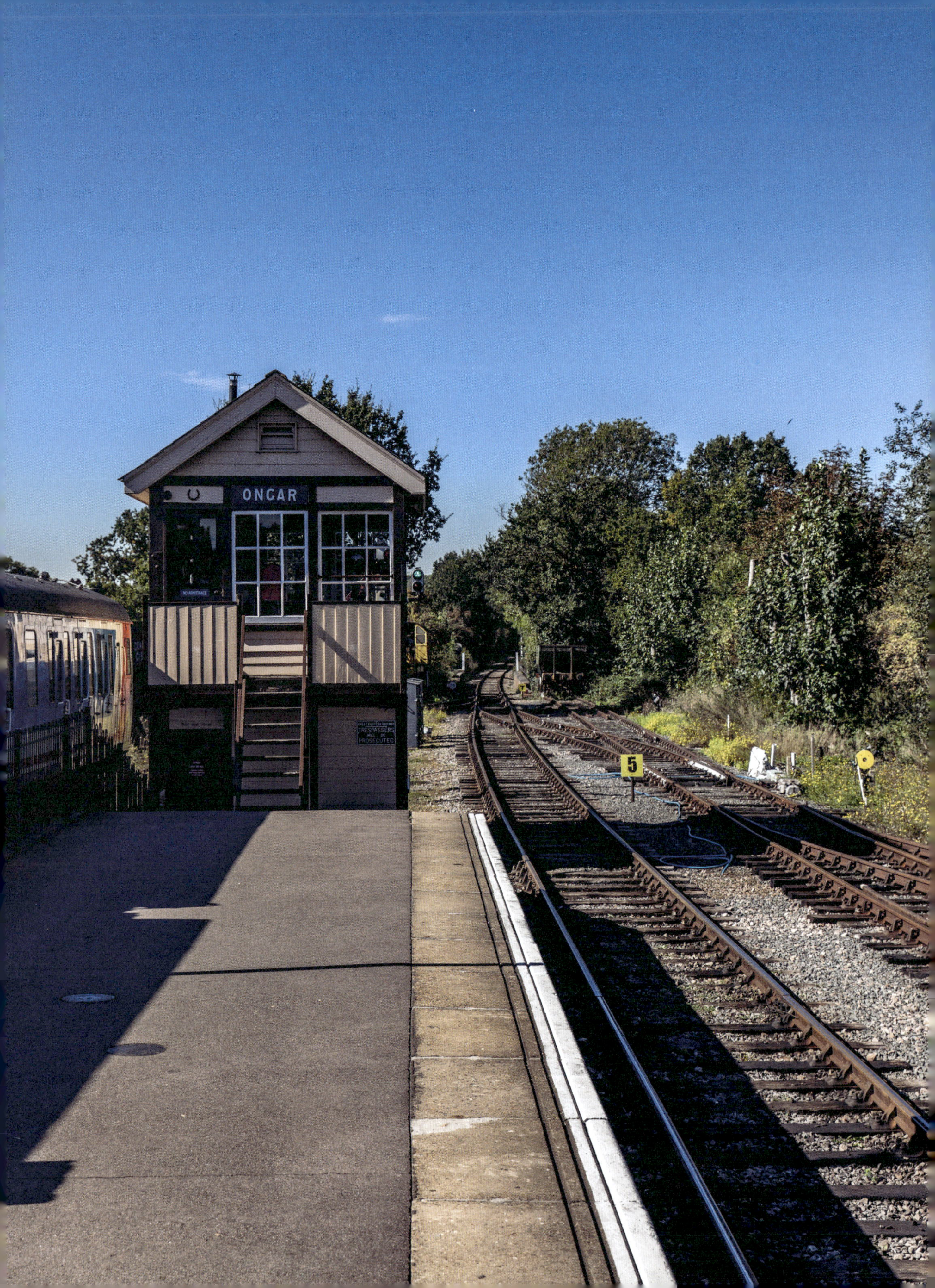
ONGAR
NO ADMITTANCE
TRESPASSERS
WILL BE
PROSECUTED
5

ONGAR & QUAINTON ROAD

FROM UNDERGROUND OUTPOSTS
TO HERITAGE RAILWAYS

ONGAR STATION, VIEW ALONG PLATFORM SHOWING ENGINE SHED. 12-5-38. 5865.

[FIG.149] PREVIOUS The manually operated signal cabin at Ongar station serves as a visual reminder of the railway's nineteenth-century origins, before it became part of London Transport. The current cabin, originally from Spellbrook in East Anglia, sits on the site of its Victorian predecessor, which was demolished some years ago.

[FIG.150] TOP Ongar photographed from the 'London end' in May 1938. Located deep in rural Essex, the station opened in 1865 as the terminus of a winding Great Eastern Railway (GER) route to London, via Epping and Loughton.[1] By the 1930s, the entire route had been incorporated into the London & North Eastern Railway (LNER), which was, at that time, in discussion with London Transport regarding the improvement of rail services across the capital known as the New Works Programme. Under this scheme, parts of east London and Essex were scheduled to benefit from an extension to the Underground's Central line, alleviating congestion and providing better connections for remote districts. Delayed by the Second World War, the scheme eventually resulted in the extension of the Central line along sections of the former GER, including the line from Loughton to Ongar, which was handed over to London Transport and electrified in stages.[2] Remote Ongar then became the unlikely terminus of one of London's busiest Tube lines, although the final stretch of railway from Epping was not electrified until 1957.[3] Before then, passengers had to complete their journey to Ongar by a steam-hauled shuttle service hired from British Railways.

ONGAR

For over 150 years, the Underground has played an important part in shaping the extent and influence of London. The presence of a Modernist-inspired Tube station, with reassuringly visible 'roundel' signage, connects the leafy outer suburbs with the city centre both physically and emotionally. Some of these now-thriving suburban communities were originally built on greenfield sites, with little historic connection to the bustling metropolis. But all were transformed by the arrival of fast and frequent Underground trains, changing forever the centuries-old agricultural and riverside communities into commuter dormitories.

Well, almost all. In the more remote corners of leafy Buckinghamshire and Essex, two Victorian railway schemes bequeathed their isolated and little-used country stations to London Transport on its creation in 1933. From the start, it was clear that no amount of rebranding would ever compensate for these stations' distance from London and lack of passengers. At Ongar, on the outskirts of Epping Forest, and Quainton Road, high up in the Chiltern Hills, London Transport inherited steam-hauled rural railways that were 40 and 74 kilometres (25 and 45 miles) from central London, respectively. Both had become part of the London Transport network for very different historical and political reasons, but both were to share the same fate when dwindling financial returns led to closure and abandonment.

Today the two stations have been reborn as part of heritage railways. Ongar sits at the terminus of a steam- and diesel-hauled branch line from Epping, with lovingly restored former London Transport stations at North Weald and Blake Hall. At Quainton Road, a working museum tells the story of how the world's first underground system, the Metropolitan Railway, sought to break out of London and develop this part of rural Buckinghamshire into a major railway junction.

[FIG.151] OPPOSITE BELOW LEFT Despite electrification, the line from Epping to Ongar was never well patronised. With passenger numbers in terminal decline, London Transport tried unsuccessfully to close the line on two occasions, in 1970 and 1980. This image of a graffiti-covered Tube train at Ongar, by the American photographer Wozzy Dias, sums up the station's forlorn appearance in the 1980s. With no sign of improvement on the horizon, this loss-making section of the Central line was finally closed on 30 September 1994.

[FIG.152] OPPOSITE BELOW RIGHT Today, the Epping and Ongar line is run as a heritage railway by a staff largely made up of volunteers.[4] The station at Ongar, seen here with a Metropolitan Railway steam-hauled train in 2017, has been faithfully restored to appear as it did in the days of the Great Eastern Railway (c.1880–1920). One notable exception to the restoration is the presence of post-war, London Transport 'roundel' name boards – a testimony to the importance of this period in the railway's history.

[FIGS 153 & 154] North Weald, on the same line as Ongar, photographed from the 'country end' by the London & North Eastern Railway (LNER) in 1938 (right), and as a preserved station today (below). By the time the line closed in 1994, North Weald was recording less than 50 passenger journeys a day.[5] It is now restored in the colours of the LNER and British Railways (Eastern Region), to represent the period from the 1930s to the 1950s.

QUAINTON ROAD

[FIGS 155 & 156] ABOVE Blake Hall, between Ongar and North Weald, had the unenviable distinction of being the least-used station on the London Transport network. Passenger services were reduced during the 1960s to save money and removed altogether in 1981, 13 years before the rest of the line closed. The photograph (above left) taken in 1955, shows the original Great Eastern Railway station virtually unchanged except for the addition of London Transport signage and posters. Fully refurbished, the building is now used as a private residence (above right).

[FIG.157] Quainton Road was closely associated with the Underground from its earliest days. Built in the nineteenth century, it became part of a bold scheme to link the urban, underground network of the Metropolitan Railway with the national rail system.[6] The architect of the scheme was the Met's chairman, Edward Watkin, who, by the 1890s, had overseen the construction of a 'mainline' from Baker Street (on the modern-day Metropolitan line) to Verney Junction, over 80 kilometres (50 miles) north of London.[7] Quainton Road was initially an important rail junction on the new line, connecting the Metropolitan with the Great Central Railway to Manchester and also providing local services to Brill via a short branch line. Ultimately, however, transport developments elsewhere saw the station's role diminish and it settled down to life as a quiet country station. After the Metropolitan Railway became part of London Transport in 1933, passenger services to stations beyond Aylesbury (including Quainton) were transferred in 1936 to the London & North Eastern Railway. Declining use saw Quainton Road close to passengers in 1963 and to goods traffic in 1966. Now fully restored, the main platform buildings look remarkably similar to how they would have appeared in the early twentieth century.

[FIG.158] RIGHT London Transport inherited a fully operational mainline railway from the Metropolitan Railway in 1933, complete with goods trains, milk churns, country stations and local delivery services. None of this aligned with the vision of the chairman, Lord Ashfield, and his deputy, Frank Pick, had of a modern urban transit system. Services in the more remote areas were quickly pruned back or removed. This 1934 poster lists the former Metropolitan stations north of Harrow-on-the-Hill, newly served by London Transport. Nowadays, the Metropolitan line terminates at Amersham and Chesham, and all the stations on the poster from Great Missenden to Verney Junction have either been transferred to national rail operators or closed.

[FIG.159] BELOW This photograph shows an antiquated London Transport train about to depart Quainton Road for the Brill branch line in 1934 – a far cry from the modern, electric Tubes normally associated with the Underground at this time.[8] The 60-year-old locomotive (now preserved at London Transport Museum) started life on the steam-hauled Metropolitan underground railway in central London. Its archaic appearance, with prominent condensing pipes to reduce emissions in the city's tunnels, would have made it a curiosity even in the 1930s. The anachronistic effect is emphasised by the use of contemporary London Transport lettering on the side of the Victorian locomotive.

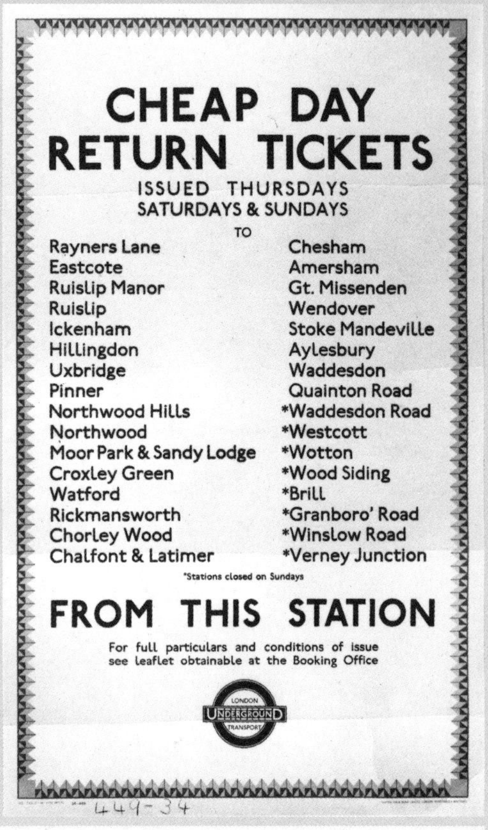

[FIG.160] ABOVE Following a financial review, the loss-making Brill Branch of the Metropolitan line was closed by London Transport on 30 November 1934, just over a year after London Transport took charge. With the track removed, the site of Brill station has returned to nature. Only a home-made sign now marks this distant outpost of London Transport's operation.

[FIG.161] RIGHT Trains on the little-used Brill branch called at five stops in total, including Westcott, shown here as photographed by London Transport in 1934.

[FIGS 162 & 163]   At Westcott station, the original Victorian wooden station building, complete with a nineteenth-century carriage, survives today.

[FIGS 164 & 165] Over 10 kilometres (6 miles) north of Quainton Road, Verney Junction (above) marked the northernmost limit of the Metropolitan Railway's empire. With interchange facilities for mainline trains to Oxford, Cambridge and beyond, the company had high hopes that the junction would one day become the 'Crewe of the south'. It was all part of the company's desire to be seen as a 'proper' railway, despite its underground origins. Such aspirations, though, were of little interest to London Transport and passenger services to this remote station were discontinued in 1936. Intermittent goods traffic kept the line alive for a few more years but, eventually, both the railway from Quainton Road and the mainline with which it connected were closed. Although there is little trace now of the line to London, the overgrown trackbed of the former mainline railway survives (right) and is set to be re-used as part of the East West Rail project, connecting Oxford and Cambridge.[9] There are no plans, to reopen the station, which remains as isolated as it was when the first trains pulled into Verney Junction over 120 years ago.

[FIGS 166 & 167] TOP South of Quainton Road, London Transport continued to run steam-hauled passenger services over the former Metropolitan Railway from Rickmansworth to Aylesbury for almost 30 years. The stations on this route were fully part of the London Transport network, complete with familiar signage and Underground staff. Following the electrification of the Metropolitan line to Amersham in 1961, the stations beyond this point, including Stoke Mandeville (seen top left, in 1955), were transferred to British Railways and are now served by Chiltern Railways trains (top right).

[FIG.168] ABOVE The Quainton Railway Society was formed in 1969 to preserve the former Metropolitan Railway station as a working museum. Now known as the Buckinghamshire Railway Centre, the greatly enlarged site houses around 170 locomotives and rail vehicles, in buildings dating from the 1870s to the 1960s. As one of the best-preserved railway stations in England, Quainton Road has appeared in several film and television dramas, including *The Jewel in the Crown*, *Black Orchid* and *Midsomer Murders*.[10]

1   For a detailed account of the history of the railway running from Loughton to Ongar, see Alan A. Jackson, *London's Local Railways* (Capital Transport, 1999), pp.381–94.
2   The Central line extension reached Leytonstone in 1946 and Loughton in 1948. Following nationalisation of the railways in 1948, the former LNER line from Leyton to Loughton was transferred to the newly formed London Transport Executive (LTE). The Central line eventually reached Epping in 1949, also taking control of the branch line to Ongar from British Railways (Eastern Region).
3   The section was electrified at a cost of £100,000 – a significant part of the Underground's annual investment budget – in 1957. Spurred on by a belief that electrification would increase traffic, the decision was questionable at best, given the small size of the local population. See Christian Wolmar, *The Subterranean Railway* (Atlantic Books, 2004), p.298.
4   For details about the Epping Ongar Railway, see www.eorailway.co.uk, accessed 16 April 2019.
5   Jackson 1999, p.393. Passenger numbers here were given an occasional boost by the air shows held at nearby North Weald Airfield.
6   The best history of the Metropolitan Railway is Alan A. Jackson's *London's Metropolitan Railway* (David & Charles, 1986). For an introduction to the background of Metropolitan Railway's northwards expansion, see David Bownes, Oliver Green and Sam Mullins, *Underground: How the Tube Shaped London* (Penguin, 2012), pp.49–53.
7   For an explanation of Watkin's grandiose, and often inconsistent, plans for the Metropolitan Railway, see David J. Hodgkins, *The Second Railway King: The Life and Times of Sir Edward Watkin, 1819–1901* (Merton Priory Press, 2002).
8   The Brill Branch, variously known as the Wotton Tramway and the Brill Tramway, ran from Quainton Road to Brill, a distance of approximately 9.5 kilometres (6 miles), with stops at Waddesdon Road, Westcott, Wotton and Wood Siding. It was originally built in 1871 as a private light railway by the Duke of Buckingham, and acquired by the Metropolitan in 1894. See Bill Simpson, *The Brill Tramway* (Oxford Publishing, 1985).
9   At the time of writing, the route from Bedford to Oxford, via the disused station at Verney Junction, is due to reopen in 2023 (see www.eastwestrail.org.uk, accessed 24 October 2018.)
10. For details about the Buckinghamshire Railway Centre, see www.bucksrailcentre.org, accessed 16 April 2019.

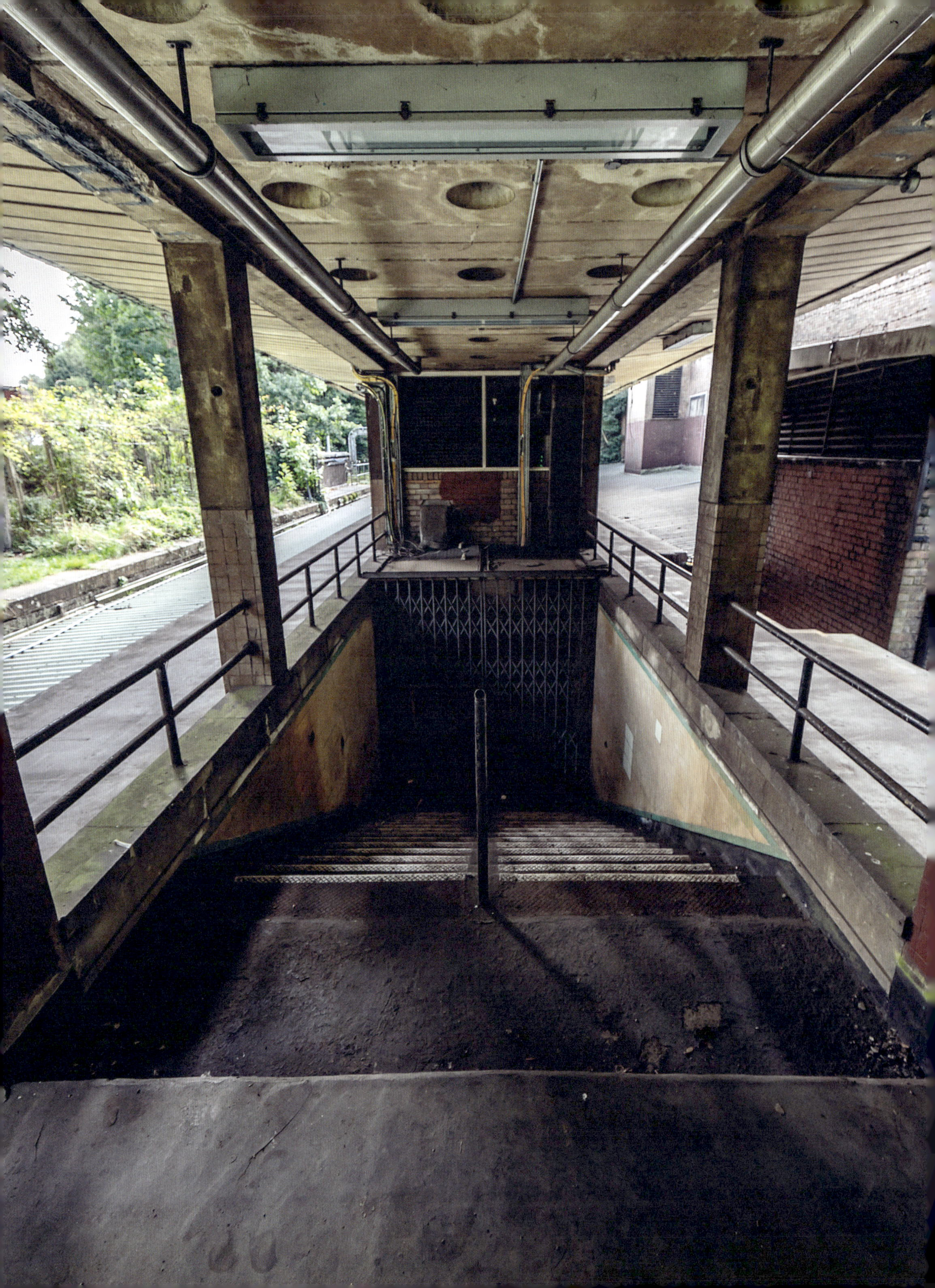

HIGHGATE HIGH-LEVEL

CHANGE FOR THE NORTHERN HEIGHTS

Highgate Station

[FIG.169] PREVIOUS The station canopy and blocked-off steps leading down to the Tube station booking hall, seen today.

[FIGS 170 & 171] Because of the hilly terrain, Highgate station was built in a deep cutting, with tunnels at either end of the platforms. These commercial postcards from the 1900s show the original station layout before and after conversion to a single-island platform, and also the very steep passenger route to the main road.

Today, Highgate high-level station is abandoned and largely overgrown. Fenced off, it has become an oasis of greenery only yards from the busy Archway Road and directly above Highgate station on the Northern line. The twin tunnels at the northern end of the platform, which once echoed to the sound of steam-hauled passenger trains, are now a protected bat sanctuary. The Modernist waiting room, with concrete canopy, stands forlorn and decaying, devoid of the 'bullseye' roundels that formerly proclaimed the station's connection with the wider London Transport network. How differently things might have turned out. In the 1930s, a government-endorsed scheme placed Highgate at the centre of an ambitious plan for modernising and expanding north London's railways. Under what was known as the Northern Heights Project, several existing routes would have come under the remit of London Transport, resulting in much improved services for local communities. Highgate was to provide interchange facilities between the deep-level Tube and overground railways. The scheme was within months of completion when the Second World War intervened and halted progress. By then, the interchange station at Highgate was more or less ready and it opened for business shortly afterwards, but in the changed circumstances of post-war Britain, the rest of the Northern Heights Project was eventually shelved and, with it, any prospect for the long-term survival of Highgate high-level station.[1]

HIGHGATE OR HIGHGATE?

Confusingly, three different stations have been named Highgate over the years. The first, and the subject of this chapter, was opened by the Great Northern Railway in 1867 on a branch line from Finsbury Park to Edgware.[2] It was never well patronised, although the surrounding low-lying hills, known as the Northern Heights, were popular with middle-class day trippers and homeowners. From the 1870s, Highgate was the junction with an even shorter branch line to the emerging suburb and recreational destination of Alexandra Palace [FIG.173]. This line, too, remained poorly used, with later passengers preferring the more direct, and frequent, tram services. Highgate retained the air of a quiet country station (rather than a suburban stop only 9 kilometres or 5 1/2 miles from Charing Cross) well into the 1920s. By now, the entire route had been absorbed into the much larger London & North Eastern Railway (LNER), although investment in services remained low.

Meanwhile, a second 'Highgate' opened in 1907 as part of the Tube network.[3] Situated at the bottom of Highgate Hill, this station was renamed Archway in 1947 and still exists today. For the sake of clarity, its modern name is used throughout this chapter. Lastly, there is the current Highgate Tube station, built by London Transport in 1941 underneath the earlier Victorian station, which was subsequently known as 'Highgate high-level' to avoid confusion.

[FIGS 172, 173, 174, 175] (clockwise from top left) The railway stations at Cranley Gardens, Alexandra Palace, Crouch End and Muswell Hill, photographed by London Transport in 1935, prior to the start of the Northern Heights Project. Scheduled to be served by Tube trains from Finsbury Park, with further interchange facilities available at Highgate, none of these locations are on the Tube map today. Only the station building at Alexandra Palace survives, now used as a community centre.

NORTHERN HEIGHTS PROJECT

In 1935 the London Passenger Transport Board (LPTB, known as London Transport) announced a £40 million 'New Works Programme' to transform the capital's Tube and rail network. It was a colossal sum and a mammoth project, made possible by the availability of government funds to relieve unemployment. The proposals covered a wide geographic area but, according to a post-war review in the *Railway Gazette* in 1946, 'the North London portion of the scheme [was] the most complex from the traffic viewpoint.'[4]

In brief, the Northern Heights Project (as it was popularly known) called for the electrification of three existing LNER branch lines that would henceforth become part of the Tube, albeit located above ground:[5]

1. Finsbury Park to Highgate, Finchley and Edgware
2. Highgate to Alexandra Palace
3. Finchley to High Barnet

In addition, a new overground line would be built from Edgware to Bushey Heath, and all would be connected to the deep-level Tube via new underground sections from Archway to East Finchley, Drayton Park to Finsbury Park, and an interchange at Edgware. Even for those who knew the area well,

[FIG.176] How the Northern Heights scheme was supposed to look. This diagram from *Improving London's Transport* (a special *Railway Gazette* publication from 1946) shows the full extent of the planned rail improvements for north London, including the interchange between the Tube and surface railways at Highgate.

the bewildering array of improved lines and complex connections must have been hard to picture. Fortunately, the *Railway Gazette* was on hand in 1946, when it still seemed possible that all the proposals would be realised, to provide readers with a clear diagram of what to expect [FIG.176].

Under the scheme, new electric Tube trains would replace the outdated and infrequent steam-hauled services, providing north London passengers with direct access to both the City and the West End. The new trains would be jointly owned with LNER, which would also retain the freehold of its stations and track. A large, poorly served, residential district was about to become part of the modern London Transport network.

The proposals were warmly welcomed in the local press, especially in the vicinity of Highgate, where an interchange station would connect the prosperous suburb of Muswell Hill with the Tube and provide greatly improved rail services for Alexandra Palace, Crouch End and Stroud Green.[6] However, things did not quite work out as planned.

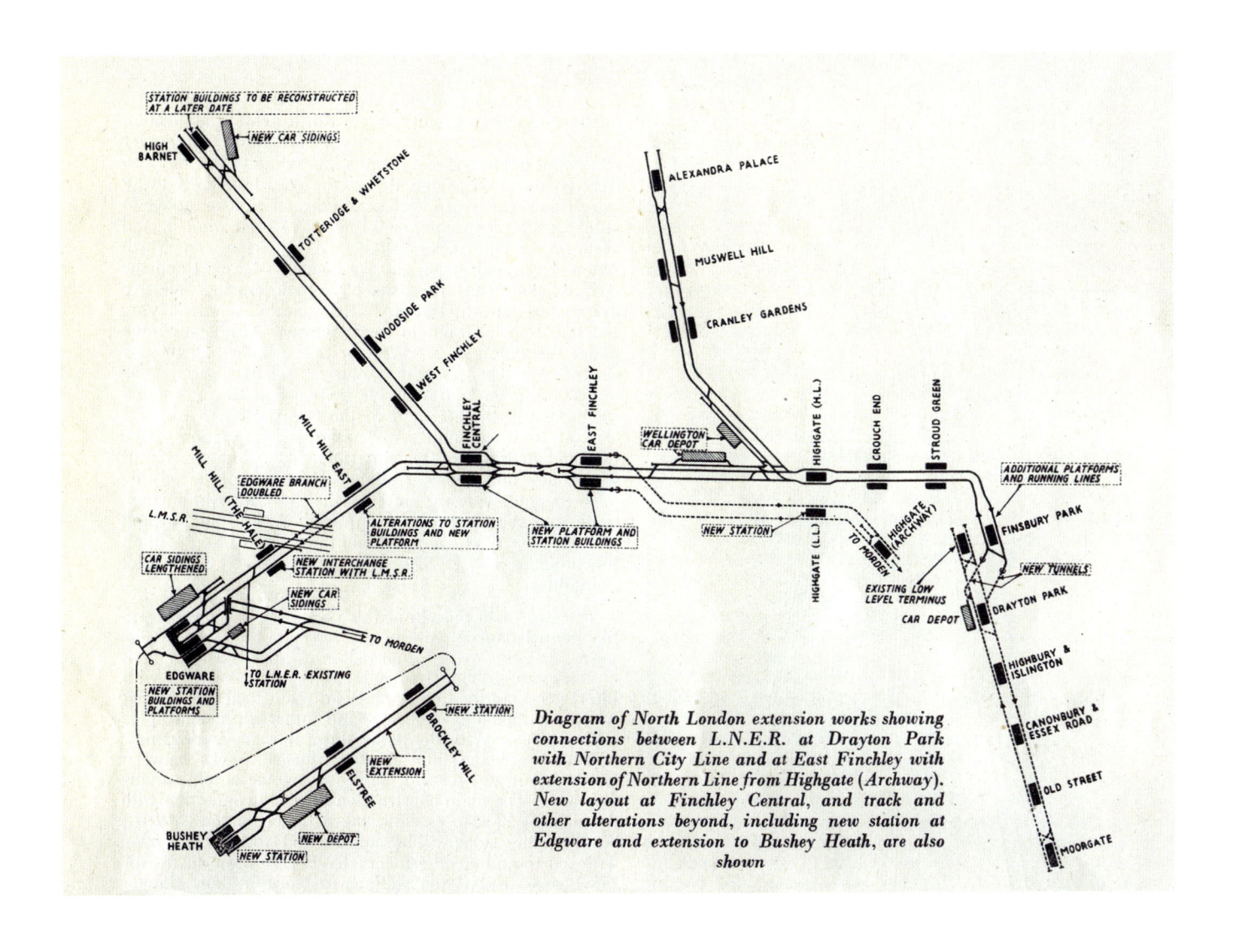

Diagram of North London extension works showing connections between L.N.E.R. at Drayton Park with Northern City Line and at East Finchley with extension of Northern Line from Highgate (Archway). New layout at Finchley Central, and track and other alterations beyond, including new station at Edgware and extension to Bushey Heath, are also shown

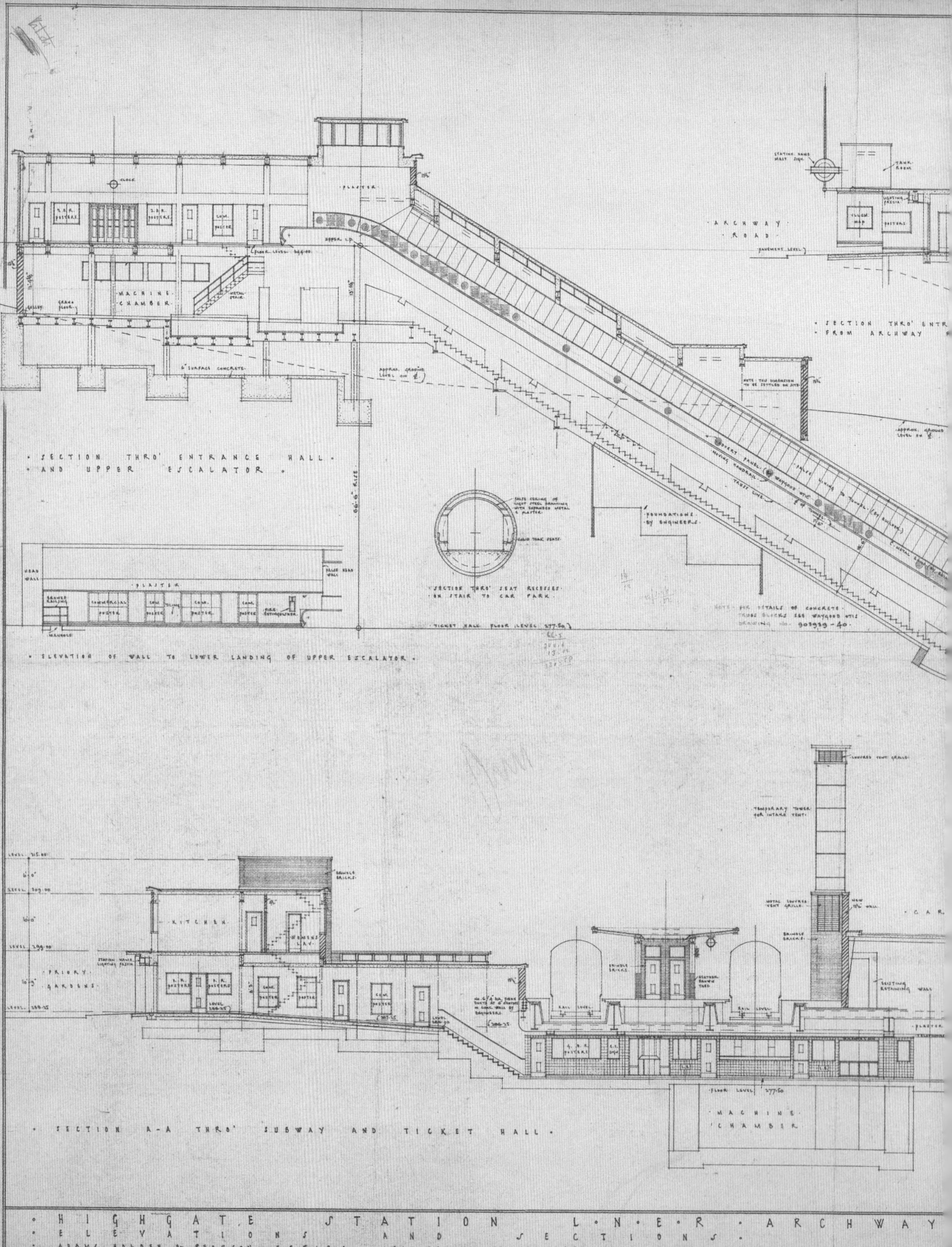
SECTION THRO' ENTRANCE HALL AND UPPER ESCALATOR
SECTION THRO' ENTR... FROM ARCHWAY R...
ARCHWAY ROAD
MACHINE CHAMBER
PLASTER
FOUNDATIONS BY ENGINEERS
SECTION THRO' SEAT RECESSES ON STAIR TO CAR PARK
ELEVATION OF WALL TO LOWER LANDING OF UPPER ESCALATOR
TICKET HALL FLOOR (LEVEL 277.50)
KITCHEN
PRIORY GARDENS
TEMPORARY TOWER FOR INTAKE VENT
FLOOR LEVEL 277.50
MACHINE CHAMBER
SECTION A-A THRO' SUBWAY AND TICKET HALL
HIGHGATE STATION L.N.E.R. ARCHWAY
ELEVATIONS AND SECTIONS
ADAMS, HOLDEN & PEARSON. F.F.R.I.B.A. ARCHITECTS NO. 26. TORRINGTON SQUARE. W.C.1.

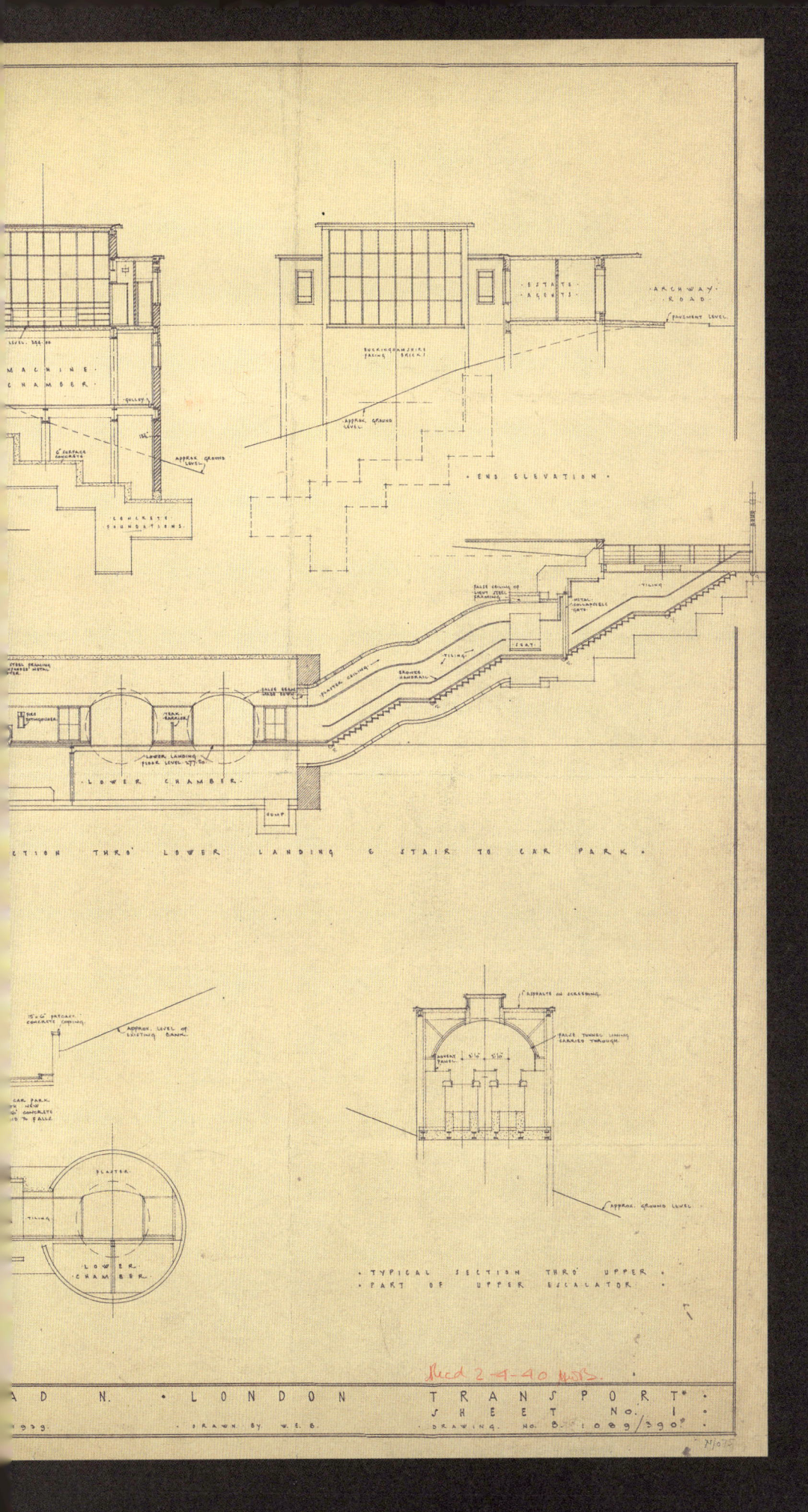

[FIG.177] An architect's drawing of Highgate station from 1939, showing the relationship between the surface platforms and the Tube station below. A high-speed lift was originally planned to take passengers to Archway Road but was rejected in favour of a dual escalator, which would have had greater capacity during rush hour had it been installed.

TRANSFORMATION

Work on the Northern Heights Project began in November 1936. At Highgate, architect Charles Holden was put in charge of the transformation of Victorian suburban station into modern transport interchange. An artist's impression prepared for the press shows the full extent of what was envisaged [FIG.180]. Stripped of its domestic-style architecture, Highgate was to be reborn, with modern concrete platform buildings dominated by a towering edifice housing the escalators leading to a new entrance on the Archway Road. The whole structure was to be topped by a statue of local legend Dick Whittington, the three-times Lord Mayor of London who allegedly returned to the city from Highgate to make his name and fortune.

Like so much of Holden's architecture for London Transport (see also 55 Broadway, pp.109–21), the planned station was both 'fit for purpose' and designed to make a statement about the modernity of public transport. From the start, London Transport planners understood that interchange traffic between the deep-level Tube and surface station would be more important than locally generated journeys.[7] Consequently, Holden's emphasis was on the smooth movement of people between the two stations, with plenty of room for circulation [FIG.177]. It was a point picked up by the local press, which anticipated 'heavy interchange [at Highgate] because at this point trains may be taken for all parts of the line: Edgware, Barnet and Alexandra Palace; the West End and the City by way of Camden Town, and the City by way of Finsbury Park'.[8]

The main ticket hall was excavated underneath the centre of the existing LNER station, with steps to the surface and escalators to the new Tube platforms 21 metres (70 feet) below ground. In addition to the planned entrance high on Archway Road, two further entrances were built from the car park and Priory Gardens, the route by which passengers had previously entered the LNER station.

The new Tube from Archway to East Finchley, via Highgate, opened in July 1939. The deep-level Highgate station was due to open soon afterwards, but difficulty securing materials caused by the outbreak of war in September, coupled with unexpected engineering difficulties, saw the work run on.[9] Frank Pick himself, vice-chairman of London Transport at this time, inspected the unfinished Tube station on 11 April 1940 to check progress, just days before his surprise resignation from the organisation. With war planning entering a critical phase, Pick may have been forgiven for paying little attention to the minutiae of works at Highgate. Instead, he issued a memo to Charles Holden asking to see progress on the Dick Whittington statue and requesting that a decorative scheme be added to the platform tiling incorporating miniature bronze versions of the Whittington motif.[10] In the event, neither were installed, as materials of all kinds grew ever more scarce.

Wartime shortages were also resulting in more practical cutbacks. The planned escalator to Archway Road was postponed until peace returned, with passengers having to make do with a temporary (and very steep) wooden stairway. The full complement of works planned for the surface station was also postponed.

The new station officially opened on 19 January 1941. The whole of the High Barnet branch from Highgate had now been electrified, and steam passenger trains were finally withdrawn on this section in 1941. To cope with the predicted traffic, LNER's former carriage depot at nearby Wellington Road was converted for Tube cars and renamed Highgate Depot. Elsewhere, however, worsening wartime conditions put paid to pre-war plans for electrification and expansion. Despite some modernisation, the route from Finsbury Park to Highgate and the branch line to Alexandra Palace remained steam-hauled. Progress on all other north London lines was similarly halted, including the extension from Edgware to Bushey Heath, where preparatory work had included a new depot at Aldenham and a viaduct near Brockley Hill [FIG.181].

WARTIME SHELTERING

From October 1940, the deep-level platforms at Highgate were used as a shelter from German air raids and V-weapon attacks on London. At first, London Transport was reluctant to open up the unfinished station to the public, as it still lacked proper access from street level. The *Daily Mirror* was unconvinced, arguing that 'if people seeking shelter were allowed to go to an unused station like Highgate, pressure on stations being used by the travelling public would be much relieved.'[11] London Transport finally relented and allowed Highgate to be used as an overflow for Archway station, with shelterers arriving each night by Tube train and departing the same way the following morning.

Sheltering became easier once the station had fully opened in January 1941, and special tickets were introduced to manage numbers. Highgate was apparently very popular with Londoners seeking deep-level shelter away from the more dangerous central areas, and also with London Transport staff looking for a safe place to rest.[12] Admission of the latter resulted in a flurry of complaints from locals, who believed that staff and their relatives were given priority over others and received special treatment [FIG.178].[13] One anonymous East Finchley resident wrote that 'the transport workers, including Bus Men, young men at that, leave their bundles and bedding on the platform all day, as many as 50 bundles, whereas the Public are not entitled to but have to take theirs home ... while the Tram, Bus and Tube men and their friends go about at ease without luggage.'[14]

The number of nightly shelterers declined after the first wave of the Blitz subsided in 1941, but rose again during the desperate V-1 and V-2 rocket attacks of the war's closing months. Less accurate than aerial bombing, these attacks struck indiscriminately across London, hitting several locations in Highgate and the surrounding area. Pregnant women were among those advised to use the Tube shelters at this time; in a much-quoted story, the American chat-show host Jerry Springer claims he was born in Highgate 'subway' on 13 February 1944.[15]

CLOSURE

In 1946 London Transport issued a new version of the famous diagrammatic Tube map for display at stations [FIG.182]. Designed by Harry Beck and with a decorative border by Charles Shepherd ('Shep'), the map optimistically showed all of the Northern Heights scheme as 'under construction'. After years of wartime austerity, it was a positive statement of intent. Passengers

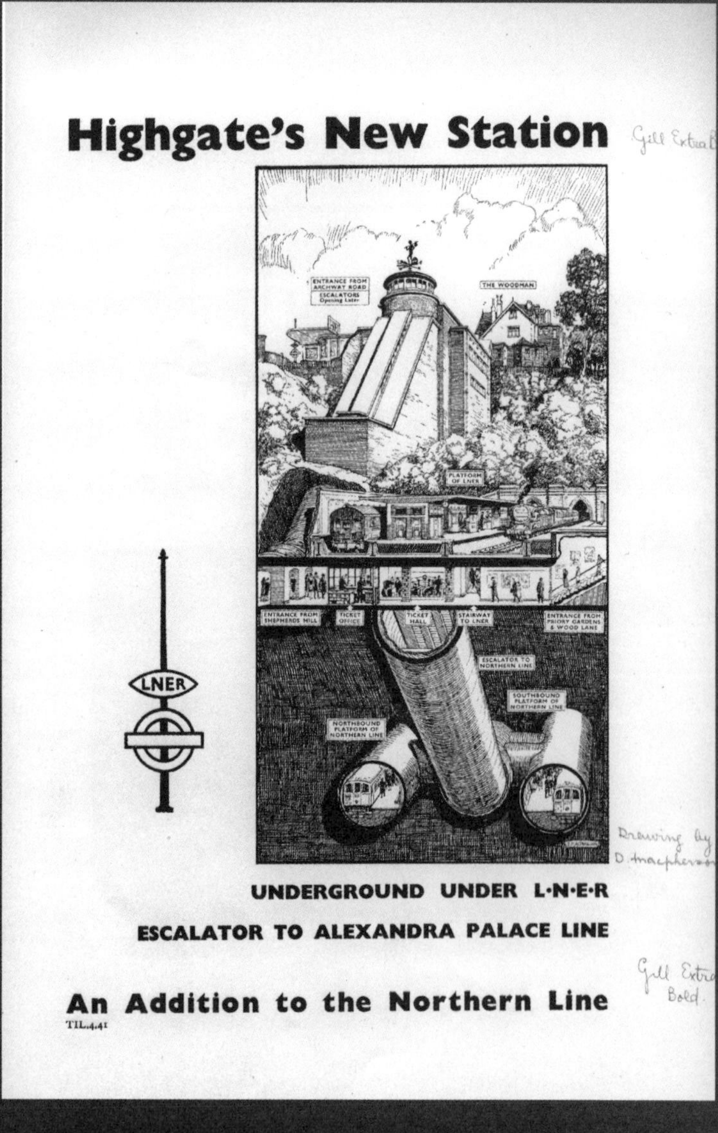

[FIG.178] ABOVE LEFT
An especially poignant photograph of children sheltering at Highgate Tube station in around 1941. This official image, released for press use, would have been much preferred to one showing London Transport staff occupying the platform spaces, as was claimed by local residents.

[FIG.179] ABOVE RIGHT
Workmen laying track in the new Tube tunnel between Highgate and East Finchley in 1938.

[FIG.180] RIGHT
An advertisement from 1941, with a cutaway impression of how Highgate interchange station would eventually look. The massive, outdoor brick escalator shaft can still be seen today, although without the planned statue of Dick Whittington, which was axed as a wartime saving.

[FIG.181]   RIGHT   Built to serve the Northern Heights Project, the unopened rail depot at Aldenham (on the route to Bushey Heath) was converted during the war to produce Halifax bomber aircraft. With the Project abandoned after the war, the site was repurposed for bus overhaul, as seen in this 1956 photograph. Aldenham Works was closed in 1986 and subsequently replaced with a business park.

[FIG.182]   BELOW   This 1946 Tube map shows the proposed Northern Heights Project as 'under construction' (top right). In fact, most work had stopped by this date and was later abandoned. Only the routes to High Barnet and a truncated line to Mill Hill East were completed.

[FIG.183] ABOVE LEFT The modest car park entrance to Highgate Tube in 1955. Unlike other Underground stations, Highgate does not have a prominent surface building, as the booking hall was built under the existing railway station as part of the interchange facilities.

[FIG.184] ABOVE RIGHT A platform direction sign manufactured in anticipation of the post-war completion of the Northern Heights scheme north beyond Edgware. In fact, none of the proposed stations listed here (Brockley Hill, Elstree South and Bushey Heath) were built.

in north London must have looked forward to the imminent arrival of London Transport services at Stroud Green, Crouch End, Cranley Gardens, Muswell Hill, Alexandra Palace, Mill Hill (The Hale), Brockley Park, Elstree, and Bushey Heath. On the map, Highgate appears at the centre of a junction of lines, with almost limitless travelling opportunities. Publicly, at least, the London Transport chairman, Albert Stanely, Lord Ashfield, encouraged this sense of renewed optimism:

> After six year[s of war], new factors have come into play. A new and better London is being planned. The programme begun before the war is vital to any improvement of the social environment and in all essentials will be completed.[16]

It was not to be. Repairing war damage and replacing worn out stock was the first priority, followed by the completion of extensions to the Central line in west and east London. Any glimmer of hope faded with the nationalisation of the transport system in 1948, which saw funding for London Transport slip even lower down the government's list compared with the task of modernising the war-ravaged railways.[17] At the same time, the Town and Country Planning Act 1947 created a 'green belt' around London, which effectively ended plans for the construction of new railways on greenfield sites, such as Bushey Heath. As a result, work on the unimplemented aspects of the Northern Heights Project was first delayed and then cancelled altogether.

The poorly used steam service from Finsbury Park to Alexandra Palace, via Highgate, was never electrified and was finally withdrawn in July 1954. Infrequent goods traffic kept the line alive for a few more years, but this, too, had gone by the mid-1960s and all stations on the line closed, including Highgate high-level. It has been calculated that if the start of the war had been delayed by just one year, the entire route from Moorgate to Alexandra Palace would have been modernised and the branch served by Tube trains today.[18] Instead, a populous part of north London is no longer on the Underground map.

With the surface station closed, ambitions for the completion of pre-war works at Highgate Tube were inevitably scaled back. The grand entrance on Archway Road was never built, and only a single 'up' escalator was finally installed in 1957 to augment the temporary wartime wooden stairway from the station to the top of the cutting.

HIGHGATE HIGH-LEVEL TODAY

With the tracks lifted in 1971 and the station tunnels partially blocked off, Highgate station was slowly reclaimed by nature. Step access from the Tube had been blocked in and a high fence erected around the site, giving Highgate high-level an isolated and forgotten feel. These measures, however, also preserved some of what was there at the point of closure, including Holden's platform canopy [FIG.185]. Remarkably, one of the former Victorian station buildings also survives at the entrance to the site and was occupied for many years as a private house. Since the 1980s, the derelict station has been regularly maintained by London Transport, and latterly Transport for London, to prevent water seepage into the Northern line booking office below – foliage is now kept at bay. One of the most surprising and unforeseen 'reuses' of the site has been the colonisation of the former running tunnels by several species of rare bats, including Natterer's and Daubenton's. Strictly protected by conservation laws, their habitat has been further secured by the installation of gates at the tunnel mouths to prevent unauthorised human access [FIG.186].

Elsewhere, the former branch line to Alexandra Palace has been turned into a pleasant public footpath known as the Parkland Walk. Opened by Haringey Council in 1984, the path passes through the remains of several stations on the line and has become a haven for local wildlife, including the elusive Muntjac deer.[19] Further afield, there is more evidence of what might have been and of the railway infrastructure taken over by London Transport during the heady days of the Northern Heights Project. Stranded pockets of abandoned architecture, such as the foundations of Brockley Hill viaduct, survive here and there. And, on the modern Northern line beyond Highgate, former Great Northern Railway buildings still retain a strong flavour of the Victorian era, especially the beautifully preserved station at West Finchley, with its original platform awnings, waiting room and benches.

As enchanting as the closed station and woodland walkways may be, Highgate high-level is ultimately a monument to failed transport planning. The Northern Heights Project would have transformed public transport in north London. Various schemes for the reopening of the branch from Finsbury Park have been mooted in recent years, but new housing on parts of the route means that such schemes are now unlikely to come to fruition.

[FIG.185] ABOVE The disused platform building at Highgate, seen today.

[FIG.186] RIGHT One of the bricked-up station tunnels at Highgate station, now a protected bat sanctuary.

1   For a general introduction to the New Works Programme, of which the Northern Heights Project was part, see David Bownes, Oliver Green and Sam Mullins, *Underground: How the Tube Shaped London* (Penguin, 2012), pp.141–7. See, also, Tony Beard's *By Tube Beyond Edgware* (Capital Transport, 2002), for a meticulous account of the planned, but unbuilt, extension from Edgware to Bushey Heath, and, for a description of the Northern Heights Project, Brian Hardy, *The Northern Line Extensions* (London Underground Railway Society, 2011).
2   Alan A. Jackson, *London's Local Railways* (Capital Transport, 1999), pp.301–13.
3   This Highgate station was opened as part of the Charing Cross, Euston and Hampstead Railway (CCE&HR), also known as the Hampstead Tube. For a history of the railway, see Antony Badsey-Ellis, *The Hampstead Tube: A History of the First 100 Years* (Capital Transport, 2007).
4   *Improving London's Transport*, a *Railway Gazette* publication (1946), p.12.
5   All three branches had been built by the former Great Northern Railway in the nineteenth century. For a history of these lines, see Jackson 1999, pp.301–33.
6   Local newspapers, such as the *Hendon & Finchley Times*, carried frequent articles about the planned works during the 1930s. Although broadly welcomed, the proposals were sometimes criticised for taking too long to come to fruition.
7   'New Interchange Station at Highgate (L.N.E.R)', Memorandum to Vice Chairman from the Station Committee, 3 February 1936, TfL Archives, LT000509/097.
8   *Hendon & Finchley Times*, 17 June 1938, p.17.
9   Reported in a letter from London Transport (Public Relations Office) to the Ministry of Transport, 13 July 1940, TfL Archives, LT000509/097.
10   Letter to Charles Holden, 11 April 1940, TfL Archives, LT000509/097.
11   *Daily Mirror*, 27 September 1940, p.2.
12   Report to Operating Manager (Railways), 23 December 1940, TfL Archives, LT000341/87.
13   Several complaints were received between October 1940 and January 1941. TfL Archives, LT000341/127.
14   Undated letter received by London Transport, 15 December 1940, TfL Archives, LT000341/127.
15   Springer's family were refugees from Nazi Europe, living at 48 Belvedere Court, East Finchley, at the time. ' Jerry Springer: Born in Highgate Underground station', BBC News, 28 May 2012, https://www.bbc.co.uk/news/av/entertainment-arts-18231560/jerry-springer-born-in-highgate-underground-station, accessed 21 September 2018.
16   *Improving London's Transport*, a *Railway Gazette* publication (1946), p.1.
17   Bownes, Green and Mullins 2012, pp.171–7.
18   Jackson 1999, p.323.
19   For a detailed analysis of the extraordinary ecology now flourishing on the disused railway, see Maria Longley, *An Ecological Data Survey for Highgate Station on behalf of TfL*, report ref. 1705, Greenspace Information for Greater London CIC, 2017.

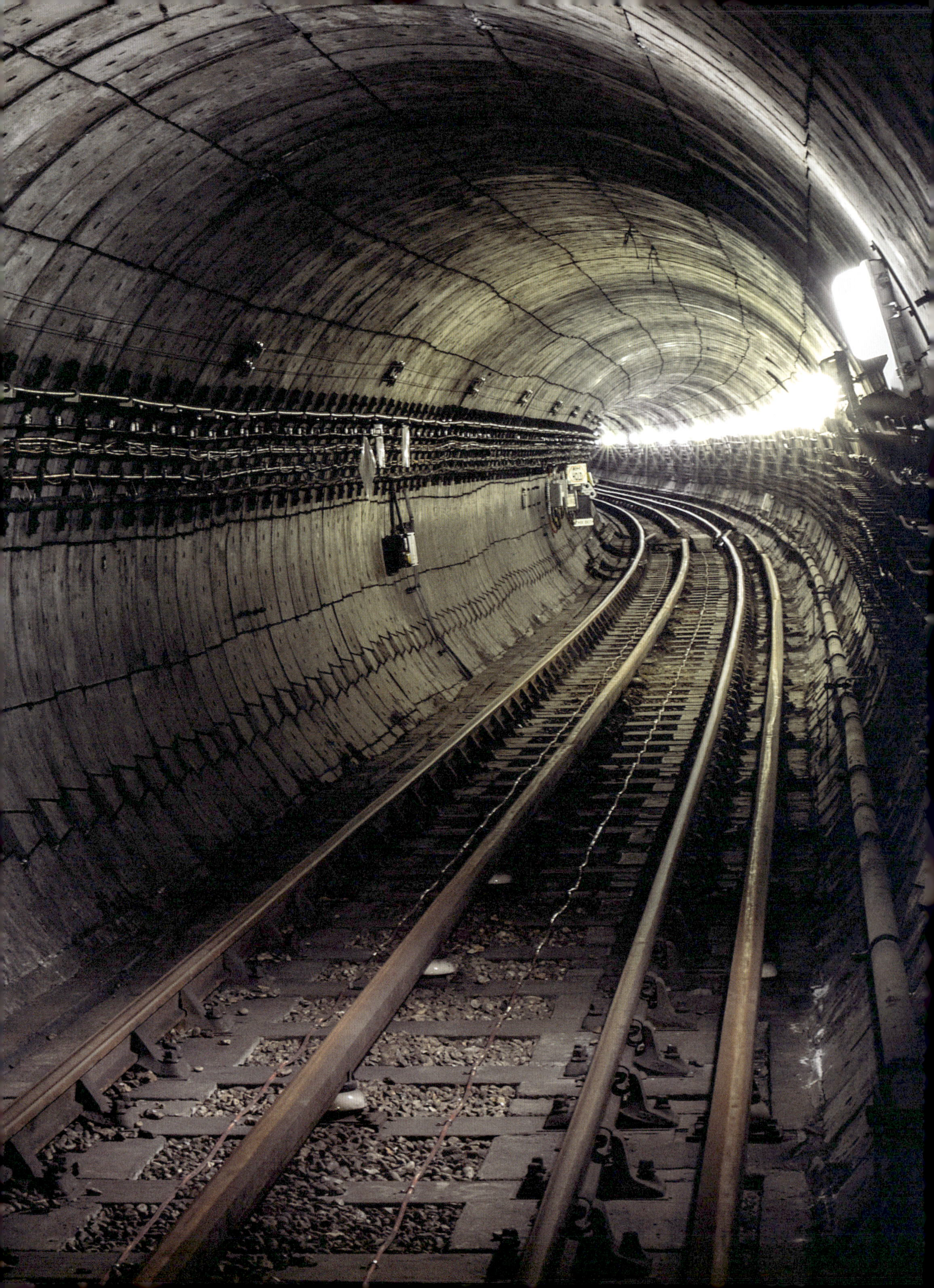

THE STRAND

HOW HOLLYWOOD CAME TO
THE UNDERGROUND

Strand Station

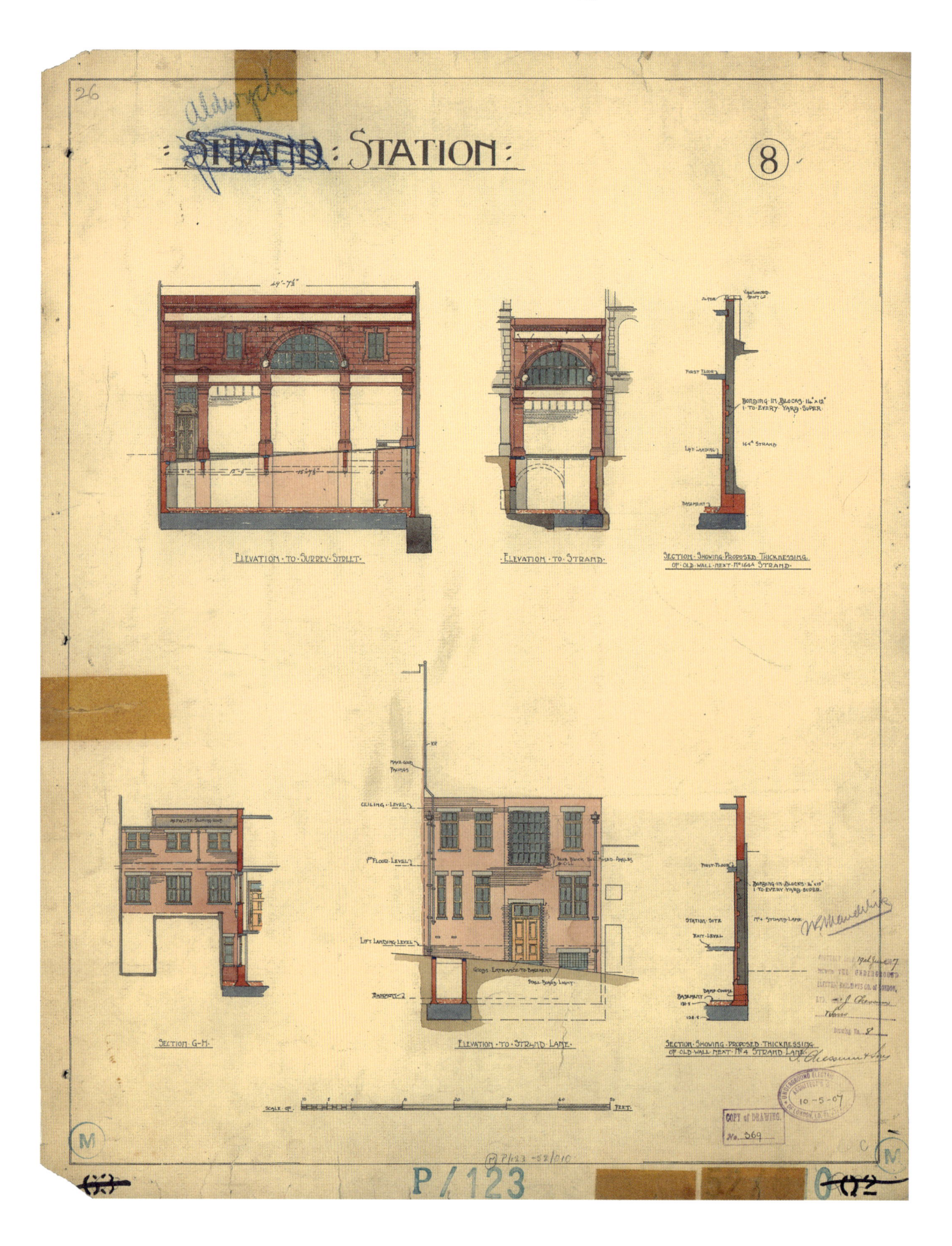

[FIG.187] PREVIOUS A section of the Jubilee line extension from Charing Cross, in the direction of Aldwych. It is now used for service vehicles, rather than passenger trains as originally envisaged.

[FIG.188] Elevation drawings of the first Tube station to be called the Strand, on the modern-day Piccadilly line, from 1907. Designed by Leslie Green, the station had two entrances, on Surrey Street and the Strand. The drawing has been crudely retitled 'Aldwych' following the station's name change in 1915.

Understanding the mysteries of Tube lore and the occasional difference between a station's name and its actual location has long been something of a badge of honour for Londoners, and a source of confusion for visitors. This was especially the case with the cluster of stations known as The Strand, Trafalgar Square and Charing Cross. In the early part of the twentieth century, travellers needed significant prior knowledge to ensure that they disembarked at the right stop. Served by different Underground lines, and subject to both name changes and closures, these stations are the key to understanding the development of the Tube in the centre of London, and their story reveals a labyrinth of disused tunnels and underground platforms – some abandoned as recently as the 1990s. They are also examples of the surprising ways in which underground spaces have been reused, from providing shelter for Londoners during the Blitz and ventilation for the Tube, to becoming film sets for Hollywood blockbusters.

COMPETING ROUTES AND CONFUSING TITLES

Two stations in the Underground's history have been named after the Strand, the famous London thoroughfare running from Trafalgar Square to Fleet Street, which includes Charing Cross railway station and the theatres of Aldwych among its many well-known landmarks. Both Tube stations were built as central termini, on lines with the potential to be extended further south. Yet only one was fully developed, while the other languished, poorly used, before being eventually closed.

The first station to be called the Strand opened on 30 November 1907 as the terminus of a short branch from Holborn, on what is now the Piccadilly line [FIG.188].[1] Built on the site of the former Royal Strand Theatre, the original red-tiled, surface-level entrances can still be seen in Aldwych and around the corner on Surrey Street. From the start, hopes were high that the route would be extended further south across the Thames to Waterloo, and the station was built with twin running tunnels and the capacity for multiple passenger lifts, to meet expected demand. This was not to be, however. Instead, the branch was operated as a shuttle service from Holborn, mainly for theatregoers. With little hope of attracting significant traffic, one of the platforms was taken out of use altogether in 1914, and work on additional lifts and connecting passageways remained unfinished.

At the other end of the Strand, the Charing Cross, Euston & Hampstead Railway (CCE&HR; the 'Hampstead Tube', now part of the Northern line) had built its own terminus at Charing Cross, directly under the forecourt of the mainline railway station [FIGS 192 & 193].[2] Like its neighbour further along the Strand, the Tube station at Charing Cross was not intended to be the final stop on the line and became a 'through' station when the route was extended to a new temporary terminus in 1914. Within a year, Charing Cross Tube station had been renamed Strand, at which point the original, but now moribund, Strand station was renamed Aldwych to avoid confusion [FIGS 189 & 190]. If that wasn't complicated enough, the next station along from the newly named Strand was rebranded Charing Cross in 1915, having opened as Charing Cross (Embankment) a year earlier. It went on to be renamed a second time, as Embankment, in 1976, and is the station currently known by that name on the Northern line.[3]

OPENS DECEMBER.
PICCADILLY TUBE
STRAND STATION

LTD. 170
PICCADILLY RLY
COLLECTIONS
PURCHASED
ALDWYCH STATION
UNDERGROUND
WHY NOT TAKE A SEASON TICKET
UNDERGROUND
FREQUENT ELECTRIC TRAINS TO ALL PARTS OF LONDON
STAINLESS
SWAN

UNDERGROUND
MAP OF LONDON
REFERENCE
Travels in time on your doorstep

[FIGS 189 & 190] OPPOSITE ABOVE The Strand entrance of Aldwych station, before (above left) and after (above right) its name change. The photograph on the left was taken shortly before the station opened on 30 November 1907.

[FIG.191] OPPOSITE BELOW The rebranding of the Strand stations in the 1910s, together with the existence of more than one destination called Charing Cross, must have caused confusion. In this 1930s photograph, passengers outside the Strand (Charing Cross) study an enamel, geographic Underground map – understood by Londoners but often bewildering for visitors.

Part of the reason for all this confusion was that the stations were originally built and operated by independent, competing companies with no reason to cooperate with one another. Although now under one management, the early Tube network in this part of London (as elsewhere) reflected a lack of strategic planning that had resulted in some oddly sited and peculiarly named stations. As the unified Tube expanded during the 1920s, a more rational approach was adopted, which inevitably caused earlier schemes to be modified, renamed or abandoned [FIG.191].

When the Hampstead Tube was extended to Charing Cross (Embankment) in 1914, for example, it was initially constructed as a single-track tunnel with a 'loop' extending under the Thames, which allowed trains to turn around for their return journey. After the route was further extended to Waterloo in 1926, this already outdated relic of operational history was bricked up and backfilled to prevent flooding.[4]

Meanwhile, at Aldwych, passenger numbers had continued to decline. Sunday services were withdrawn in 1917, initially as a wartime economy measure, and by the early 1920s the original booking office had been closed, with tickets sold by the operator in the lift instead, to reduce costs. The contrast with the 'new' Strand station at Charing Cross could not have been greater, as passenger numbers there rose in response to improved services. Instead, Aldwych was one of several poorly used stations considered for closure in 1926. It in fact remained open until September 1940, when the entire branch from Holborn was temporarily transferred to Westminster City Council for conversion to create a public air raid shelter for the duration of the war.

THE ALDWYCH SHELTER AND POST-WAR CLOSURE

With train services suspended and the track boarded over to provide extra accommodation, Aldwych became probably the best-known wartime Tube shelter, occasionally featuring in morale-raising propaganda to show the world that Londoners could 'take it'.[5] Conditions here were rather better than elsewhere, with Westminster City Council eventually providing bunks for 1,500 shelterers, together with medical and catering facilities. Before long, there was even an underground library and lecture programme, with additional entertainment provided by the Entertainments National Service Association (ENSA) and the shelterers' own amateur dramatics society [FIG.195]. Aldwych station had never been so busy.

As in the First World War, parts of the disused station and associated tunnels were also used to store the nation's most important artworks and treasures – most notably, the British Museum's Parthenon Marbles – transferred from museums and galleries 'for the duration' [FIG.196]. The shelter remained under the control of Westminster City Council until June 1946, when it was handed back to London Transport and train services resumed.

There was to be no post-war resurgence in passenger traffic however [FIG.194] and, in 1958, London Transport tried unsuccessfully to close the branch.[6] Instead, the station closed on Saturdays and trains only ran in peak hours during the week. By the 1990s, urgent repairs to the lifts (by then almost 90 years old) and much-needed maintenance work on the station building triggered a final, and

[FIGS 192 & 193] TOP The Craven Street entrance to the Strand Tube station at Charing Cross, seen here in 1930. Platform signs originally read 'Strand for S.E.& C.R.', assuming that passengers knew Charing Cross railway station was owned by the South Eastern & Chatham Railway. 'Strand for Charing Cross' would perhaps have been a better title.

[FIG.194] ABOVE The Aldwych shuttle in 1958, arriving on a near-deserted platform.

[FIG.195] ABOVE Members of the Entertainments National Service Association (ENSA) performing to shelterers at Aldwych station during the Blitz.

[FIG.196] RIGHT The disused platform and connecting tunnel at Aldwych were allocated to the Victoria and Albert Museum and British Museum for deep storage under pre-war air-raid precaution plans. Both museums moved thousands of irreplaceable artefacts to the station in 1939–40, including the Parthenon Marbles (seen here in transit).

fatal, review of its future. With just 450 return trips being made on the branch each day, the estimated costs of refurbishment, put at nearly £9 million over ten years, could not be justified, and the branch was permanently closed from 30 September 1994.

ALL CHANGE (AGAIN) AT CHARING CROSS

There had, though, been a glimmer of hope for the Aldwych branch in the 1960s, which would have seen the original, 1907 Strand station connected with its namesake at Charing Cross. In the event, the connection was never made, but the scheme created a new and short-lived underground terminus at Charing Cross whose history was to have uncanny parallels with that of Aldwych and whose existence would lead to yet more name changes.

In the years after the Second World War, several unsuccessful schemes for relieving congestion on the Underground had looked at potential east–west routes through the Aldwych area. In March 1965, a report jointly authored by British Rail and London Transport proposed the construction of a new Tube, originally called the Fleet line but later renamed the Jubilee.[7] It was to join the Bakerloo line at Baker Street and then run via Bond Street, Green Park, Charing Cross, Aldwych and the City stations before heading into south-east London to Lewisham. Under the scheme, Aldwych would have become an interchange and the Piccadilly line branch from Holborn extended to Waterloo.

Although plans to extend the Holborn branch were quickly dropped, work on the rest of the Jubilee line began in 1971, with a temporary southern terminus at Charing Cross. The scheme called for the complete remodelling of all underground facilities at Charing Cross, to accommodate the new terminus and provide improved ventilation, a central booking hall and passenger walkways connecting the Jubilee with the existing Bakerloo and Northern line platforms at Trafalgar Square and Strand [FIG.197]. It was a mammoth task. The Strand station closed to passengers on 16 June 1973 to enable construction and didn't reopen until 1979 when, along with Trafalgar Square, it was rebranded as Charing Cross. The revamped Charing Cross now incorporated both the former Bakerloo and Northern line stations, as well as the new Jubilee line platforms [FIG.198]. A unified visual identity for all three was provided by the artist David Gentleman, who designed a series of murals based on local landmarks for the platforms.

Meanwhile, work had already begun to extend the Jubilee line from Charing Cross to Lewisham in south-east London, with new tunnels almost reaching Aldwych station. The regeneration of Docklands in London's East End during the 1980s and 1990s, and the creation of the Canary Wharf financial district, however, resulted in a change of plan. The route south-east was drastically altered to bypass Charing Cross altogether in favour of a new line from Green Park, providing interchanges at Westminster, Waterloo and London Bridge stations and then heading on east to the new financial district at Canary Wharf on the Greenwich Peninsula and to Stratford (later the site of the 2012 Olympic Park).

Like Aldwych before it, the Jubilee line terminus at Charing Cross was left stranded due to changes in transport policy and the platforms were closed to passengers on 20 November 1999, just 20 years after the station had opened.

[FIG.197] TOP LEFT As this 1977 London Underground poster shows, the new Charing Cross Tube station provided interchange facilities between the Northern, Bakerloo and Jubilee lines and incorporated the existing stations at the Strand and Trafalgar Square with the new Jubilee terminus.

[FIG.198] TOP RIGHT A battery-powered maintenance train stabled at a disused Charing Cross (Jubilee line) platform in 2018. Kept in operational condition, the platforms are frequently used for train movements that would otherwise interfere with the running of the network.

[FIG.199] ABOVE Filming at Aldwych station in 2015 to commemorate the 75th anniversary of the Blitz.

[FIG.200] One of the platforms at Aldwych as seen today, retains posters from the mock up of South Kensington in 1973, and part of the original 'STRAND' lettering on the platform wall.

NEW USES FOR CLOSED STATIONS

As the case studies in this book demonstrate, disused underground spaces are valuable plots of subterranean real estate, rarely allowed to slumber undisturbed. The various station closures and track reroutings in the Strand area released former operational sites for a variety of new uses.

Even when services were still running at Aldwych, one of the platforms (which had been closed to the public since 1914) was used by London Transport to provide mock-up facilities for new station decor ideas. In the 1960s, it became 'Oxford Circus' to evaluate the tiling scheme for the Victoria line, and a decade later became 'Bond Street' on the Fleet (Jubilee) line. More recently, the closed branch has been used for emergency services training, and the track and infrastructure are maintained in operational condition, complete with a train of ex-Northern line, 1972 Tube stock stabled in the tunnels. Similarly, the Jubilee line platforms at Charing Cross are kept in working condition and routinely used as sidings to allow trains to be reversed, or, if defective, taken out of service and stored [FIG.198].

The operational capacity of these disused stations has also resulted in a lucrative, and unforeseen, reuse, with the sites used as locations for film and television makers [FIG.199]. Managed by TfL's Film Office, both stations have appeared on the big screen, often 'reskinned' as real or imagined locations. Edwardian Aldwych is especially popular with directors seeking to recreate a period atmosphere. The station featured in *The Krays* (1990), *Atonement* (2007), *The Edge of Love* (2008) and *Mr Selfridge* (2013–16).[8] The disused tunnels have also provided an ideal backdrop for more dystopian dramas, such as *28 Weeks Later* (2007) and the music video for The Prodigy's *Firestarter* (1997), while a much-modified and expanded version of the station appears as a level in the video game *Tomb Raider III* (1998).

In contrast, the contemporary look of the disused Jubilee line platforms and concourse makes this station perfect for modern and futuristic dramas and it was chosen for James Bond film *Skyfall* (2012), *Thor: The Dark World* (2013) and *The Woman in Black: Angel of Death* (2014), among many other TV and film productions.[9]

WHAT REMAINS TODAY

Today, the facade of Aldwych station is a listed building, part of The Strand Conservation Area. Both entrances, in the Strand and Surrey Street, retain their original, oxblood-red terracotta tiling, with dark-grey lettering on white tiled bands. Thanks to low passenger numbers and the consequent reluctance of London Transport to finance upgrade work, the booking office [FIG.201] retains many original features, including the only surviving example on the Underground of a terrazzo floor finish, a vintage ticket office, and even a complete Edwardian ladies' washroom. Most surprising of all, the lifts installed by the Otis Elevator Company in 1906–7 are, uniquely, still in situ, together with their Art Nouveau-style ventilation grilles [FIG.202].

Underground, Aldwych is eerily silent, undisturbed by the sounds of nearby trains and with little air movement. Although littered with the evidence of continual reuse, the overall impression is of an isolated time capsule, disconnected from the busy street above. This atmosphere is made all the more marked by the survival of patches of Edwardian tiling in the lower passageways and platforms, including ghostly traces of the original Strand name [FIG.200], together with early, enamelled direction signs featuring pointing fingers instead of the more usual arrows.

[FIGS 201 & 202] The booking office (below left) and interior of one of the original Otis lifts (below right) at Aldwych.

[FIG.203] The construction tunnel for the Jubilee line at Charing Cross, built in 1973 to facilitate underground construction without disturbing traffic on the Strand above. The tunnel, which extends beneath Trafalgar Square, was used to move spoil to a surface shaft. The shaft has now been backfilled and the site developed as the Sainsbury Wing of the National Gallery.

By contrast, much of the early-twentieth-century Charing Cross/Strand site has been modified beyond recognition. The more recently disused Jubilee line platforms and concourse look much as they did in the 1990s, complete with escalators, signage and the decorative panels designed by David Gentleman. The environment here is bright and clean, with the distant sounds of the operational Jubilee line adding to the sense that the station has only been temporarily closed and will spring back to life at any moment.

Beyond the working passageways, it is still possible to see the contractors' tunnels, built during the construction of the original Jubilee line [FIG.203]. One of these was used to remove spoil and extends from Charing Cross station under Trafalgar Square, although the exit shaft to the surface is now filled in. Most surprising are the running tunnels, built as part of the abandoned Jubilee line route, which stretch far from Charing Cross, beneath the Strand, to within touching distance of Aldwych station. These tunnels are now used by the Underground to stable trains and for emergency services training.

1   For an excellent overview of the Piccadilly line, including the Aldwych branch, see Mike Horne, *The Piccadilly Tube: A History of the First 100 Years* (Capital Transport, 2007).
2   For a description of the station's construction under Charing Cross, see Desmond F. Croome and Alan A. Jackson, *Rails Through the Clay: A History of London's Tube Railways* (Capital Transport, 1993), p.67. For a history of the Charing Cross, Euston & Hampstead Railway, see Antony Badsey-Ellis, *The Hampstead Tube: A History of the First 100 Years* (Capital Transport, 2007).
3   All this must have made sense to the planners at the Underground Group, which owned both routes, but would have caused bewilderment for many travellers trying to find the best way to Charing Cross mainline railway station. The situation was not helped by the existence of yet another Underground station, already called Charing Cross, on the sub-surface District Railway. Opened in 1870, this station was a less convenient means of accessing the mainline than the CCE&HR Tube station, as it required passengers to walk the last part of their journey up Villiers Street to the Strand, where they entered Charing Cross railway station at surface level. The naming anomaly here was not resolved until 1976, when Charing Cross on the District line also became an 'Embankment'.
4   The sealed-off loop was hit by a German bomb just before midnight on 9 September 1940 – it was the only section of the Tube under the Thames to be struck during the Second World War. Some repair work was carried out at the time, although the tunnels remain partially flooded.
5   See John Gregg, *The Shelter of the Tubes: Tube Sheltering in Wartime London* (Capital Transport, 2001), pp.27–9, and David Bownes, Oliver Green and Sam Mullins, *Underground: How the Tube Shaped London* (Penguin, 2012), pp.164–6.
6   The closure was successfully opposed by the London Area Transport Users' Consultative Committee. Croome and Jackson 1993, pp.305–6.
7   Originally named after the Fleet River, the line was renamed in honour of the Queen's Silver Jubilee in 1977, although the first section didn't open until 1979. For a history of the Jubilee line, see Mike Horne, *The Jubilee Line: An Illustrated History* (Capital Transport, 2000), and Bob Mitchell, *Jubilee Line Extension: From Concept to Completion* (Thomas Telford, 2003).
8   The disused platform at Aldwych meant the station could be used for filming before complete closure in 1994. Other notable films to have been shot here include *Conspirator* (1949), *A Run for your Money* (1949), *The Clouded Yellow* (1950), *Ghost Story* (1972), *Death Line* (1972) and *Superman IV: The Quest for Peace* (1987).
9   These include episodes of the BBC television series *Spooks* (2002–11) and the films *Creep* (2004), *The Deaths of Ian Stone* (2007) and *The Bourne Ultimatum* (2007).

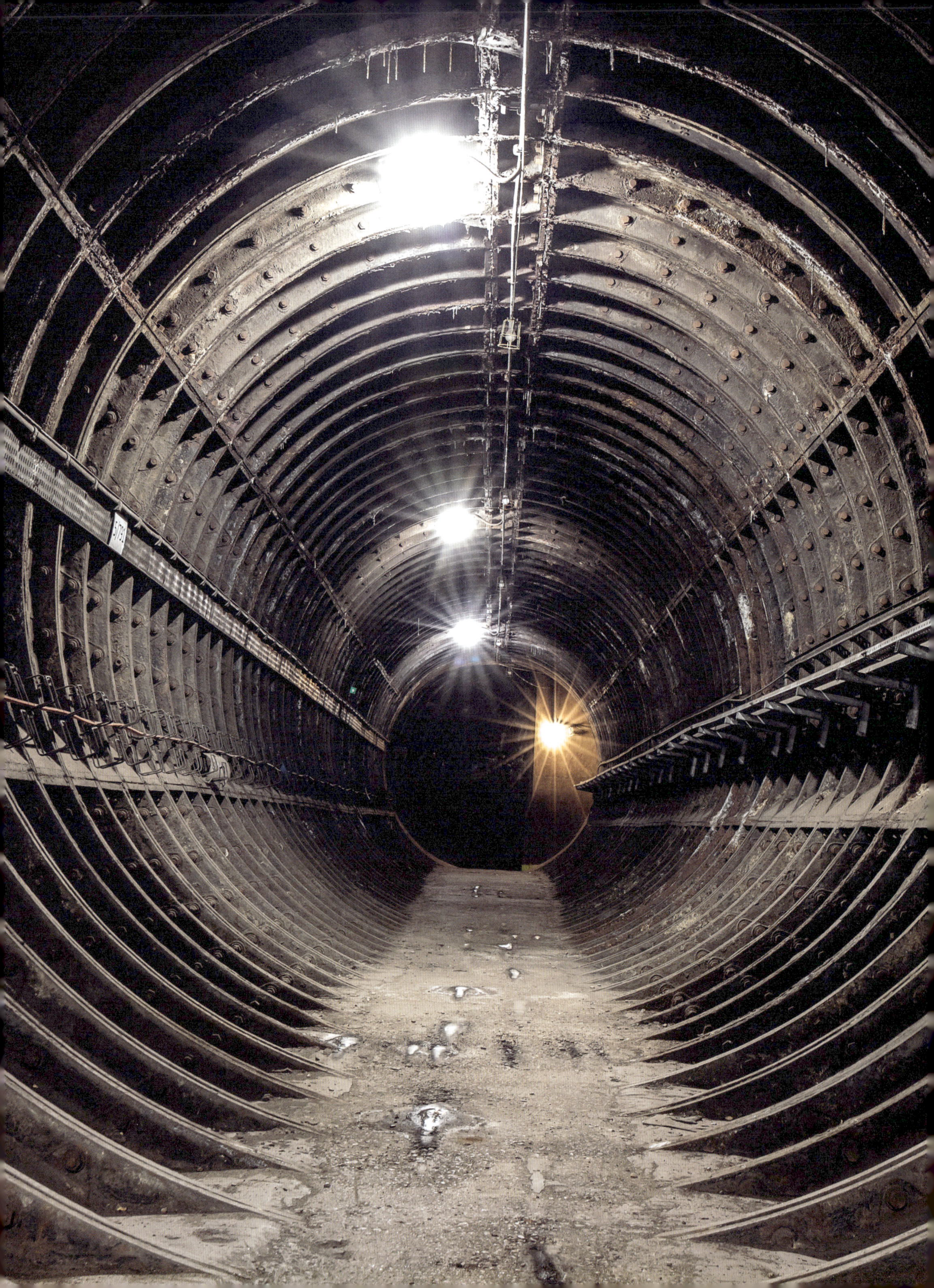

EUSTON

GATEWAY TO THE NORTH

QUICKEST AND BEST ROUTE TO
LONDON BRIDGE RAILWAYS. ELEPHANT.
QUICKEST & BEST ROUTE TO THE CITY
SOUTH OF LONDON
BOOK HERE FOR
RAILWAY
CITY AND SOUTH
LONDON RAILWAY
SOUTH LONDON
EXIT
EXIT
ICES

[FIG.204] PREVIOUS
The ventilation tunnel, purpose-built at Euston to serve the Victoria line.

[FIG.205] OPPOSITE ABOVE
Melton Street in 2018, when the former Hampstead Tube station was still visible but fenced off, awaiting demolition. It is making way for platforms and a brand-new concourse for High Speed Two. The vital ventilation function provided by the structure will be relocated, as will the power supply from the brick electricity substation on the right, which feeds the Northern line below.

[FIG.206] OPPOSITE BELOW
City & South London Railway (C&SLR) station at Euston, opened in 1907.

Euston is London's gateway to the north of England and Scotland. Tides of passengers ebb and flow through its Brutalist, 1960s 'dingy, grey, horizontal nothingness'.[1] Most of the 120,000 daily passengers use the Underground below to reach the station or for their onward journeys. The mainline terminus station opened in 1837, was rebuilt for electrification in the 1960s and will accommodate High Speed Two (HS2) as that transport project opens in phases over the next decade. Two rival Underground stations, serving two separate Tube lines, were opened beneath in 1907 to cope with the traffic generated by the terminus. As the mainline station developed above and the Tube system advanced below, the tide of change left disused a series of entrances and passageways, unknown to commuters and long-distance passengers both. Many of these spaces are about to be absorbed and lost to the expansion that is demanded by HS2.

On the corner of Melton Street and Drummond Street, next to Euston mainline railway station, is a former Tube station building, which was opened as part of the Hampstead Tube (formally, the Charing Cross, Euston & Hampstead Railway, or CCE&HR, owned by the Underground Electric Railways of London, or UERL). The surface building opened in 1907 [FIG.206] and closed only 7 years later, in 1914. Its distinctive glazed, oxblood-red tiling marks it out as one of the many in central London designed by architect Leslie Green. Its passageways survive, hidden from public view, and its platforms continue to serve the Northern line. The surface building at Melton Street – the last remaining visible relic of the two original Euston Tube stations – will be swept away by HS2 in 2020.[2]

CATCH THE TUBE TO EUSTON

Euston was London's first intercity railway station. It was built on the edge of the expanding city and opened in the first month of Queen Victoria's reign, in July 1837. As railway travel boomed and the capital grew, the streets became more and more congested and traffic frequently ground to a halt. A solution had to be found, and so the world's first underground railway, the steam-hauled Metropolitan, was opened in 1863 to connect the railway termini on the edge of the city to the commercial centre of the City of London.[3] Because of the limitations of cut-and-cover construction in the 1860s, some underground stations had to be constructed some distance away from the terminus they were intended to serve; the cut-and-cover method, whereby a road is dug up, tracks laid down in the cutting and then the whole recovered with a brick arch, limited the construction of early Underground routes, as the road above needed to be wide and straight – a rare occurrence in Victorian London. Euston terminus station was theoretically served by Gower Street station (renamed Euston Square in 1909), on the Metropolitan Railway, but this station was inconveniently located, nearly 500 metres away on Euston Road. When the deep-level Tube railways were planned and built in the early twentieth century, the railway companies took the opportunity to build connections closer to Euston. The City & South London Railway (C&SLR) was the first deep Tube electric railway in the world and the first to reach Euston in 1907.

On 12 May 1907, the C&SLR opened their new northern terminus at Euston. The station building, designed by architect Sidney Smith, was located on the corner of Seymour Street and Drummond Street and its facade was clad with ornate white and green tiles. From the ticket hall, two lifts and an emergency staircase gave access to an island platform [FIG.207]. Beyond the platform, the tunnels extended 70 metres (230 feet) before joining to form a 7.6-metre (25-foot) tunnel, where an engine traverser was located for the purpose of transferring locomotives between tracks [FIG.210].[4]

A month after the C&SLR opened its station at Euston, the new CCE&HR opened, on 22 June 1907 [FIG.209]. Soon known as the Hampstead Tube, all of the stations on this line were designed by architect Leslie Green. Two lift shafts were dug when the station was constructed, though only two lifts were installed – the other shaft was used for ventilation. A brick substation built next to the station itself supplied power to the railway [FIG.208].

In addition to the two station buildings on either side of Euston, there was a third entrance to the Underground, located within the mainline station concourse. The Tube companies had reached an agreement in December 1905 with the London & North Western Railway (LNWR), who owned the land around the station, under which the two companies were authorised to construct stations and connecting subways and lifts for an annual payment of £1,100.[5] The idea was to spread the load of local traffic and prevent congestion on the mainline station concourse.

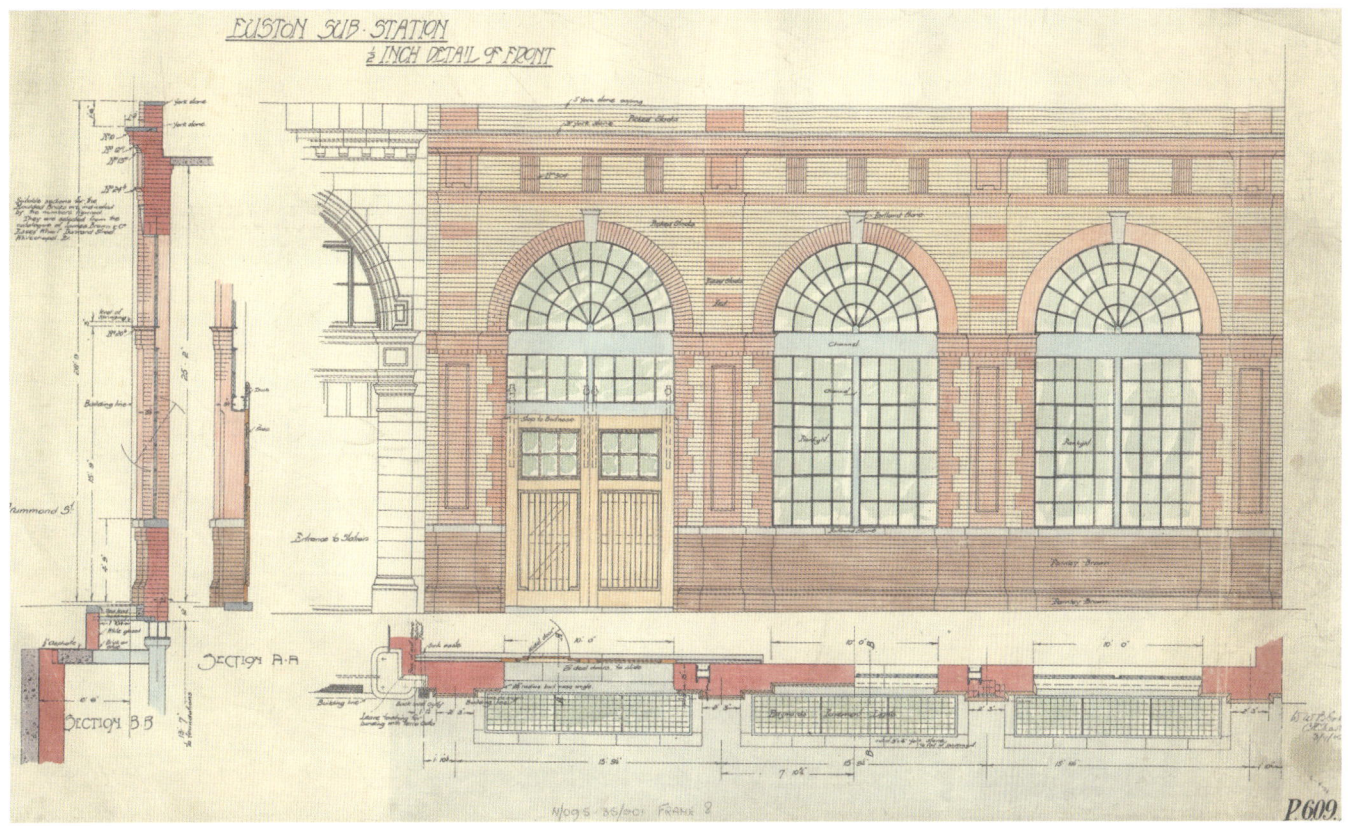

[FIG.207] OPPOSITE The City & South London Railway island platform at Euston in 1908, lined with brilliant-white glass tiles that reflected the dim gas and, later, electric light.

[FIG.208] TOP
A contemporary drawing of the electricity substation at Euston, designed to complement Hampstead Tube station next to it.

[FIG.209] ABOVE LEFT The Hampstead Tube station at Euston in 1907, shortly after opening.

[FIG.210] ABOVE RIGHT The widened tunnel once housed the engine traverser used to transfer locomotives from one track to the other on the City & South London Railway at Euston. This was an efficient and cost-effective way of reversing trains at the terminus station, as it did not require a long-loop tunnel to be built. The tunnel seen ahead is the former Northbound tunnel, decommissioned in 1967.

ONE COMPANY, ONE ENTRANCE, ONE LINE

In 1913 the two companies were united under the management of Albert Stanley and the Underground Electric Railways of London Ltd (UERL). On 1 October 1914, the two separate station buildings were closed as a cost-saving measure and Underground customers were thereafter diverted to the entrance inside Euston station [FIG.211]. The lifts were removed from both stations and the shafts and passageways used instead for ventilation.

As the lines were now operated by the same company, it made sense to integrate them, and plans were made to modernise the older C&SLR. The platforms and running tunnels had to be enlarged and modified [FIG.215] and a project was put under way to connect the two railways at Camden, allowing customers to travel to both the City and the West End, and thus forming what we today know as the Northern line. Work was delayed until 1922 due to the First World War, but was then funded by a government loan, and Euston Underground station closed from August 1922 to allow the works to take place.

The first section of the modernised tunnels opened on 20 April 1924, running from Moorgate to Euston and through the new Camden Junctions to both Hendon and Highgate. Euston had not been modernised with escalators like many other stations due to site restrictions within the mainline concourse; therefore, the three passenger lifts and mutual ticket hall remained the only way to enter the Underground [FIG.213].

ALTERATIONS AND PREPARATIONS

Traffic through Euston station steadily increased throughout the 1920s and 1930s, and by the mid-1930s it was clear that the three passenger lifts and staircase were no longer adequate. The ticket hall often became very congested with customers trying to reach the Underground. In 1935, the Railways (Agreement) Act was passed, granting government loans to railway companies to upgrade their networks and, in so doing, relieve the country's unemployment problem. As a part of the London Passenger Transport Board's New Works Programme, a plan was made to replace Euston's lifts with escalators, but it did not progress – as the railways had started preparing for a more sinister possibility: that of war.

SHELTERING AT EUSTON

As the clouds of war started gathering over Europe in the late 1930s, vital services, including Britain's railways, sought ways to defend themselves against potential aerial bombardment. The London Midland & Scottish Railway (LMSR) began making its own preparations in 1937.[6] By July 1938, a contract had been issued by London Transport to build a nearly 5-metre (16-foot) iron-lined tunnel, as well as a passage and stairway, at the south end of the lower lift entrance at Euston station, to shelter staff and keep vital services running.

20 permits were issued to members of LMSR control staff in August 1939, two months before war was declared, giving them access to this newly built tunnel. The passes permitted staff to enter their new control room from the platforms, via the substation on Melton Street. This arrangement was unfavourable, since

[FIG.211] TOP LEFT Entrance to the Underground inside Euston mainline station, 1915.

[FIG.212] TOP RIGHT View of the joint Underground ticket hall in 1927. A sign points to the three lifts that took passengers to the platforms below. An emergency staircase is seen on the right.

[FIG.213] ABOVE The two connecting subways running between the Hampstead tube platforms and the C&SLR island platform were lined with deep blue and cream tiling. This ticket window allowed passengers to purchase a ticket to travel with both Tube companies – a unique feature only found at Euston.

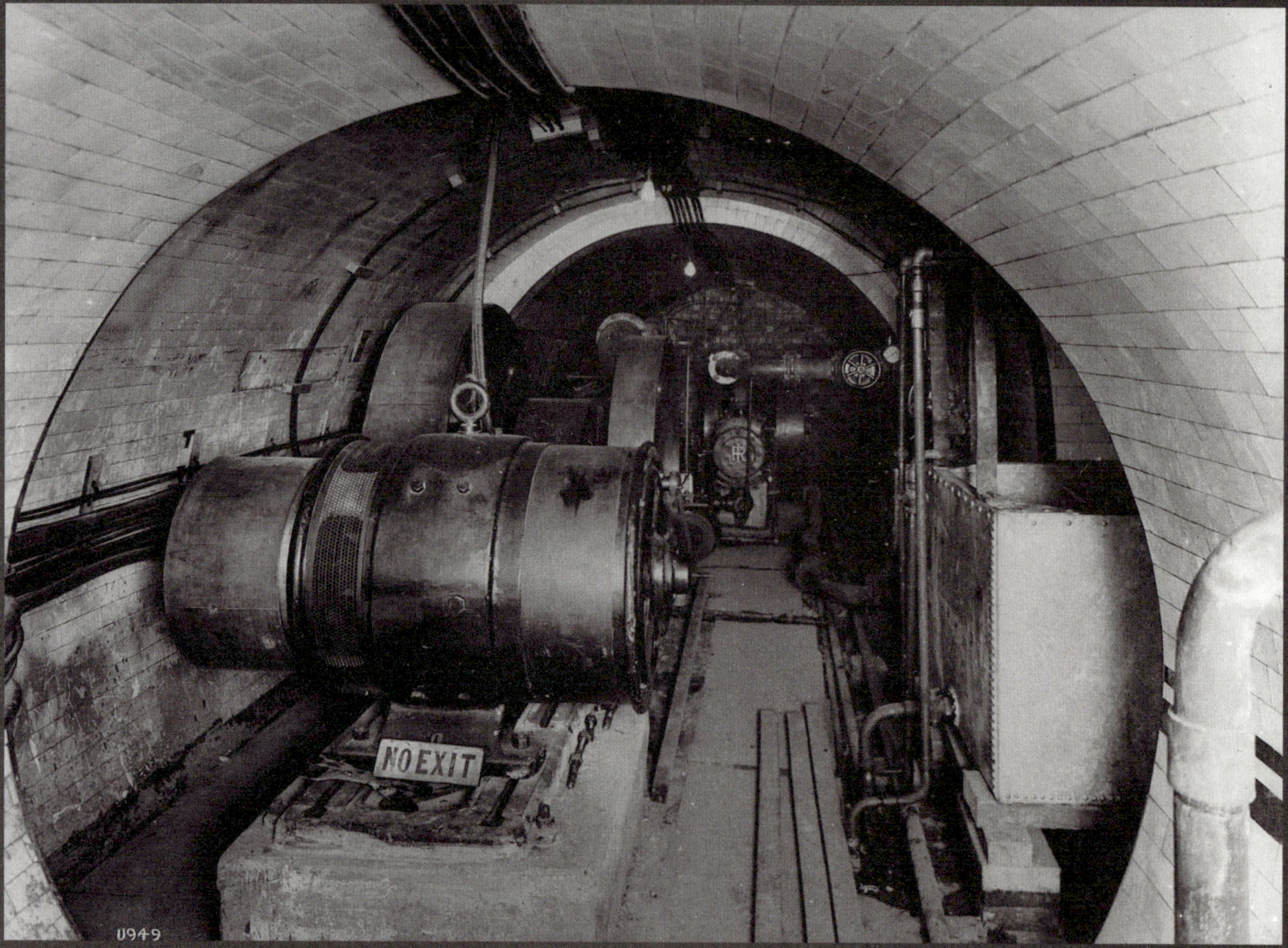
NO EXIT
U949

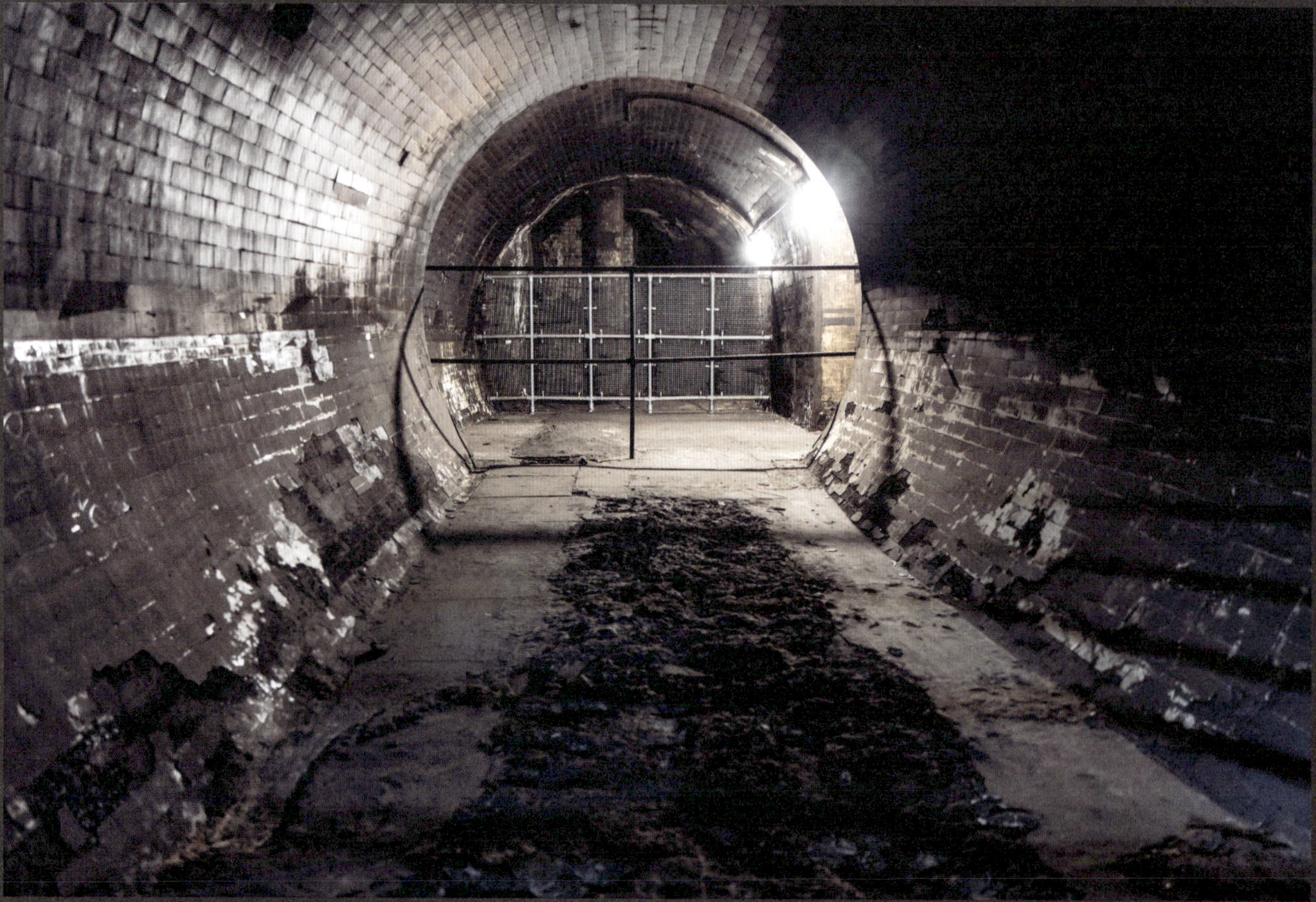

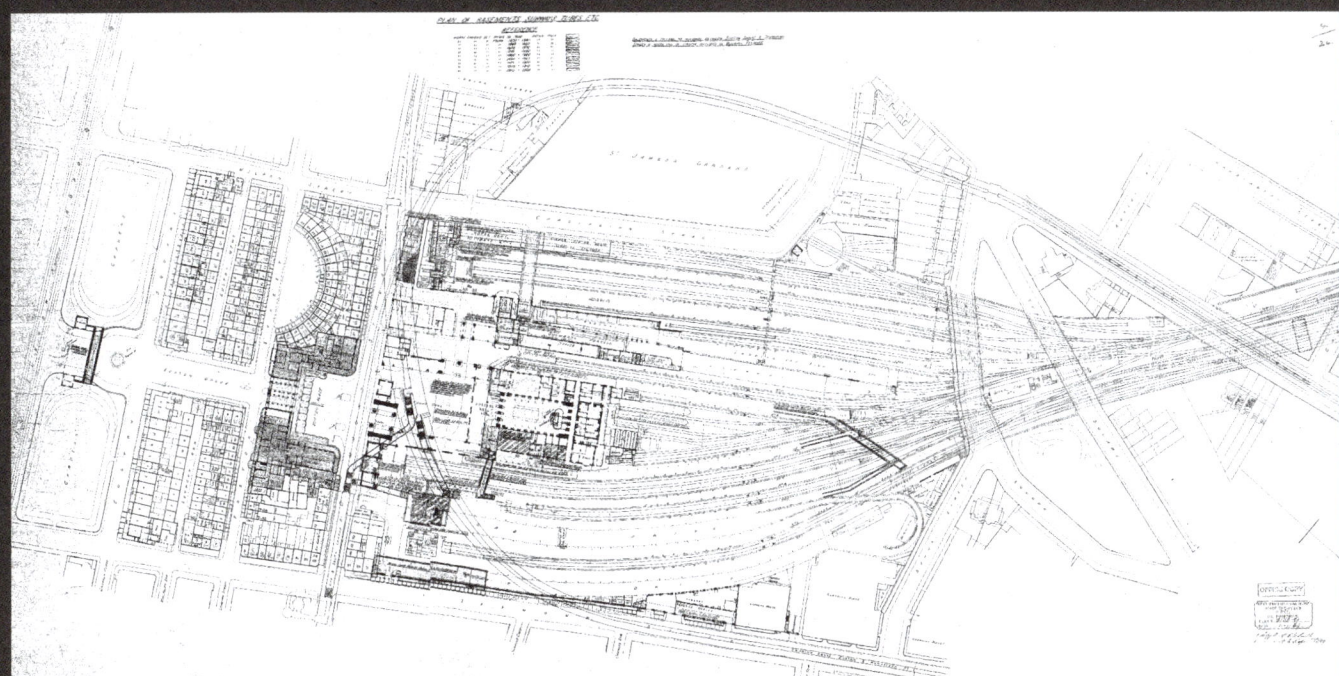

[FIG.214] OPPOSITE ABOVE The disused City & South London Railway passageways as seen in 1922, being used to house the compressors needed to enlarge the tunnels. Note the distinctive thin glass tiling on the walls, unique to the company's stations.

[FIG.215] OPPOSITE BELOW The same passageways seen in fig. 214, above, were emptied after the enlargement project to provide ventilation for the City branch of the Northern line. The lift and stair shafts were capped and, in 1934, the former City & South London Railway station building was demolished to make way for Euston House, the headquarters of the London Midland & Scottish Railway.

[FIG.216] ABOVE This plan from 1939 shows the layout below ground of the two Tube railways and the subways connecting these to Euston mainline station.

[FIG.217] RIGHT A poster by Charles W. Baker, illustrating the newly built Camden Town junctions. It was produced for the 1924 opening of the reconstructed City & South London Railway, running between Moorgate and Euston stations.

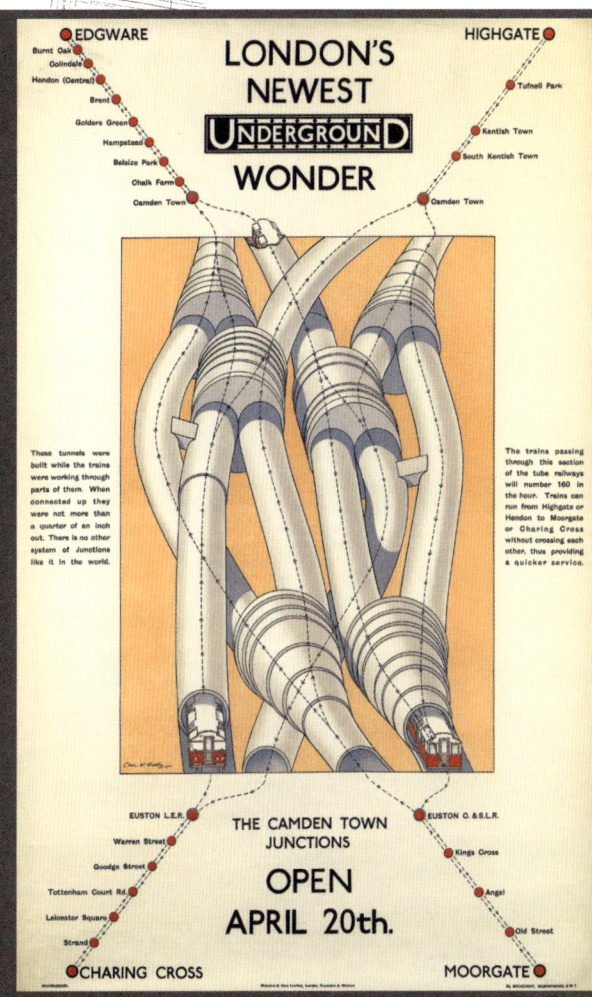

LONDON TRANSPORT. EUSTON STATION.
Control Room for L.M.S. Railway.
Scale. 1/20" = 1 foot.

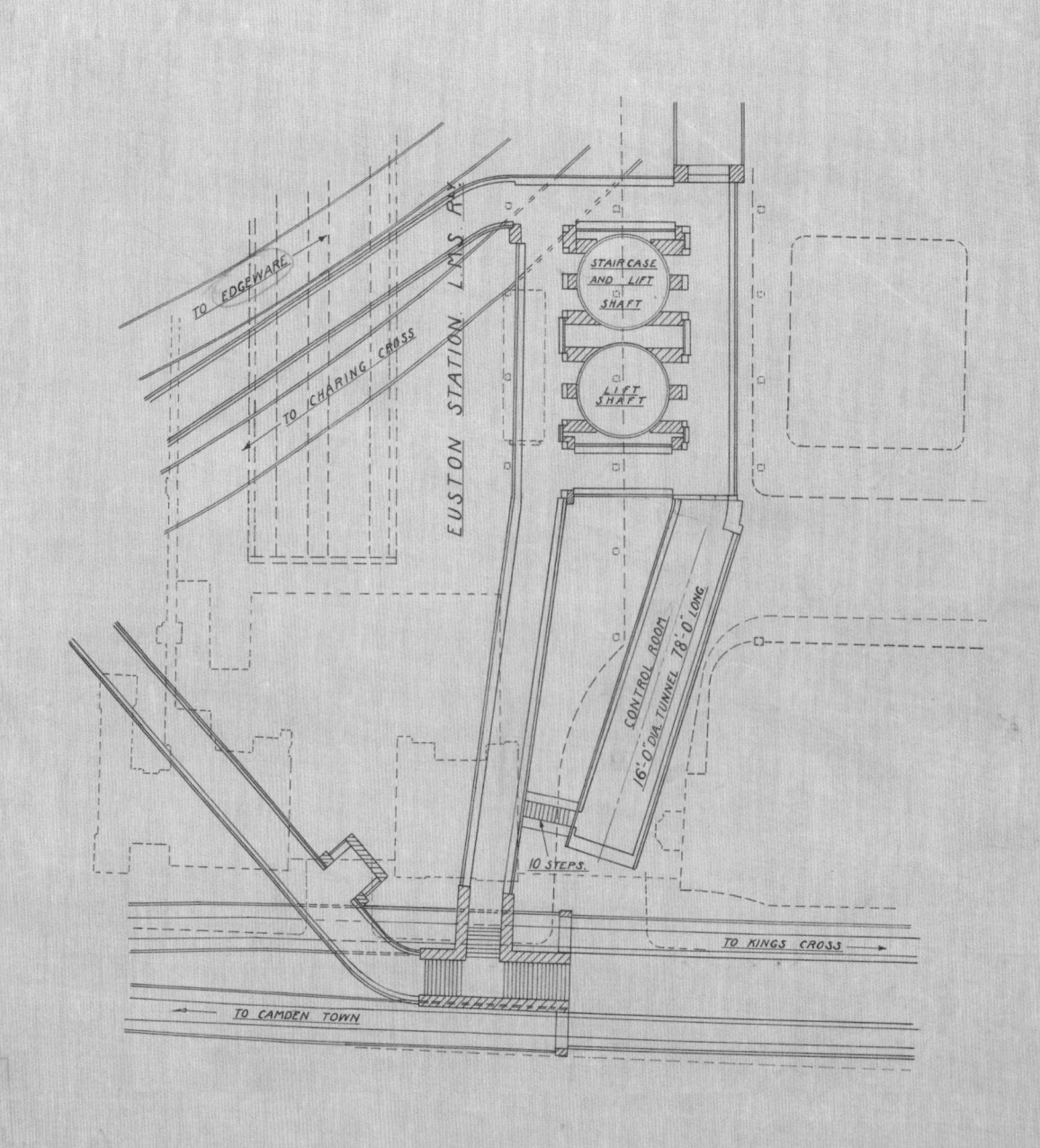

[FIG.218] OPPOSITE A diagram from 1938 showing alterations proposed to the subways at Euston. The alterations are marked as a control room for the London Midland & Scottish Railway. Other diagrams from 1937 and 1940 show a cable shaft linking the tunnel to surface level.

[FIG.219] ABOVE
A view down the additional tunnel constructed at Euston in 1938. Today this is part of the ventilation system at Euston, but some traces of its former use can be seen on the left-hand side, with mustard-yellow and green paint still faintly visible on the wall.

[FIG.220] BELOW
Disused passageways of the Hampstead Tube now serve as ventilation shafts for the Charing Cross branch of the Northern line.

most of the staff would have been working in Euston House, from which the quickest way to enter the Underground was through the public entrance on the main station concourse. In July 1940, further permits were issued to allow staff to enter via the main entrance. Later, in 1942, London Transport renewed and issued a total of 50 staff permits, allowing staff to enter the shelter. On plans, this accommodation was referred to as a control room; however, in various papers from the Railway Executive Committee (REC) based at Down Street (see pp.79–107), the Euston control room was said to contain a telephone exchange for use as a backup if the one at Down Street station were to be compromised.[7]

INADEQUATE CONDITIONS

When the Blitz started, on 7 September 1940, the public flocked to the Underground for shelter. Conditions were generally dreadful, and Euston was no exception, with no services or medical facilities for shelterers injured in raids or taken ill. In November 1940, medical officers from the borough of St Pancras visited Euston to inspect the conditions and identify a site for a first-aid post. Eventually, a small medical post was assembled in the passage adjoining the lift shaft on the C&SLR side. Later that year, on 27 December, Clementine Churchill, wife of the prime minister, visited Euston and King's Cross to inspect the conditions of the stations after having received countless letters from civilians informing her of the distress and discomfort of the Tube shelters (see Clapham South, pp.123–43).[8] As a result of the visit to Euston and visits to several other Tube stations, Clementine wrote to government ministers to stress the importance of better facilities for shelterers. She also wrote to Albert Stanley, Lord Ashfield, chairman of London Transport on 3 January 1941, stating:

> We visited Euston and King's Cross Tube stations. I was told how much the food which is provided by the London Passenger Transport Board is appreciated by the shelterers. But I was shocked at the inadequate number of latreens [sic], and more especially by the fact that there are no doors or screens to them. Do you think this could be remedied? I understand that many people are disturbed and unhappy about this.[9]

Conditions rapidly changed in the Tube stations after the interventions made by Lady Churchill, and heaters, beds, disinfected bedding and other improvements were supplied to shelterers across London. The standards that Clementine set for shelters in London were later implemented for the building and fitting out of deep-level shelters. Euston was heavily used throughout the War for sheltering, with the interchange subways, in particular, often becoming very crowded.

POST-WAR IMPROVEMENTS

After the war, London Transport revisited the improvements planned in 1935. Despite the immense destruction and loss of life that the Second World War brought upon London, it was essential to rebuild the city and reinvigorate the economy. One of the upgrades discussed at length was the possibility of connecting Euston, via subway, to Euston Square Underground station. This would have required a 411.5-meter (1,350-foot) tunnel, to connect the Metropolitan line with National Rail services and the Tube at Euston. These plans were drawn up and circulated to the Railway Joint Committee.[10] The general opinion was that the works would not be beneficial, and the plans went no further. Other upgrades considered included the installation of escalators, for which a plan was drawn up in 1945 [FIG.221]. This would have involved moving the entrance to the Underground within the mainline concourse and significantly rearranging the station. At the time, other upgrades across the network were also being considered and were favoured over the Euston upgrade works, due to the amount of rebuilding required. In the end, two improvements were made. In 1951, the emergency staircase was removed from Melton Street to provide better ventilation, and an additional tunnel was constructed to connect to the running tunnels of the Northern line.

THE VICTORIA LINE AND VENTILATION

Euston mainline station was completely rebuilt and modernised in the early 1960s. This finally allowed the upgrade to the much-debated, improved entrance to the Underground to proceed. The rebuilding coincided with the construction of the first new Underground line to be built for 60 years, the Victoria line. The new line was to be built next to the City branch of the Northern line (the former C&SLR), to allow easy interchange between the two lines. To achieve this, the island platform arrangement on the City branch was altered and the northbound track diverted to the other side of the newly built Victoria line, creating a very wide southbound platform that covered the former running tracks. Escalator shafts and new passageways leading to this altered arrangement were built, rendering the old lift shafts and interchange subways connecting the two branches unnecessary.

The works began in 1962 with the closure of one of the two interchange subways [FIG.223], the second subway closing in 1967 when the new escalators were switched on and the lifts were decommissioned. The final stage of construction was that of building a large ventilation tunnel, which connected the newly built Victoria line platforms to the original lift shafts to provide draught relief. The closed-off subways were then left as they were, and now represent a fascinating time capsule of peeling posters from the 1960s and earlier [FIG.224].

MODERN DAY EUSTON AND HS2

Euston station has gone through further upgrades since the major overhaul of the 1960s. The old tiling on the Hampstead Tube platforms has been covered with decorative enamel panels and the booking hall was retiled in the 1980s. Now the station is primed for its next transformation – the coming of HS2. This will be the second High Speed line in the United Kingdom, providing a rapid link to the Midlands and, later, to Manchester, Liverpool, Sheffield and Leeds – a route similar to that run by Euston's original 1837 railway. In 2018,

PLAN AT TUBE PLATFORM LEVEL

NOTE: DATUM TO WHICH ALL LEVELS ON THIS PLAN
REFER IS 100 FEET BELOW ORDNANCE DATUM.

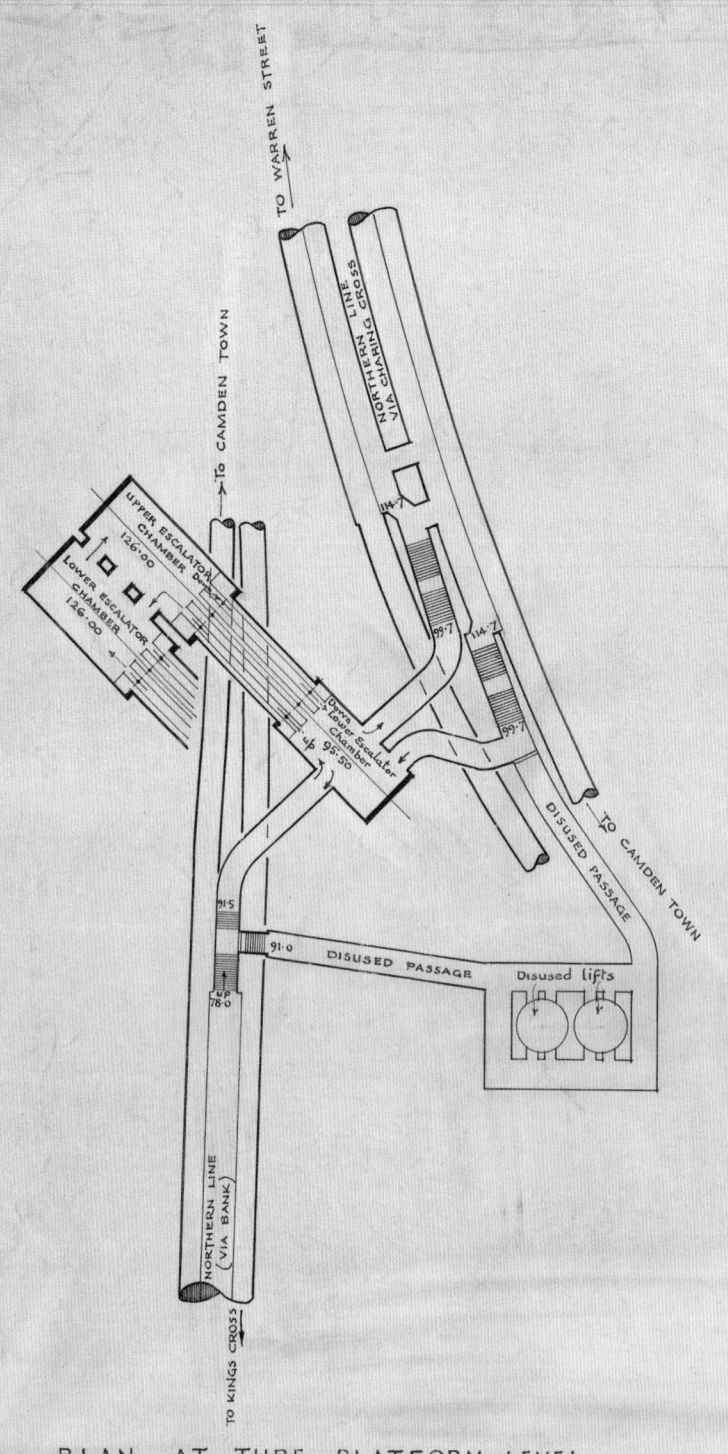

PLAN AT

AMENDMENTS	DATE

EUSTON STA

· NEW · TICKET · HALL · & · ESCALATORS · TO · SUIT

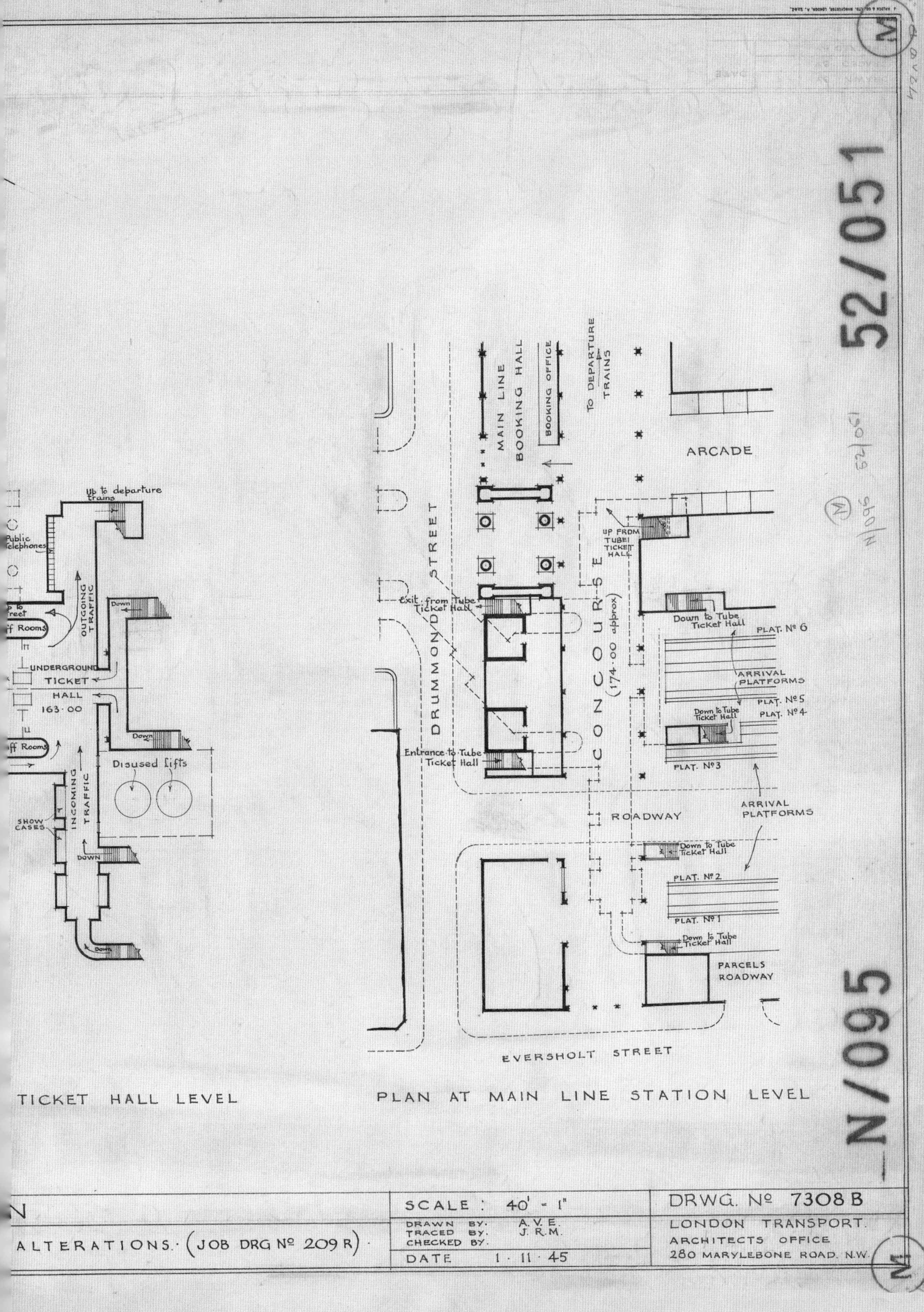

TICKET HALL LEVEL   PLAN AT MAIN LINE STATION LEVEL

	SCALE: 40' = 1"	DRWG. No 7308 B
ALTERATIONS. (JOB DRG No 209 R)	DRAWN BY. A.V.E. TRACED BY. J.R.M. CHECKED BY.	LONDON TRANSPORT. ARCHITECTS OFFICE 280 MARYLEBONE ROAD. N.W.
	DATE 1·11·45	

[FIG.221] PREVIOUS From 1945, this plan shows proposed escalators for Euston Underground station. The new escalators were to intersect one of the interchange subways, leaving the other to become disused.

[FIG.222] TOP LEFT One of Euston's many unusual features, deep within its maze of passageways, is a tunnel-lining dome. Built from cast iron segments, this elegant way to terminate a tunnel is a rare sight compared with the more usual technique of using a large plug of cast concrete.

[FIG.223] TOP RIGHT Poster from one of the interchange passages at Euston, which connected the two branches of the Northern line, notifying passengers of the impending reconstruction in 1962.

[FIG.224] ABOVE Abandoned lift landings at Euston, where posters from the 1960s can still be viewed.

Euston mainline station was used by 44 million passengers. This number is set to double with the completion of HS2, with the site redevelopment also creating new homes, shops and improved public spaces. The platforms for HS2 will be constructed in the area to the west of the current station, causing the demolition of the old Hampstead Tube building. A new connection with Euston Square Underground station is also planned, finally bringing the three railway services – mainline, sub-surface and deep-level Tube – together.

MOORGATE

Euston Underground station exemplifies a station shaped by the needs of the mainline station that it serves – a driver so powerful that, as these needs changed over a century, whole station buildings, lifts and passageways have been abandoned and repurposed. Moorgate station is another example of a station that has gone through progressive design evolutions in response to its growing need for capacity. Moorgate has experienced extensions and upgrades over the years and has recently undergone another big refurbishment ahead of the opening of the planned Elizabeth line. It too has many hidden gems that evidence its past, including the pioneering deep-tube tunnelling of the C&SLR.

Moorgate opened as Moorgate Street in 1865 as an extension of the Metropolitan Railway. In 1900, the C&SLR extended to Moorgate, opening a separate station close by [FIG.227]. Four years later, the Great Northern & City Railway (GN&CR) opened their line from Finsbury Park to Moorgate, where the company shared a booking hall, lifts and emergency staircase with the C&SLR. The GN&CR was built to a bigger scale than the other Tube services of the time. Their tunnels were just under 5 metres (16 feet) in diameter, enabling

[FIG.225] The subways and lift shafts at Moorgate were converted for ventilation after closure. Despite the change of use, posters still survive in the passageways, showing advertising from 1934–6.

mainline-size trains to run directly to the City of London from Finsbury Park. When the line opened, there were plans to extend it nearly half a kilometre to Lothbury in the heart of the City, and the Greathead tunnelling shield used to dig the tunnels was left in situ, waiting to begin construction of the extension. The plans were abandoned due to financial problems and the Greathead shield is still there, a unique survival, hidden beyond the platforms at the end of the tunnel [FIG.228].

On 2 September 1912, a new subway connection was opened between the C&SLR, GN&CR and Metropolitan Railway booking hall. These subways and the passenger lifts were in use until the station was extensively reconstructed in 1936 to cope with increased passenger numbers [FIGS 225 & 226]. Moorgate has been re-tiled and renovated since 1936, but the latest upgrade will transform the station once again. The Elizabeth line platforms at Moorgate connect directly with Liverpool Street station, thus merging the two stations together underground and providing two brand new, sub-surface ticket halls for both sites. The platforms, just over 200 metres (656 feet) long, have been excavated carefully between all the existing services in the ground nearby, with the closest being the Post Office Railway, only 0.5 metres (just under 2 feet) away from the Elizabeth line tunnels. When it opens, the Elizabeth line is projected to add 10 per cent capacity to central London's rail network, bringing an extra 1.5 million people to within 45 minutes of central London.[11] Despite this immense undertaking, the old passageways and the Greathead shield will remain in place underground, at least until Moorgate goes through its next transformation.

[FIG.226] LEFT These subways and lift shafts at Moorgate were converted for ventilation after closure, with a large fan in a former subway at Moorgate.

[FIG.227] ABOVE The Metropolitan Railway and the City & South London Railway (C&SLR) extended their lines to Moorgate station in 1865 and 1900 respectively, to establish a better foothold in the City. The C&SLR station building was designed by Thomas Phillips Figgis and featured decorative stone carvings of wings and lightning bolts to highlight the speed of the new electric railway.

1   Andrew Martin, 'So, what would you burn?', *New Statesman*, 13 December 2004, https://www.newstatesman.com/node/161150, accessed 16 April 2019.
2   'London Euston', HS2 website, https://www.hs2.org.uk/stations/london-euston/, accessed 4 January 2019.
3   *St James's Gazette*, 6 January 1900, p.15.
4   Desmond F. Croome and Alan A. Jackson, *Rails Through the Clay: A History of London's Tube Railways* (Capital Transport, 1993), p.27.
5   TfL archives, LT001249/003/017.
6   The London Midland & Scottish Railway (LMSR) took over the LNWR in 1923 and became one of the 'Big Four' major railway companies.
7   National Archives, MT 6/2728.
8   Sonia Purcell, *First Lady: The Life and Wars of Clementine Churchill* (Aurum Press, 2015), p.245.
9   Churchill Archives, CSCT 3/33.
10   The Railway Joint Committee was a post-war name for the Railway Executive Committee (see Down Street, which still held powers until 1 January 1948.
11   'Delivering Economic Benefits in London, the South East, and Across the UK', Crossrail website, http://www.crossrail.co.uk/route/wider-economic-benefits, accessed 27 November 2018.

[FIG.228] NEXT The Greathead tunnelling shield, used to create the Great Northern and City Railway line, still guards the end of the tunnel at Moorgate since 1904. This is the only known surviving Greathead shield, a key innovation in the creation of deep tube railways.

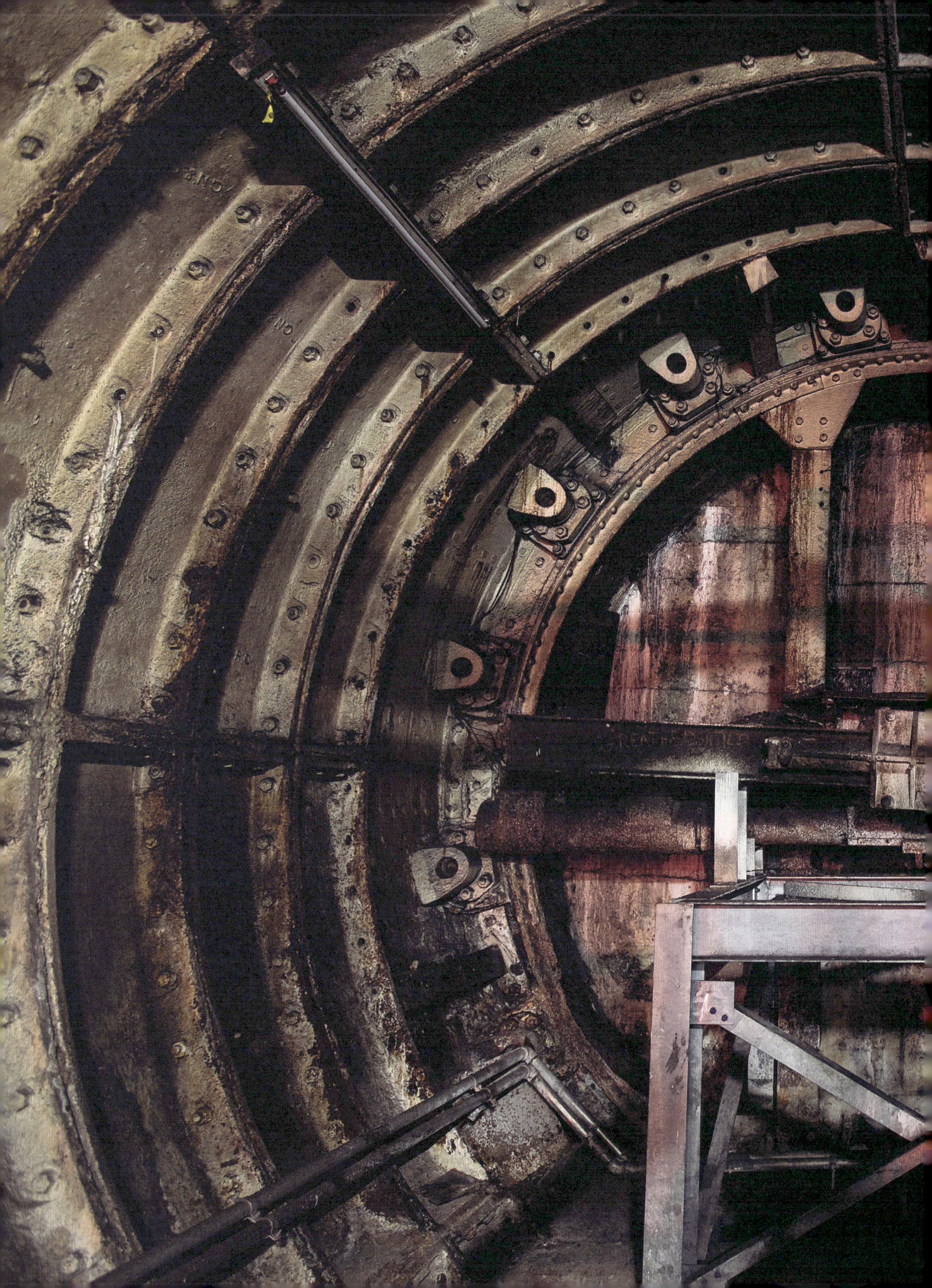

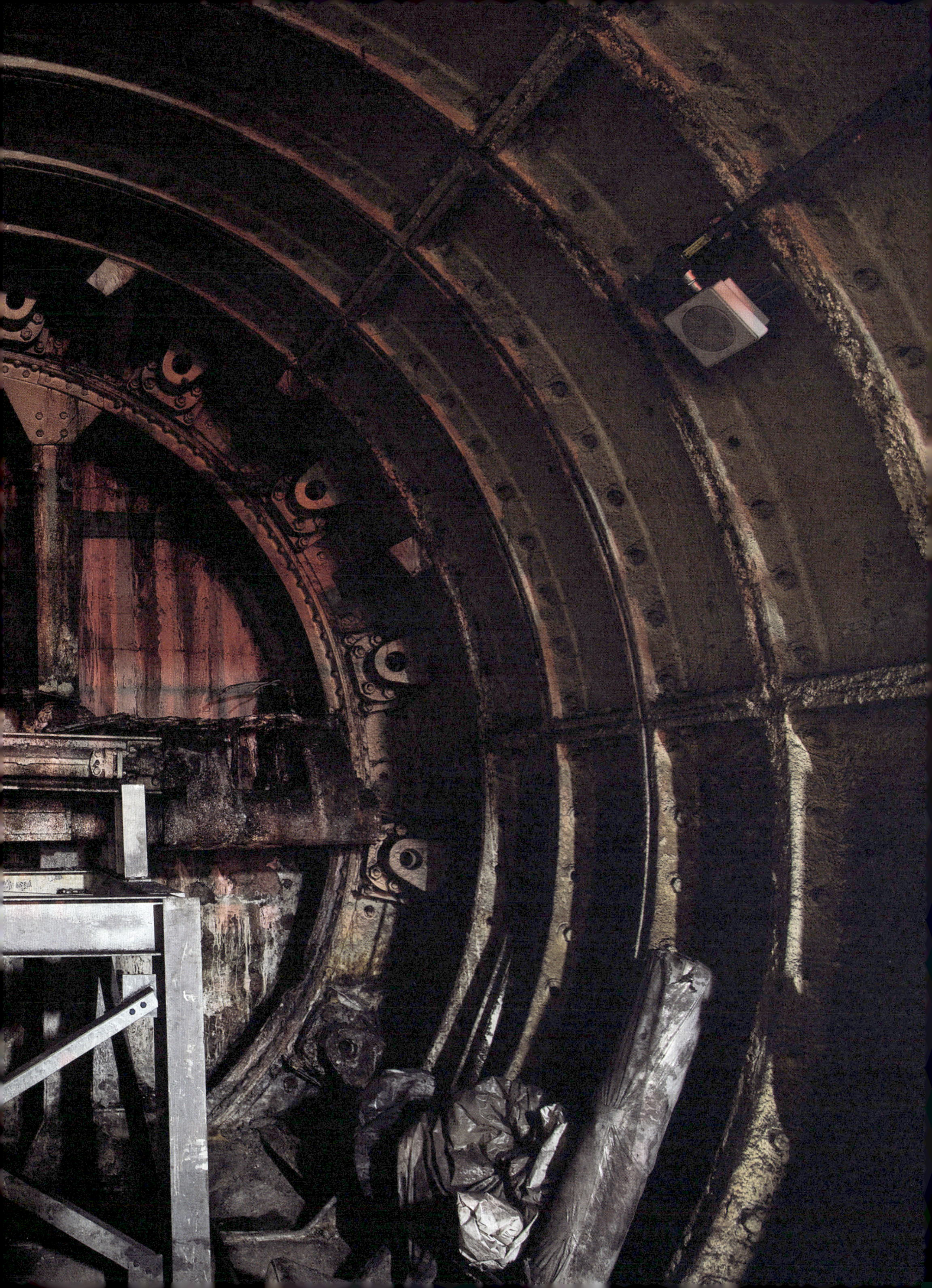

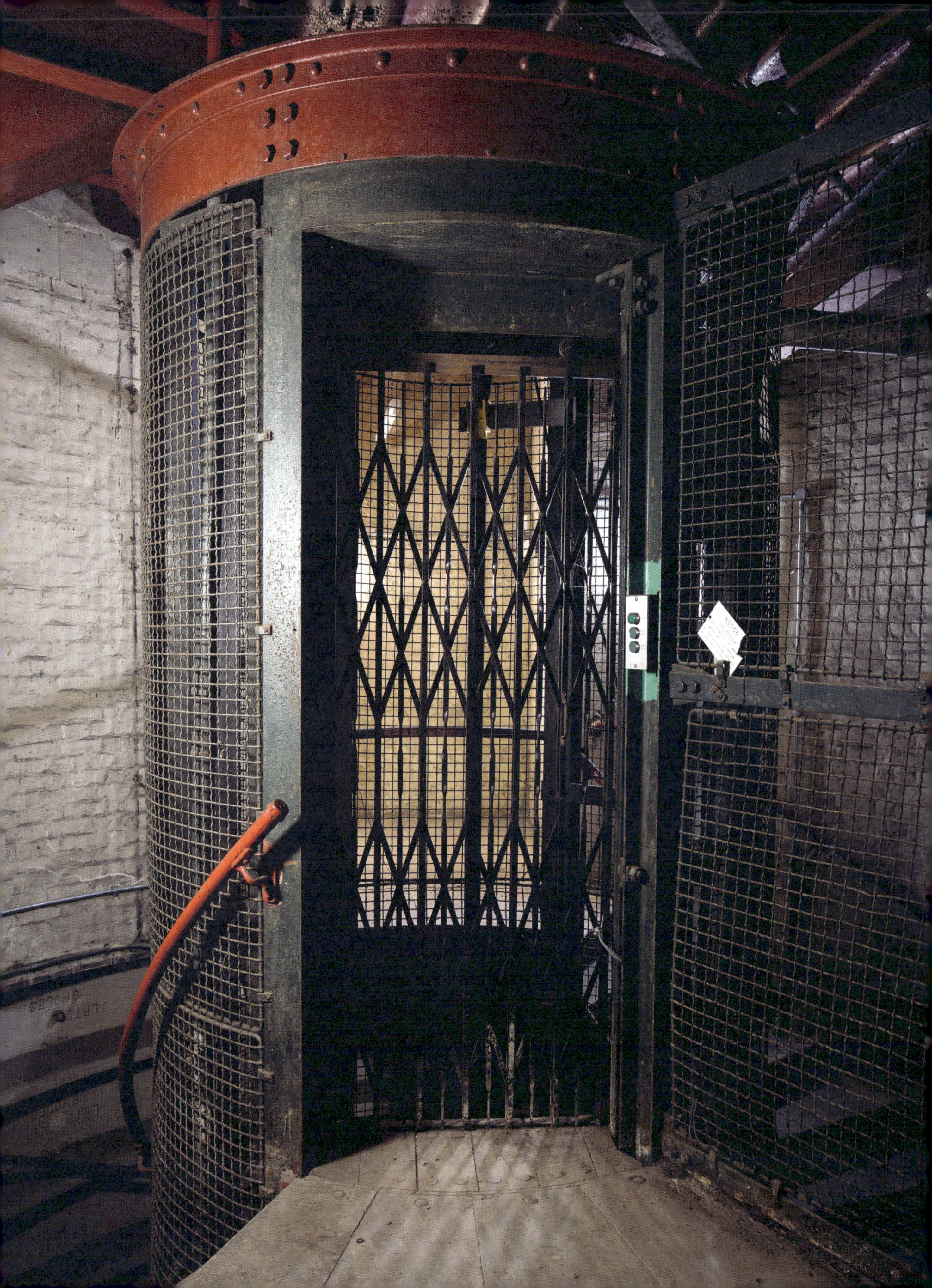

SELECT BIBLIOGRAPHY

Anon, 'The Secret Underground Railway Executive HQ', *After the Battle*, no. 12 (1976)

Anon, 'Underground Stations Closed & Partly Closed Part I', *Underground News*, no. 238 (1981)

Badsey-Ellis, Antony, *London's Lost Tube Schemes* (Capital Transport, 2005)
The Hampstead Tube: A History of the First 100 Years (Capital Transport, 2007)
Building London's Underground: From Cut-and-Cover to Crossrail (Capital Transport, 2016)

Badsey-Ellis, Antony, and Mike Horne, *The Aldwych Branch* (Capital Transport, 2009)

Bancroft, Peter, *The Railway to King William Street and Southwark Deep Tunnel Air Raid Shelter* (Nebulous Books, 1981)

Barker, T. C., and Michael Robbins, *A History of London Transport, Vol. 1: The Nineteenth Century* (Allen & Unwin, 1963)
A History of London Transport, Vol. 2: The Twentieth Century to 1970 (Allen & Unwin, 1974)

Beard, Tony, *By Tube Beyond Edgware* (Capital Transport, 2002)

Bownes, David, Oliver Green and Sam Mullins, *Underground: How the Tube Shaped London* (Penguin, 2012)

Catford, Nick, *Secret Underground London* (Folly Books, 2013)

Catford, Nick, and Peter Kay, 'North End (Bull & Bush)', *London Railway Record* (January 2013)

Churchill, Winston, *The Second World War 4: The Commonwealth Alone* (Cassell, 1964)

Colville, John, *The Fringes of Power: Downing Street Diaries 1939–1955* (Weidenfeld & Nicolson, 2004)

Connor, J. E., *London's Disused Underground Stations* (Capital Transport, 2011)

Connor, J.E., and B.L. Halford, *The Forgotten Stations of Greater London* (Connor & Butler, 1991)

Croome, Desmond F., and Alan A. Jackson, *Rails Through the Clay: A History of London's Tube Railways* (2nd edn, Capital Transport, 1993)

Emmerson, Andrew and Tony Beard, *London's Secret Tubes* (Capital Transport, 2009)

Follenfant, H.G., *Reconstructing London's Underground* (London Transport, 1975)

Gilbert, Sir Martin, *Winston S. Churchill, Volume 6: Finest Hour, 1939–1941* (Hillsdale College Press, 2011)

Glancey, Jonathan, *Twentieth Century Architecture* (Carlton Books, 1999)

Greathead, James Henry, 'The City & South London Railway', *Proceedings of the Institution of Civil Engineers*, vol. cxxiii (1896)

Green, Oliver, *Frank Pick's London* (V&A Publishing, 2013)

Gregg, John, *The Shelter of the Tubes: Tube Sheltering in Wartime London* (Capital Transport, 2001)

Halliday, Stephen, *Underground to Everywhere: London's Underground Railway in the Life of the Capital* (Sutton Publishing, 2001)

Hardy, Brian, *The Northern Line Extensions* (London Underground Railway Society, 2011)

Henrey, Robert, *A Village in Piccadilly* (J.M. Dent, 1942)

Hodgkins, David J., *The Second Railway King: The Life and Times of Sir Edward Watkin, 1819–1901* (Merton Priory Press, 2002)

Holman, Printz P., *Amazing Electric Tube: History of the City and South London Railway* (London Transport Museum, 1990)

Horne, Mike, *The Jubilee Line: An Illustrated History* (Capital Transport, 2000)
The Piccadilly Tube: A History of the First 100 Years (Capital Transport, 2007)

Izzo, Julian, 'Surplus to Requirements', *London Lines* (1993)

Jackson, Alan A., *London's Metropolitan Railway* (David & Charles, 1986)
Semi-Detached London: Suburban Development, Life and Transport, 1900–39 (Wild Swan Publications, 1991)
London's Local Railways (Capital Transport, 1999)
London's Metro-land (Capital History, 2006)

Karol, Eitan, *Charles Holden: Architect* (Shaun Tyas, 2007)

Kirkland, R. K., 'Closed Tube Stations', *The Electric Railway*, vol. 1, no. 6 (1946)

Laurie, Peter, *Beneath the City Streets* (Harper Collins, 1979)

Longley, Maria, *An Ecological Data Survey for Highgate Station on behalf of TfL*, report ref. 1705, Greenspace Information for Greater London CIC, 2017

Miller, Mervyn, *Hampstead Garden Suburb: Arts and Crafts Utopia* (The History Press, 2006)

Mitchell, Bob, *Jubilee Line Extension: From Concept to Completion* (Thomas Telford, 2003)

Ovenden, Mark, *London Underground by Design* (Penguin Books, 2013)

Pedroche, Ben, *Do Not Alight Here: Walking London's Lost Underground and Railway Stations* (Capital History, 2011)

Purnell, Sonia, *First Lady: The Life and Wars of Clementine Churchill* (Aurum Press, 2015)

Rose, Douglas, *Tiles of the Unexpected Underground: A Study of Six Miles of Geometric Tile Patterns on the London Underground* (London [self published], 2007)

Sherwood, Tim, *Charles Tyson Yerkes: Railway Tycoon* (The History Press, 2009)

Simpson, Bill, *The Brill Tramway* (Oxford Publishing, 1985)

Slack, Kathleen M., *Henrietta's Dream: A Chronicle of Hampstead Garden Suburb 1905–1982* (London [self published], 1982)

Taylor, Sheila (ed.), *The Moving Metropolis* (2nd edn, Laurence King Publishing, 2015)

Treby, Edward, 'Closed London Underground Stations', *Railway World*, vol. 35, no. 409 (1974)

Trench, Richard and Ellis Hillman, *London Under London: A Subterranean Guide* (John Murray, 1993)

Wilson, (Mrs) Arthur, 'Wyldes and Its Story', *Transactions of the Hampstead Antiquarian and Literary Society* (1902–3)

INDEX

Page numbers in *italics* are for figures.

air raid shelters *see also* Clapham South station; deep-level shelters
   Aldwych station 28, 30, 193, *195*
   Clementine Churchill's campaign for conditions in 125–6, 214
   Euston station 214
   Highgate station 30, *180*, 183
   King William Street station 39, *42*, 45–50, *46*
   Knightsbridge station 67
   Piccadilly Circus station *64*, 65
   planning for the Blitz 28, 81–2, 125–6
   post-war uses of 133–4
   reuse of abandoned Underground spaces 27–30
   Stockwell station *138*, 139
   storage of artworks in 65, 193, *195*
   Whitechapel St Marys *26*
Aldwych station *see also* Strand station
   as an air raid shelter 28, 30, 193, *195*
   booking office 199, *199*
   closure of 193, *196*
   Edwardian tiling 199, *199*
   Jubilee line extension *188*
   lifts 199, *199*
   mock-up facilities 198
   passageways *34*
   storage of artworks in 193, *195*
   as TV and film location *197*, 198–9
Alexandra Palace 175, *176*, 184, *185*
Anderson, David 125
Angel station
   adaptation for escalators *72*
   island platform *72*
Archway (Highgate) 175

Baker Street station *76*
Balham station *124*, 125
Bank station
   access shaft *22*, *25*
   as replacement for King William Street station 44
   shrine to Saint Barbara *28*
   upgrade of *22*, 24, 39, 50–4
Barnett, Henrietta 148, *149*
Belsize Park deep-level shelter *127*, *138*
Bethnal Green station 30
Betjeman, John 22
Blake Hall station *165*
Brill Branch, Metropolitan line *166*, *167*
Brompton Road station
   as anti-aircraft operations command centre 99, *100*
   briefing room *100*
   station building *99*
   tiles *100*

calthemite straws 32, *33*, 39
Camden Town station *211*
Chancery Lane deep-level shelter *138*, 139–40
Charing Cross, Euston & Hampstead Railway (CCE&HR) 187, 191
Charing Cross Tube station
   interchange with the Jubilee line 196–8, *197*, *200*, 200
   operational platforms *197*, 198
   renamed as the Strand 191
Churchill, Clementine 125–6, 133, 214
Churchill, Winston 23, 81, 90, *91*, *93*, *96*
City & Brixton Railway 44
City & South London Railway (C&SLR) 24, 27, 38, 39, 44, 52, 204, 205–6, *210*, 219
Clapham North deep-level shelter 140, *142*
Clapham South station
   as accommodation for Jamaican migrant workers 134, *136*
   as an air raid shelter *122*
   civilian uses *131*
   Clementine Churchill's visit to 133
   as hydroponic farming site 24, *138*
   layout of the deep-level shelter *130*
   post-war use as a hostel 133, *134*
   rotunda entrance *131*
   stairways *131*
   surviving original features 140, *140*
   as temporary labour exchange 134, *136*
Cold War-era bunkers 23
Cole Deacon, Gerald 84, 85, 90
Colville, John 90, *91*
construction techniques
   cut-and-cover method 24, 205
   Greathead tunnelling shield 27, 59, *222*
   at King William Street stations 38, 40, *40*
Cranley Gardens *176*
Crouch End station *176*, 177, 184
cut-and-cover method 24, 205

deep-level shelters *see also* Clapham South station
   Chancery Lane *138*, 139–40
   Clapham Common 129, *130*, *131*
   Clapham North 140, *142*
   construction of *129*
   provision of 126–8
   Belsize Park *127*, *138*
   Goodge Street *135*, 136, *137*, 139
   layout of *127*, *129*
   location map *127*
   post-war uses of 139–40
disused/abandoned Underground spaces
   during the expansion of the Tube network 81
   Hidden London tour programme 34
   narratives of 23–5
   new uses for 198–9
   physical evidence 30–2
   repurposed stations for ventilation 27, 81
   during the Second World War 27–30, 81–4
Dover Street station 104, *104*, *106*
Down Street station
   closure of *80*, 84
   Railway Executive Committee (REC) 92, 214
   secret Second World War bunker 28, 32, 81, 84–5, *86*, 90–1
   stairways *78*
   station building *80*, *98*
   station plan *83*
   telephone lines 81, 84, 85, *88*, *93*, *94*
   ventilation systems *98*
   water drip pattern *33*
   Winston Churchill's use of 23, 81, 90, *91*, *93*, *96*

Earl's Court station 59
Elizabeth line 220
Embankment station 191
Epping and Ongar line *162*, 163
Epstein, Jacob *116*
escalators
   Angel station *72*
   Euston station 215, *216*
   Hyde Park Corner station *68*
   Oxford Circus station *69*, *70*
   Piccadilly Circus station 59, *66*
   South Kensington station *102*
Euston station
   additional tunnel (1938) *213*
   as an air raid shelter 214
   alterations diagram (1938) *212*
   backfilled passageway *31*, 32
   below ground layout plan (1939) *211*
   City & South London Railway (C&SLR) 204, *210*
   Clementine Churchill's visit to 125, 214
   disused lift landings *221*
   electricity substation 206, *207*
   engine traverser *207*
   entrance to *209*
   as the first underground railway station 205–6, *206*
   High Speed Two (HS2) 205, 215, 219
   information poster *218*

joint ticket hall *209*
Melton Street (Hampstead Tube station) *204*, 205, 206, *207*, 213
modernisation of (1914) 208
post-war improvements 214–15
proposed escalator plans 215, *216*
as staff shelter, Second World War 208, 214
terminus building 205–6
ticket window *209*
tunnelling dome *218*
ventilation system *202*, 213

55 Broadway
aerial view *115*
bomb damage *119*
carved reliefs *116*
central tower *116*
contemporary use *120*
cruciform structure *114*
early proposal for 'Traffic Buildings' *112*
ground-floor concourse *115*
as London Transport's headquarters *113*
1980s revamp *120*
office areas *117*
staff leisure areas *118*
street entrance *108*
Finsbury Park station 72, *74*, 176, 219–20
First World War 27, 84
flood control 153–6

Goodge Street deep-level shelter
ceiling graffiti *135*
closure of 139
as the Eisenhower Centre *136*
Lamson tube pneumatic system 136, *137*
street entrance *137*
Great Northern & City Railway (GN&CR) 72, 219–20
Greathead, James Henry 40
Greathead tunnelling shield 27, *59*, *222*
Green, Leslie 29, 30, *58*, 80, 190, 205, 206

Hampstead Garden Suburb 147, 149, *150*, *151*, 153
Hampstead Heath Extension project 148–9
Hampstead station *192*, *204*, 205, 206, *207*, 213
Hidden London tour programme 34
Highgate station
as an air raid shelter 30, *180*, 183
as a bat sanctuary *172*, *173*, 185, *186*
impact of wartime shortages 182–3
interchange function 175, *180*, 182
within the Northern Heights Project 176–7, 184–5

platform canopy 185, *186*
station layout *174*
three stations as 175
Holborn station
disused platform *81*
tiles *101*
wartime adaptation *101*
Holden, Charles 64, *113*, 114, *115*, 116, 182
Hyde Park Corner station
adaptation for escalators 68
exterior *29*
ventilation system 68

Jubilee line *188*, 196–8, *197*, 200, *200*

King William Street station
as an air raid shelter 39, *42*, 45–50, *46*
attempted reuse 44–5
and the Bank Station upgrade 22, 24, 39, 50–4
closure of 44
emergency stairway *52*
engineering drawings *40*
engineering techniques 38, 40–1
entrance tunnel *36*
as the first electric underground railway 40
original single-track bay *41*, 41
street entrance *41*
as a time capsule 44–5, *46–7*, 50
tunnels under the Thames 49–50, *54*
uses for 24
ventilation systems 51
Knightsbridge station
adaptation for escalators 67
as an air-raid shelter 67
step-free adaptation 67
ventilation systems 67

Lee, Charles 44
lifts
adaptation for step-free route, Knightsbridge station 67
adaptation of for ventilation systems 26, 27
Aldwych station 199, *199*
Baker Street station *76*
Dover Street station 104, *104*, *105*
Euston station *218*
Finsbury Park station 72, *74*
hydraulic, Great William Street station 39, 45
importance of 59
North End station 149
Piccadilly Circus station 59, *60*, *62*, 66
St Paul's station conversion *156*, 158

York Road station *103*
London and North Western Railway (LNWR) 206
London Midland & Scottish Railway (LMSR) 208
London Passenger Transport Board ('London Transport') 30, 33
London Underground, history of 24–30

MacPherson, Douglas 63
Maw and Company *29*
Melton Street (Hampstead Tube station) *204*
Metropolitan line 165, 170
Metropolitan Railway 24, 33, 166, 169, 170, *170*, 205, 219
Moorgate station 41, 44, 219–20, *219*
Morrison, Herbert 125, 128, 133
Muswell Hill station *176*, 177, 184

North End station
as the Bull and Bush Emergency Control Headquarters 23, *152*, 153–5
as a civil defence flood-control bunker 153–4
emergency stairway *144*, 148
flood control office *155*
and the Hampstead Garden Suburb 147, 149, *151*
lifts 149
passageways *154*
proposed construction of *146*, 147–8, *151*
unopened status of 148–52
North Weald station *164*
Northern Heights Project
cancellation of 184
planned rail improvements under 175, 176–7, *177*
platform direction sign *184*
on the Tube map *181*, 183–4
Northern line 27, 208

Ongar station
closure of 163
incorporation into the Central line 162
restoration of *162*, 163
signal cabin *160*, 162
Oxford Circus station
adaptation for escalators 69, *70*
station building *69*
ventilation system *71*

Parkland Walk 185
Pemberton, Thomas 41, *41*
Piccadilly Circus station
adaptation for escalators 59, 66
as an air raid shelter 64, *65*

booking hall *62, 63, 64*
entranceways *58*
lift shafts *59, 60, 62, 66*
old passageways *56, 66*
storage of artworks in *65*
tiling *29*
ventilation system *66*
Piccadilly line 27, 81
Pick, Frank 28, 30, 59, 84, *92*, 103, *113*, 116, 166, 182
Post Office station 158, *158*

Quainton Railway Society 170
Quainton Road station 163, *165, 170*

Railway Executive Committee (REC) 84, *92*
Railway Magazine 44–5

Saint Barbara 28
Second World War *see also* air raid shelters; Clapham South station; Down Street station
bomb crater, Balham *124, 125*
bomb damage, 55 Broadway *119*
bomb damage, Balham station *124, 125*
Brompton Road station adaptation 99, *100*
Dover Street station 104, *104, 106*
flying bombs 128–33
Holborn station adaptation *101*
impact on the Highgate interchange plans 182
Thames flood-control measures 153
York Road station 103
South Kensington station
engineering control services 102
escalator conversion *102*
South Kentish Town station *22*
St James's Park station *110*
St Paul's station 155, *156*
stalactites 32
stalagmites 32
Stanley, Albert, Lord Ashfield 104, 126–7, 166, 184, 208
steam trains 24–7, 39, *166*, 177, 183, 184
Stoke Mandeville station *170*
The Strand station *see also* Aldwych station
the Aldwych shuttle *194*
alternative names for 191–2
Charing Cross Tube station as 191
Craven Street entrance *194*
elevation drawings *190*
first station *190, 191, 192*
renamed as Aldwych *190, 191, 192*

10 Downing Street 85, 90
tiles
Brompton Road station *100*
Down Street station 80
Edwardian tiling, Aldwych station 199, *199*
Holborn station *101*
King William Street station *52*
maker's tiles *29*, 32
Piccadilly Circus station *29*
on station facades *29*, 30
in ticket halls *29*, 30
use throughout the London Underground 30
York Road station *29*
Transport for London 33

Underground Electric Railways of London Ltd (UERL) 33, 208
urban myth 23

ventilation systems
adaptation of lift shafts *26, 27*
Down Street station 98
Euston station *202, 213*
Hyde Park Corner station *68*
King William Street station *51*
Knightsbridge station *67*
Moorgate station *220*
Oxford Circus station *71*
Piccadilly Circus station *66*
repurposed stations for 27, 81
for the Victoria line 215
Whitechapel St Marys *26*
Verney Junction *169*
Victoria line 215

W.B. Simpson & Sons 29
Wedgwood, Sir Ralph 84, *92*
Westcott station *167, 168*
Whitechapel St Marys *26*
witness marks 32
Wyldes Farm *146, 147, 148, 149, 150*

Yerkes, Charles Tyson *147*, 151
York Road station
fan impeller *26*
lift shafts *103*
Second World War use of 103
tiling *29*

IMAGE CREDITS

Illustration Details

pages 2–3: Witness marks of original tiles at South Kensington station, showing their rectangular and herringbone keystone designs.

pages 4–5: The air flow in tunnels caused by train movement or fans can sometimes influence the falling of water to create unexpected patterns on the floor, as here at Down Street where a single drip from the ceiling has gradually drawn what appears to be London Underground 'bullseye' roundel.

pages 6–7: Original signage and wayfinding detail, such as direction arrows, were often fired into the glaze of tiling. Wartime conversions also resulted in new information, such as office locations and exit ways, applied by hand on tiled or nearby painted surfaces.

pages 8–9: In some disused areas, peculiar stencilled marks such as this 'S' can be found. However, their former function remains a mystery.

pages 10–11: A unique survivor, this wafer-thin glassmaker's tile was discovered broken on the floor at Euston. Now fully conserved, it is part of the London Transport Museum collection.

pages 12–13: Strong internal wall partitions had been built within the old station passageways by pouring concrete into the void between two sheets of plasterboard. When demolished this type of construction leaves a distinctive witness mark.

page 16: Extensive surviving witness marks in the war-time bunker conversion of the disused lift shafts of Dover Street station (now Green Park). Marks like these were corroborated with surviving plans and helped to determine the layout of a similar conversion at Down Street for which plans no longer exist.

page 18: The 1925 reconstruction left this emergency staircase of the Central line disused. This space now functions as a ventilation shaft and storage area, and the original tile finishes and fittings can still be seen.

pages 20–21: A Northern line train rejoins the original northbound tunnel at Angel. The line originally travelled through the point where the photographer is positioned.

page 224: Pair of staircases in a double helix around a service lift at Clapham South. The two entrances allowed a flow of up to 8,000 people to enter the building in less than an hour.

Image Credits
References relate to figure numbers, unless stated otherwise

Epping & Ongar Railway: 152

Keystone / Stringer/Getty Images: 196

Harry Todd / Stringer/Getty Images: 27,

Kim Rennie: 200

London Metropolitan Archives, from the collection of Hampstead Garden Suburb Archives Trust: 138, 139

Mirrorpix: 24

Nigel Thompson: 167

National Archives: 114 (MT 6/2728)

Network Rail Archives, 214

Courtesy National Museums Liverpool, Walker Art Gallery: 140

RIBA Collections: 98

TfL/London Transport Museum:
18 (LTM 2018/5279), 19 (LTM 1999/3638), 20 (LTM 1998/84315), 21 (LTM 2010/8054), 22 (LTM 2003/22363), 23 (LTM 1999/77778), 25 (LTM 1998/75394), 26 (LTM 1998/77770), 28 (LTM 2018/5083), 34 (LTM 2004/9507), 35 (LTM 1998/81403), 36 (LTM 1997/6622), 37 (LTM 1999/6809), 38 (LTM1999/11838), 39 (LTM 1999/24941), 40 (LTM 2004/12547), 41 (LTM 1999/19646), 42 (LTM 2015/10187), 43 (LTM 1998/84649), 47 (LTM 2000/20843), 50 (LTM 1998/97753), 52 (LTM 2000/2205), 53 (LTM1998/84907), 54 (LTM 1997/6622), 55 (LTM 1983/4/1881), 59 (LTM 1998/84379), 65 (LTM 2000/20846), 66 (LTM 2007/6690), 67 (2018/4830, PA4 J), 68 (1997/6622), 69 (2018-5683), 70, 71 (LTM 1998/59849), 72 (courtesy of Sau-Fun Mo), 74, 75 (2018/5277), 78 (LTM 1998/85250), 79 (LTM 2001/10104), 82 (2018/5627), 84 (1998/36463), 85 (1998/46756), 88, 90, 91 (LTM 1994/1875), 92 (LTM 2017/3229), 93 (LTM 1998/24727), 94 (LTM 1998/84961), 95 (LTM 1998/80014), 96 (2002/9230), 97 (1998/75514), 99 (LTM 2004/13385), 100 (LTM 2007/7673), 101, 102 (1999/10361), 103 (1998/55453), 104 (1998/48753), 105 (LTM 1998/84659), 106 (LTM 2018/5634), 107 (1951), 108 (1998/34822), 110 (LTM 1989/159), 112 (LTM 1998/84797), 113 (LTM 1998/35630), 115 (LTM 1998/51199), 116 (LTM 2018/5632), 117 (LTM 2015/6951), 118 (LTM 2000/7789), 119 (LTM 2018/2546), 120 (LTM 2006/398), 122, 123 (LTM 2006/417), 141 (1997/1506), 142 (1996/1899), 143 (1998/26738), 146 (2018/5682), 147 (1998/78775), 153 (2010/24167), 155 (LTM 1998/69503), 158 (2007/11891 part231), 159 (LTM 1998/25270), 161 (LTM 1998/48238), 162 (LTM 1998/84863), 164 (LTM 2010/24683), 166 (1998/84878), 168 (2010/24398), 170 (LTM 2006/14157), 171 (2008/2429), 172 (LTM 1998/57986), 173 (1998/87185), 174 (1998/87186), 175 (1998/57971), 176 (LTM 1998/108982), 177 (LTM 1998/91826), 178 (1998/36136), 179 (LTM 2005/106), 180 (LTM 1999/21775 Part 45), 181 (LTM 1998/62539), 182 (LTM 1983/4/6015), 183 (LTM 1999/35051), 184 (LTM 2001/53308), 188 (LTM 1994/3442), 189 (LTM 2000/20851), 190 (1998/58819), 191 (LTM (1998/51631), 192 (LTM 1998/79083), 193 (LTM 1998/81330), 194 (LTM 1998/87900), 195 (LTM 2004/5150), 197 (LTM Y481), 199, 206 (LTM 1998/86931), 207 (LTM 1998/84312), 208 (LTM 1998/92315), 209 (LTM 1998/83764), 211 (LTM 1998/58672), 212

(LTM 1998/85056), 214 (LTM 2014/2062), 215 (LTM 1983/4/1649), 218 (LTM 1998/92207), 220 (LTM 1998/92379),

TfL/London Transport Museum/Andy Davis: p.18, pp8–9, pp.20–21, 5, 8, 10, 11, 33, 44, 45, 46, 48, 49, 51, 56, 57, 58, 60, 61, 62, 63, 83, 133, 149, 154, 156, 157, 160, 165, 169, 185, 186, 187, 198, 201, 202, 203, 204, 205, 210, 213, 215, 217, 219, 221, 222, 223, 224, 227

TfL/London Transport Museum/Chris Nix: pp.10–11, 77, 127, 128, 132, 148, 163

TfL/London Transport Museum/Toby Madden: pp.2–3, pp.4–5, pp.6–7, pp.12–13, p.16, 1, 2, 4, 6, 7, 9, 12, 13, 14, 15, 16, 29, 30, 31, 32, 64, 73, 76, 80, 81, 86, 87, 89, 109, 111, 121, 126, 129, 130, 131, 134, 135, 137, 144, 145, 226, 228

TfL/London Transport Museum/Toby Madden and Andy Davis: pp.6–7, 3,

TfL/London Transport Museum/Yale University Press: 17

TfL/London Transport Museum/Wozzy Dias: 151

TopFoto: 124, 125

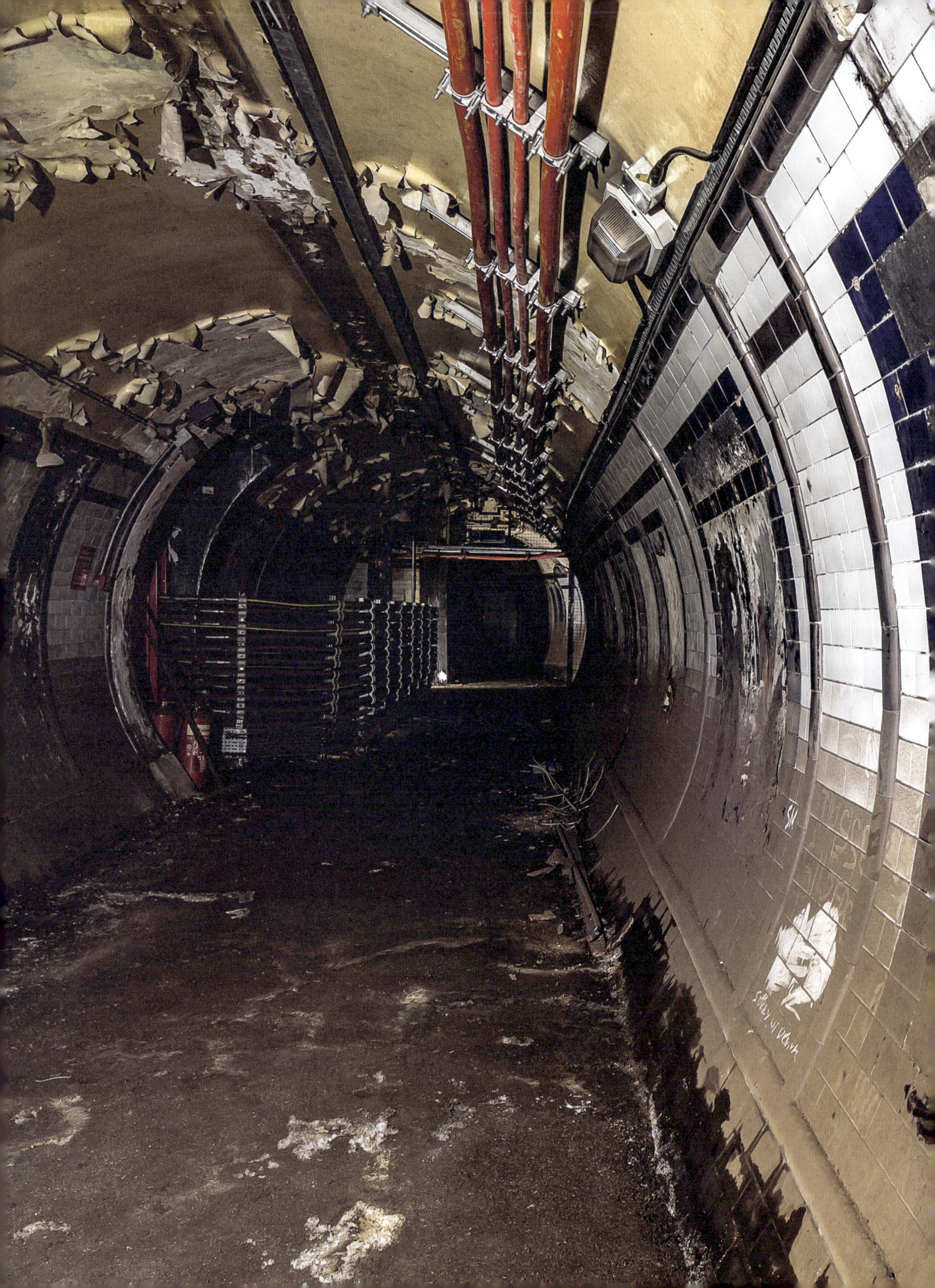

This is the age of

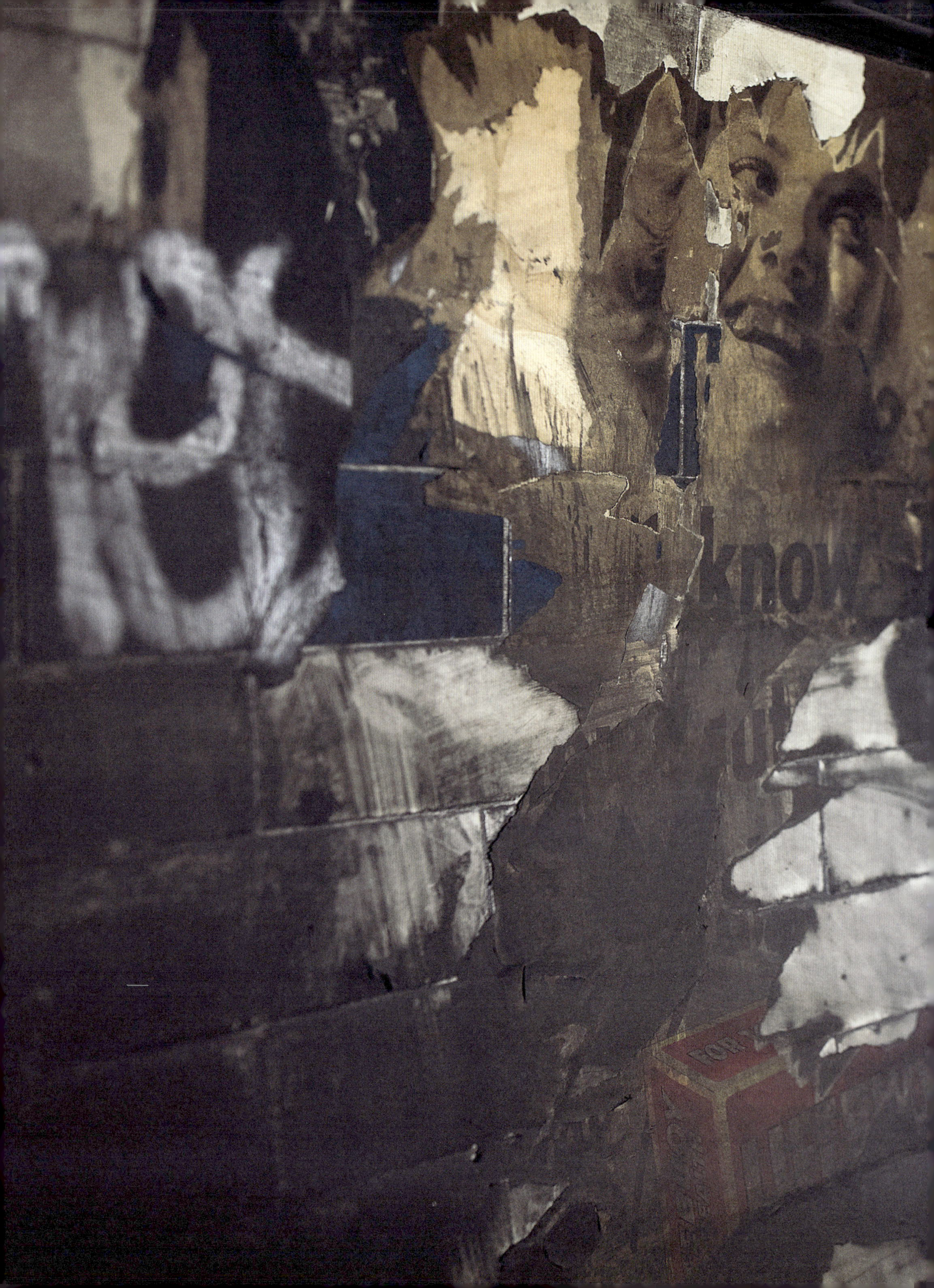
know

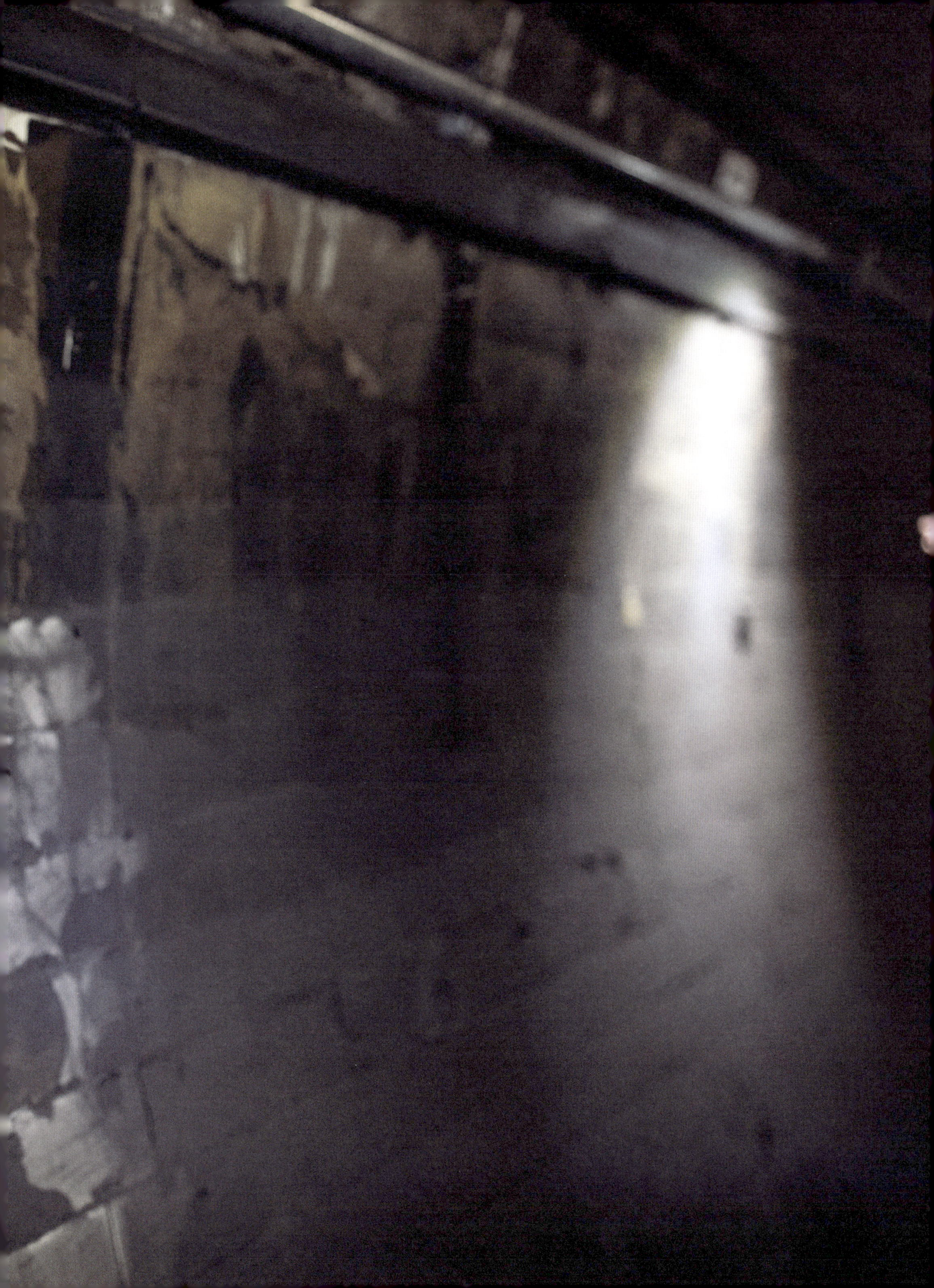

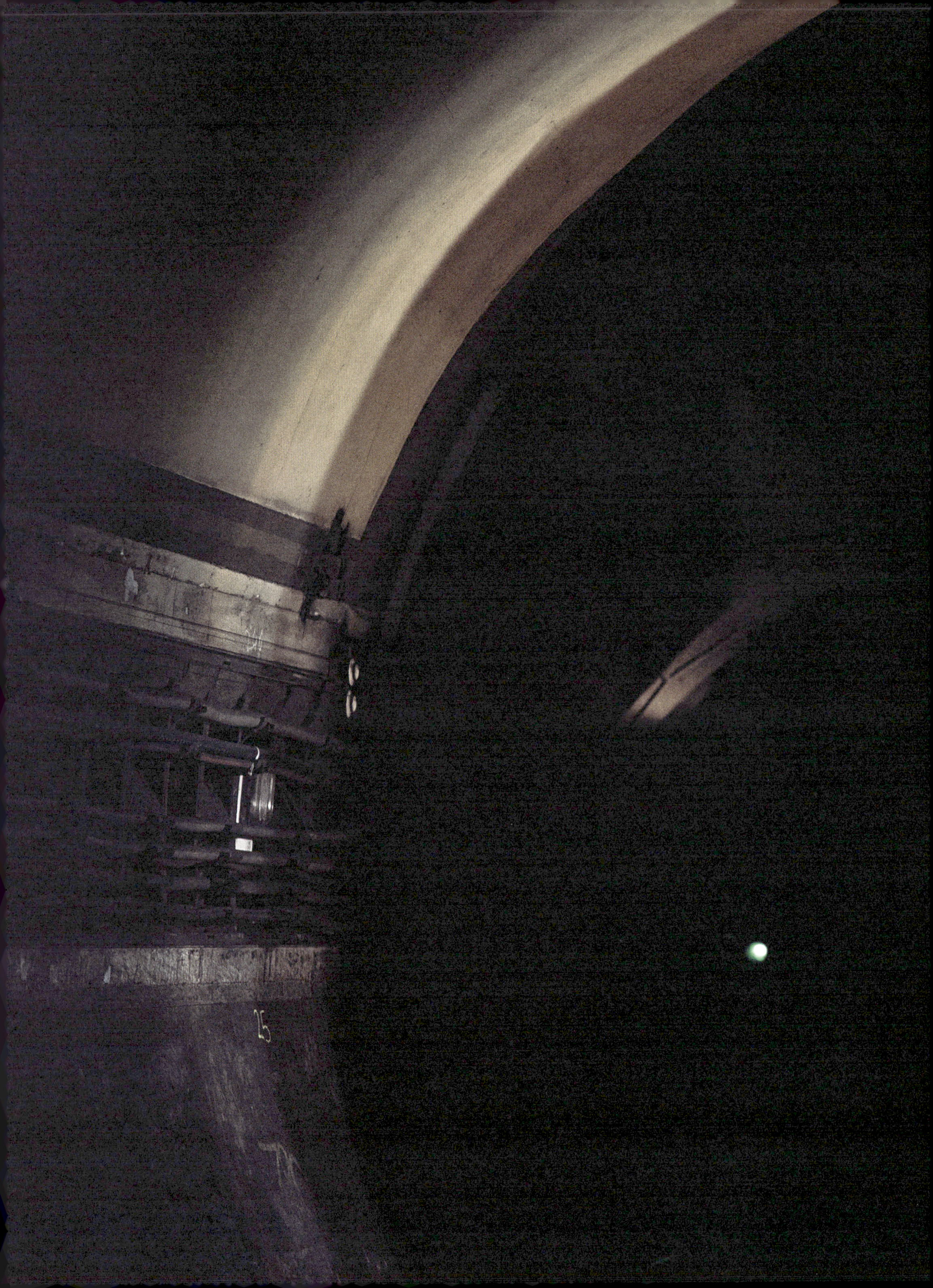

Fire point